The Apple Branch

The
Apple Branch

A Path to Celtic Ritual

Alexei Kondratiev

CITADEL PRESS
Kensington Publishing Corp.
www.kensingtonbooks.com

CITADEL PRESS BOOKS are published by

Kensington Publishing Corp.
850 Third Avenue
New York, NY 10022

First edition published in 1998 by Collins Press, Ireland.

All Kensington titles, imprints, and distributed lines are available at special quantity discounts for bulk purchases for sales promotions, premiums, fund-raising, educational, or institutional use. Special book excerpts or customized printings can also be created to fit specific needs. For details, write or phone the office of the Kensington special sales manager: Kensington Publishing Corp., 850 Third Avenue, New York, NY 10022, attn: Special Sales Department, phone 1-800-221-2647.

CITADEL PRESS and the Citadel logo are Reg. U.S. Pat. & TM Off.

First printing: July 2003

10 9 8 7 6 5 4 3 2 1

Printed in the United States of America

Library of Congress Control Number: 2003100140

ISBN: 0-8065-2502-9

In memory of
Eileen Campbell Gordon

CONTENTS

CHAPTER ONE

The Tale of the Celts

L ong ago, in that indefinite, ever-present past that belongs to
cultures with no written documents, a community of peoples
in central Europe, bound by a shared language and institutions
and by geographic proximity, took on a separate group identity.
Because of their silence in the records of civilization we know little
of the detailed pattern of their movements and its precise relationship to our dated history, but archaeological evidence provides us
with a few milestones we can follow as their tale begins to unfold. A
people noted for their stone battle-axes and tumulus burials moved
into central Europe across the Carpathians from the Russian steppe
at about the close of the third millenium B.C., just when the Beaker
traders, bringing beer and light metals from the south, were beginning to explore the same region. The two cultures appear to have
fused, or the former simply absorbed the more cosmopolitan aspects
of the latter. In any case, a distinct ethnic community became securely established in the central European area as the second millenium (B.C.) progressed. More and more proficient in the use of metals,
they also perpetuated the Beaker folk's acumen for commerce and
grew quite wealthy through trade, as the hoards of metal ornaments
found in their burial-mounds attest. Slowly they established new
settlements along the river valleys to the south and east, but did not,
as yet, go on quests far beyond their old borders.

In the last quarter of the second millenium B.C. these people made a sharp change in their burial practices. No longer were the dead placed under tumuli and surrounded by the treasures they had owned in life; instead, the bodies were cremated, and the ashes placed in urns that were buried together in cemeteries. Did they perhaps become anxious about the fate of the soul trapped in the body, and discover that it could be liberated by flame? Did they have, even then, a class of people among them whose main function was to speculate about the fate of the soul and the workings of the unseen world? What certainly did emerge at the time was a strong and ambitious warrior class, whose expeditions took them farther and farther afield to the west, even to the shores of the Atlantic and its islands.

Those western lands had, generations before, seen the flowering of a great and original culture. Its stone monuments remained, as they do today, to commemorate its mysterious obsession with mathematics and the stars, and with the sleep of the dead. Surely, despite the transformations of the Bronze Age and the ubiquitous passage of the Beaker traders, that older culture's unique vision remained strong in the traditions of the land. Surely it could not fail to impress the central European warriors who first sought to put down roots in the West. A new merging of cultural perspectives would begin, and with it the crystallization of a new civilization.

With the turn of the first millenium B.C. a new factor emerged to upset the cultural map of Europe: iron. Iron technology, first developed in the East, spread rapidly as its advantages became known. Iron-using warriors made short work of bronze-using warriors, unless the latter converted to iron weapons in time. The vigorous, wealthy culture of the central European warriors, positioned as it was on the main trade routes, quickly adopted the new technology and used it to its full potential. Warrior-bands easily conquered territories throughout the west of the Continent and in the British Isles, and established themselves everywhere as an aristocracy, ruling the autochthonous peasantry from walled hill-towns.

As their power and territory increased, again there seems to have been a change in their religious perspective. The dead—at least, the wealthy or well-born dead—were again placed, uncremated, with their most prized possessions in burial-chambers under tumuli. Was this solely due to the vaingloriousness of the chieftains, who desired eternal memorials to their careers? Or, could there have been a deeper, more spiritual reason for the change, proceeding from the culture's westward expansion? The old Atlantic tradition of the megalith-builders was greatly concerned with the proper burial of the dead, perhaps akin in this respect to Egyptian culture, assigning a local habitation to the departed and expecting the body's resurrection at the end of time's cycle. It may be that, as this ancient substratum was absorbed into Iron Age culture, there was a reversion to older ideas about death.

At this point the literate societies of the eastern Mediterranean became aware of these northern conquerors, and gave evidence of them in their records. The Greeks called them Keltoi or Galatai, certainly a version of the name the people themselves used, since it seems to reflect the Irish word *gal*, (valor). Thus it appears that they thought of themselves as the Heroic People, an apt name to express their ambitious and adventurous genius. Even the Mediterranean city-states were not always safe from the incursions of their glory-seeking bands. Celts appeared as mercenaries in regional conflicts. In 390 B.C. they plunged down into Italy and sacked the young city of Rome. In 279 B.C. several bands launched a wild expedition through Macedon and Greece, where their bemused reaction to Hellenic religious art shows how alien the Greeks' anthropomorphic representation of the gods was to Celtic conceptions. This invasion fizzled out as the Celts' short-term energy was overcome by the Greeks' careful strategy, but three Celtic tribes were allowed to settle in Asia Minor, where they founded the town of Ancyra (now Ankara) and the territory was renamed Galatia after them.

While the Celtic enthusiasm for going on raids and taking long voyages sporadically led to such violent confrontations with their neighbors, most Celtic communities were content to indulge in their old penchant for lucrative trade. Beginning in 400 B.C., a stepped-up interchange with many different cultures led to an extraordinary flowering of Celtic civilization. While foreign concepts, both technological and aesthetic, were adopted eagerly, they were recast in a uniquely Celtic synthesis. Celtic metal work achieved exquisite artis-

tic sophistication, developing a tense abstraction completely unrelated to classical canons, even when Greek models were occasionally
used. The Crater of Vix, a huge vessel made by Greeks or Etruscans
for a queen of the Sequani—a vessel larger than anything the Greeks
would have liked, which reflected the Celts' love of spectacle and
excess—shows the Celts as customers appreciative of Greek products. The Gundestrup Cauldron, found in a Danish bog, but probably made by Scordiscan silversmiths in what is now Yugoslavia,
demonstrates the prestige of Celtic art outside the Celtic lands—as
well as the eclectic genius of Celtic artists, borrowing from Thracian,
Near Eastern, and possibly even Indian models.

However, for all their international links through trade, the Celts
remained fundamentally different from their Greek neighbors. Their
rejection of writing as a primary means of keeping records—even
long after they were well acquainted with the concept—and use of
Greek letters instead for commercial transactions and monumental
inscriptions best illustrates the dichotomy. As they refused to be
ruled by objective records, the Celts resisted being dragged into the
continuum of history, and held on to the Dreamtime, the eternal
present, and the certainty of an unchanging pattern. That pattern
was sacred, related to the Otherworld in which our own world has
its origins—origins that could be seen as remote in the past, or as a
process still (and forever) underway. The Otherworld was always
there, just beyond perception, secretly empowering human actions,
giving meaning to events. Because the barrier between the worlds
was tenuous, it could, according to tradition, be breached in appropriate circumstances.

We are told, by Julius Caesar and others, that the ban on writing
was initiated and enforced by the priestly caste of the Celts, the
druids. Even tribal kings derived their authority from the druids,
whose own authority was, in practical terms, higher. Because they
communicated with the Otherworld, the supreme reality, druids
could be relied on to deliver fundamental judgments on events, and
to reveal patterns that should be followed. Perhaps it is from their
guidance that the Celtic tradition has acquired its distinctive structure: an "outer" side that innovates boldly and freely, and an "inner"

side that remains stubbornly unchanging, certain of its eternal value. Throughout the history of the Free Celts basic notions concerning society, the land, and the Otherworld underwent little transformation. Always we see the threefold structure of the tribe that Georges Dumézil considered typical of the Indo-Europeans: a priestly caste (and a sacred king) focusing authority through their association with the Otherworld; a warrior-aristocracy, defending the tribe; and a farmer class, to feed the tribe.

The priestly caste—the druids and bards—had a great variety of functions. Originally shamans who received messages from the Otherworld in a trance state, they found, in their reliance on memory, a natural ally in the art of poetry. What had come out of the visions in a torrent of words could be remembered more easily when patterned by meter and alliteration. So the craft of versemaking became intimately associated with magical practice and Otherworld power, and has remained so throughout Celtic history. Perhaps, in their origins, members of the warrior-aristocracy who were physically or psychologically unfit for combat, the druids and bards took upon themselves so many crucial roles that they became central to the cohesion of the society, and far exceeded the warriors in authority. Their persons were inviolate. Their training took many years. They alone were the ultimate experts on matters of genealogy, and of law: theirs was the last word in settling disputes. As scryers or diviners of the Otherworld they knew what sacrifices were necessary to maintain the world balance, and sometimes required human messengers to the gods. Having a curious and active intellect, they observed the natural world around them, studied the properties of herbs, and practiced healing, both shamanic and medical. And, not least, they were responsible for teaching the youth of the tribe, for imparting to them the nature of the universe and the rules by which they would have to live. Since they refused to write down any of their teachings, we can only guess at much of it, but the broad outline is clear.

The Land, they taught, was a living entity, aware of and responsive to human activity, but quite inhuman in its nature and requirements. It was an ultimate reality before which the purely human consciousness of the tribe had to bow. Personalized, she manifested herself as a Goddess whose favor had to be won. Her consort, the God, embodied all the concerns and ideals of the tribe at all its social levels, and served as a mediator between the human and inhuman spheres. Through sharing his identity with a human individual—the Sacred King—he made possible a sacramental, cosmically binding marriage between a tribal member and the Goddess. As kin of the King, the entire tribe became kin to the Land, could settle in her embrace, and derive sustenance from her body, but only as long as they respected her person and did no violence to her. Even the King's marriage remained valid only if he continued to be a proper representative of the God, unblemished in either body or character. He was to incarnate the specific virtues of the three functions: piety, bravery, and generosity.

This all-important balance between Tribe and Land was but one instance of the vast interplay between God and Goddess, which embraced the entire universe. It was a marriage of time and space, change and permanence, activity and passivity, the bound reality of our world and the inexhaustible potential of the Otherworld. Every facet of existence was in some measure a response to the shifting balance between those two polar principles. But in order for the balance to shift, to prevent the two equal powers from reaching a stalemate, thus putting an end to the cycle of events, a third element had to be introduced, a projection of either the God or the Goddess that would constantly upset the balance in favor of one or the other and set them in perpetual motion. The most complete model of universal process was a triadic one, and the Celts incorporated the threefold pattern into many of their artistic creations, whether visual or verbal. The three functions of society were one more manifestation of the three-in-one, on the level of the human community.

In the polarity between our world and the Otherworld, the disruptive third element consisted in the conditional merging of the two, either at specific points in time or in specific places where the boundaries between worlds were thinner. Time was defined by the yearly cycle, itself divided into four quarters, each quarter inaugurated by a period in which the Otherworld's influence spilled over into the human realm. The druids again played a crucial role in defining the rituals best suited to channel the exchange of energies between the worlds on the quarter-days, for the greatest good of all three classes in the tribe.

Although they deferred to the druids in matters of ultimate authority, the warrior-aristocracy were the core of the tribe's life, its most visible agents, the main focus of its admiration, and setters of trends and fashions on a more superficial, worldly level. They asserted their kin-group's right to the territory that incarnated the spirit of their Land-goddess, and kept out intruders by a show of bravery and determination. But theirs was not a tightly disciplined, militaristic organization, aiming at long-term gains through a planned strategy. They rarely sought territorial expansion through conquest, except in unusual periods of economic hardship. They had no real concept of war as it is now understood. Warriors pursued highly individualistic careers, and gained social standing by attracting attention to themselves in daring, small-scale expeditions in enemy territory, which would invite reprisals on a similar scale. Cattle constituted the primary wealth of each tribe, so cattle-raids were an especially popular form of mutual provocation. During the raid each warrior would try to engage a particularly reputed enemy warrior in combat, make a show of his prowess and fearlessness—and even, in the best circumstances, would take the enemy's head as a trophy. Competition was fierce for first place in the warriors' hierarchy: the most highly regarded, most experienced warrior could claim the champion's portion at feasts, and be shown other signs of deference. Warriors also vied with each other in the quality and ornateness of their clothes and weapons. All had the ambition to be remembered in the epic recitations of the bards.

The occupations of the third-function people—the free landholders, who functioned as farmers—did not invite celebration in song and story, but were vital to the life of the tribe; this group displayed the same ingenuity and creativity that characterized all aspects of the Celts' culture. At the height of their development, the Free Celts were prosperous and comfort-loving. They were as eclectic in matters of technology as they were in matters of art. Their achievements as cartwrights, masons, cheese-makers, preparers of smoked meats and sausages, to name a few diverse occupations, compared favorably with, and in some cases surpassed, anything to

be found among their literate, "civilized" neighbors to the south. There
was plenty of wealth to be traded for foreign goods, such as wine
and expensive bright dyes.

On the fringes of tribal society there existed some groups of
people who fell outside the trifunctional system. There were landed
bondsmen—perhaps descendants of pre-Celtic peasants—and slaves,
unprotected by kinship with tribal members. Kinship, true or assumed, was the only social cement in the Celtic world. One's only
unquestionable allegiance was to one's family, and the tribe was a
vast extended family, a family of families all recognizing descent
from a common ancestor. One could, for political reasons, extend
kinship through adoption, so the system was not without flexibility.
Children were fostered by families unrelated to them in order to
create new kinship ties not based on blood. In theory, even bondsmen and those who, for whatever reason, were "kinless" and without
rights in the tribal community could be adopted as kin, if they were
not criminals or otherwise undesirable. An outstanding personal talent for craftsmanship or music, for example, might single one out for
such promotion.

The reliance on kinship rather than social institutions as a source
of authority and the strong individualism encouraged by the warrior
class made it impossible for the Free Celts to envision anything like
a centralized state. Indeed, the whole pattern of the Celtic way of life
tended to be centrifugal. People went to market-towns for fairs, to
sacred centers for rituals, and to walled forts for protection in troubled times, but lived their personal lives in privacy, on their own
ground, far from the places of assembly. Only in their southernmost
territories did the Celts experiment (modestly) with urban living;
elsewhere they preferred to settle in isolated farmsteads, each house
separated from the others by stretches of field and pasture, each four-
generation family following, in most respects, its own rules. Kings
were ritual leaders first and foremost: what secular authority they
wielded depended on their personal charisma. The range of power
acquired by a chieftain with a forceful personality could shrink dras-
tically in the hands of an unimpressive successor. There was the ideal
of the High King, the man with enough charisma to unite many
tribes under his authority—rather like the Indian ideal of the *cakra-*

vartin, the World Ruler—but only rarely would a historic High King come close to fulfilling the expectations raised by his mythic role. Even at the height of Celtic expansion, when they ranged from Ireland and Spain in the West to the Black Sea and Asia Minor in the East, and from northern Italy in the South to (probably) the banks of the Elbe in the North, the Celts owed their cultural cohesion to language and religion rather than to any central political institution. They never could have imagined forming an empire.

This was, unfortunately, not true of some of their neighbors. Rome, which the Celts had humiliated in the city's early days, developed a quite different philosophy of social institutions, one much more suited to the concentration of power. Instead of evaluating an individual by his personal qualities alone, the Romans gave an increasing importance to the fixed role he played in society, and to the title or "label" that defined the role. Society was no longer viewed as a fluid range of interacting personalities, but as a rigid structure of interlocked, titled roles, each title carrying its own appropriate authority regardless of the individual bearing it. Such stability in the concept of authority produced an ideal of discipline; while the theoretical dissociation of institutions from the personalities operating them allowed a completely new entity, the state, to arise out of human activity. The state created a pattern of relationships not based on kinship, and, as the centuries went by, there was less and less reference to the living specificity of the Land in which it originated. The titled occupations became nodes of power in society, and the whole state structure evolved into a vast machine used to amass and preserve power for its own sake, at the expense of any rival entities. So it has remained down the ages; but the Celtic tradition was ill-equipped to understand such a concept.

The Romans never forgot their defeat at the hands of the Celts. The *Dies Alliensis*—July 18, 390 B.C.—when, just before the invasion of Rome, the Roman army had been routed by a horde of painted Celtic warriors on the banks of the river Allia, was commemorated as a day of national mourning by the Roman state. As the Roman Republic grew and affirmed its power—and clashed with equally ambitious foreign states—it encountered the Celts again and again. Celtic adventurers served as mercenaries in the Punic Wars of the third century B.C., in which the Romans successfully passed their first test as a major international power. Areas of former Carthaginian influence in Spain, which the Romans coveted for new territory, were inhabited by Celts protective of their independence. And Celtic-speaking tribes lived on the borders of Tuscany, dangerously close to the Romans' home soil.

The development of the Roman army as an efficient, hierarchical military machine, second to none in Europe, spelled the doom of the Free Celts. The Celts of northern Italy (Cisalpine Gaul) were the first to fall under its might, at the battle of Telamon in 225 B.C. Within another century Roman colonization would extend across the Alps, into the southeast of what today is France. As they obliterated the Etruscan culture that had served as a buffer between Latins and Celts, the Romans easily exported their language and values into their new Celtic territories. But for another three or four centuries the Cisalpine Gauls maintained a certain feeling of ethnic separateness within Italy, as *Transpadani*. Latin writers like Virgil, Titus Livy, and Catullus, however much they may have identified with the Roman state, came from Celtic-speaking backgrounds and expressed certain aspects of that background in their works. Virgil's wit and tenderness, like the exuberantly personal voice of Catullus, brought a new, exotic tone to the Latin tradition. And, the spoken Latin of the region preserved a distinctive sound, as evidenced by the later evolution of the Romance dialects of the Gallo-Italic area, which are much closer to those of France than to those of southern Italy.

In Spain, Roman occupation met with fierce resistance. During the years 153–133 B.C., the Numantines led the region's Celts in a long and costly rebellion. Besieged in their fort of Numantia, the rebels held out proudly to the bitter end, eating the flesh of their dead before they would acknowledge defeat. But in the summer of 133 their defense collapsed. For all the bravery of its opponents, the Roman war machine ground on.

It was another century, however, before the Romans dared to undertake any serious venture into the Celtic heartlands, Transalpine Gaul and Britain. Spain, northern Italy, and the south coast of Gaul had, after all, been on the international Mediterranean trade routes, and were influenced enough by surrounding cultures to seem somewhat familiar to invading Roman forces. *Gallia comata*, "the land of the 'long-haired' Celts," was, by contrast, something quite foreign and mysterious, a place of deep forests and treacherous hills inhabited by a people with alien customs, who knew the terrain while the Romans did not. Memory of the *Dies Alliensis* kept ancient fears alive and confidence in check, as well as providing an incentive to conquer. In the end it was the political ambition and military prowess of one man, Julius Caesar, and an unfortunate historical coincidence—the territorial expansion of the Germans—that took the Romans north and brought an end to the First Golden Age of the Celtic world.

The Germanic-speaking peoples had their heartland in Scandinavia, but ranged southward into coastal areas along the North Sea and the western Baltic, where they mingled with the Celts and absorbed many elements of their culture. It is not absolutely clear what happened around the turn of the first century B.C. to send the Germans out in conquering bands far beyond their traditional borders, but climatic changes and a jump in population must have played a part in it, as has happened several times in the history of northern Europe. In any case, a wave of Germanic invaders swept through the territories of Celtic tribes, often pushing tribes into the territories of their neighbors, creating a political turmoil unprecedented in Celtic experience.

When the Helvetii were pushed out of what has since become Switzerland into the territory of the Aedui, an eastern tribe generally friendly to the Romans, Julius Caesar seized the opportunity that was offered to him. The Aedui appealed to the Romans for help. Their leader, the druid-trained Divitiacos, who had become a friend of Caesar, warned against the ambitions of his fellow tribesman Dumnorix, a wealthy and powerful aristocrat intent on using the political turmoil to extend his own authority throughout the Celtic lands. Did Dumnorix, "King of the World," in fact aspire to be a High King, the spiritual and temporal ruler of many tribes? It seems likely; and the prospect of a strong, united Celtic realm potentially allied to or in control of the German tide was not to the Romans' advantage. Caesar easily won funding in the Senate for his expedition, which initially beat back the Helvetii and neutralized Dumnorix's allies, but which, under the pretext of consolidating military positions to fend off the German invasion, then turned into a full-scale conquest of all the tribal territories in Gaul. Caesar's horror stories of Celtic "barbarism" served to fuel support for his venture, and reports of his victories consolidated his popularity at home. He was named "protector of the Gauls," with the mission to "pacify" the wild northern lands, and to make them safe, predictable neighbors for Rome. In effect, all Celts on the Continent had been declared a part of the Roman continuum. Their destiny had been subsumed by the apparatus of the Roman state.

Celtic resistance was fierce and passionate, but the individualism of Celtic warriors and their reluctance to bow to any unconditional authority made it impossible for them to withstand the disciplined mechanism of the Roman army. There were many displays of personal heroism, many daring exploits undertaken spontaneously by well-known champions, but without coordination they had no strategic value against a true conquering force. The Romans were not fighting for glory: they were fighting to win—to grasp and to keep. They would stop at nothing to get what they sought. No aristocratic code of honor, no sense of humanity held them in check, to the Celts' dismay. Roman atrocities spurred a number of revolts in already "pacified" areas. The greatest challenge to Caesar was offered in 56 B.C. by the Veneti of Armorica, who engaged the Romans in a great naval battle in the Gulf of Morbihan. A combination of Roman strategy and sheer bad luck resulted in a crushing defeat for the Celts. There was a genocide of the Veneti: centuries later, their territory was still depopulated.

By 55 B.C., scarcely three years after the beginning of his campaign, Caesar had forced all of Gaul into submission to the Roman state. But Britain and Ireland remained free. Not only was Britain a welcoming refuge for the Continent's political malcontents, but the entire Celtic world regarded it as a spiritual homeland. To them it was the ideal training-ground for druids and bards, who gave Celtic culture its soul and conscience. To destroy the spiritual cohesion of the Celtic world and deprive the Celtic identity of its source, the intertribal bardic order had to be destroyed, and for that, Britain had to be crushed. It would have been a logical, elegant conclusion to his campaign if Caesar had added Britain to his conquests, and he certainly made the attempt. But his expeditions across the Channel were too poorly provided for to yield conclusive results. Satisfied that he had discouraged British tribesmen from giving aid to Gaulish rebels, he turned his attention back to the Continent. Britain had won breathing space for another century.

The Celts of the Continent, however, had not accepted defeat. In 52 B.C. a warrior-aristocrat of the Arverni, Vercingetorix son of Celtillos, became the charismatic focus of a new, widespread rebellion. Many tribes were awed into accepting his leadership; his commands were obeyed from one end of Gaul to the other. Here, it seemed, was a true High King at last, an individual with enough spiritual power to unite all people in a redemptive liberation of the Land. Vercingetorix was indeed a master strategist who understood the Roman mind and could anticipate his enemy's moves. The crushing defeat of the Romans at Gergovia in Vercingetorix's own Arvernian territory should have been the turning point, the launching of the rebellion's final leap to success. But recurring disunity among the tribes, the impossibility of true discipline within the Celtic warrior tradition—even the romantic dedication of those warriors, which led them to rash acts in the name of their cause— thwarted the realization of Vercingetorix's plans. At last, besieged in the fort of Alesia, Vercingetorix and his followers were shown the full measure of Roman ruthlessness. When the noncombatants on the Celtic side—those too old or too young to fight—were released and appealed for mercy, the Romans made them starve to death under the eyes of their kin in the fort. A huge coalition of Celtic tribes attempted to break the siege and free their leader, and for a while their onslaught proved a real challenge to Caesar. With the help of German auxiliaries, however, and by exploiting the usual Celtic weaknesses, he was able to fragment, and finally rout, the relief effort. Vercingetorix, walled up in Alesia with no hope of rescue, saw his vision die: he had no choice but to surrender.

His surrender, as recounted by Plutarch, is a pathetic symbol of the Celtic confrontation with Empires through the ages. Wearing his chieftain's regalia, Vercingetorix rode into Caesar's presence, dismounted, divested himself of his armor and weapons—and, with them, of all his earthly ambitions—and placed himself in Caesar's power. Having acknowledged defeat, he had a right to expect honorable treatment. But to Caesar he had become no more than an object to be used for political advantage. He was taken to Rome, where he languished in a dungeon for six years. Then he was dragged out, emaciated and weak, to march in Caesar's triumphal procession, and at last was strangled, a sacrifice to the omnipotence of the Roman state.

Thus passed Vercingetorix son of Celtillos, prince of Arvernia, and perhaps, last High King of Keltia. There was no one left to take up his standard and carry on the rebellion. Roman occupation of all the Celtic lands on the Continent became an inescapable reality. Roman citizenship—and with it a complete surrender to the apparatus of the state—was made accessible to the warrior-aristocracy and the wealthier landholders: a sore temptation where no other hope seemed possible. It was not long before many succumbed to it.

But the druids remained. Still the most prestigious class in society, they upheld a view of the world quite unlike Roman reality, and were adamantly opposed to any foreign adulteration of their creed. They rejected the Roman state's pretensions to religious authority. Of course, the state mounted a powerful counterattack. Where earlier classical writers had marveled at the druids' knowledge and wisdom, Caesar and his followers wrote of bloody sacrifices, of victims burned alive in wickerwork images. The druids, in popular thought, were equated with oppressive savagery. No self-respecting Roman citizen could be associated with such barbarism, or indeed tolerate its continued existence. Sensing the persecution to come, the druids of Gallia Lugdunensis—centered on Lugudunon, the sacred heartland of southern Gaul—decided, in their assembly of 18 B.C., to recognize Roman sovereignty over the Land in exchange for religious toleration. While such a compromise saved them from outright extermination, it really amounted to an admission of defeat: Roman citizens were still forbidden to take part in druidic rituals, and many Celts, drawn into the Roman system by social ambition, chose to distance themselves from their spiritual roots. Little remained to prevent the implantation of Roman cultural attitudes and the Latin language.

Even for the druids, the period of grace lasted only a little over half a century. The eventual conquest of Britain, and the destruction of the sacred core of druidical organization there, made the toleration of druids by the state unnecessary and undesirable. But before their final eclipse, the druids under Roman rule did some fascinating experiments with their tradition. The taboo on writing, it appears, was lifted. The famous calendar found at Coligny, not far north of Lugdunum, (what the Romans called Lugudunon), is an ambitious attempt to fuse native Celtic methods of measuring time, based on the lunar cycle, with prevalent Mediterranean concepts, based on the solar year. This was the first—and last—written document the druids consigned to posterity. Then their voice was silenced, and their tradition sank out of sight into the depths of the countryside, beyond the awareness of mainstream civilization.

The Roman conquest of Britain followed a pattern painfully familiar in Celtic history. In 43 A.D. the Atrebates, a tribe of Britain's south coast, appealed to the Romans for help against the Catuvellauni, a large and powerful Midlands tribe. As had happened in Gaul, the Roman military machine did not stop after achieving its first objective, but went on to "pacify" the entire area. The defeat of the Catuvellauni intimidated many tribes into submitting to Roman rule, although there was an attempt at organized resistance. For some ten years after Britain's official absorption into the Roman system, a Catuvellaunan nobleman, Caratacus son of Cunobelinos—or Caradog ap Cynfelin, in the Welsh of today—harried the Romans from his strongholds in western Britain. Caratacus was a charismatic warrior-hero, perhaps even High King material. It was through the treachery of the Brigantian chieftainess Cartismandua—remembered and cursed in later Welsh tradition as Agarwedd, the "Graceless One"—that he was delivered into Roman hands and taken as a prisoner to Rome. Whether the Emperor Claudius was of a more humane nature than Julius Caesar had been, or times had simply changed, Caratacus did not suffer the fate of Vercingetorix; after having acknowledged Rome's victory, he was allowed to live out his life in exile.

Still, the druidic centers in the west of Britain survived, inviolate, and influential. In 59 A.D. the Roman state appointed Suetonius

Paulinus, a ruthless and brutal man, to be military governor of the new province. He dealt quickly and radically with the druid problem. In 60 A.D. he led two legions in the assault on the island sanctuary of Mona (present-day Anglesey). There, though the Celts resisted with the passion of desperation, the holiest place in their world to which the druids and bards of many tribes had come for their training, psychically charged by hundreds of years of ritual activity, was utterly destroyed.

The Massacre of Mona is yet another vivid and tragic icon whose symbolism resonates throughout Celtic history. Tacitus tells us that the chanting druids wove a spell of real power over the advancing Roman troops. It was a triumph of psychic energy, impelling warriors to battle-frenzy, striking enemy soldiers with paralysis. But the mechanical, reflexive habits of Roman military training took over even when each individual soldier's consciousness was frozen with terror; the ability to cancel out all subjective participation in their surroundings eventually made the attackers immune to Celtic magic. The black-clad druidesses, figures of awe at first, became mere women who would crumple at the end of a spear. In their eyes, the glamour of the sanctuary was seen as nothing. Sacred trees were cut down and burned, people whose minds had stored the lore and wisdom of generations were hacked to pieces. The soul of the Celtic world was extinguished at last, crushed by superior force. Although the culture of the Free Celts would linger in marginal areas, this Roman "final solution" to the problem of Celtic religion can be said to mark the true end of the First Golden Age of the Celts, or "Keltia One" as the Breton musician Alan Stivell has called it.

It was almost as a negligible footnote to this work of destruction that Paulinus turned back east to crush the rebellion of Boudicca, consort of Prasutagus, King of the Iceni. Boudicca had been mortally humiliated by the agents of the Roman State. A physically imposing woman of passionate character, she easily rallied her tribesmen to her cause, which was, in essence, the avenging of her honor, a notion that at once compelled their imagination. Although women in Celtic society could not become Land-rulers (the consort of the Goddess had to be an image of the God), there was no obstacle to their becoming charismatic leaders. The Iceni rose en masse behind their queen and, joined by the neighboring Trinovantes, swept south like a wave of consuming fire over Roman settlements in the London area. But, like so many Celtic risings, it was a grass fire: bright, fearsome, and irresistible at first, but quickly spent. Again, the disciplined mechanism of the Roman legions endured when the battle-madness of the Celts could not. Boudicca, it is said, committed suicide amidst the ruins of her vision, while Paulinus launched massacre after massacre to cow the British tribes into submission.

Luckily for the Britons, Paulinus was removed by the Senate a year later, and Petronius Turpilianus replaced him as military governor. Paulinus had wielded the stick; now Turpilianus held out the carrot. The rich were offered commercial incentives to assimilate into the Roman system. As had already happened in Gaul, Roman colonists established urban centers that grew quickly and set a new pattern for the life of the country. Hierarchy, bureaucracy, and the pursuit of money came to dominate the minds of people who hitherto had been ruled by the laws of kinship and by awe for the mysterious reality of the Land.

The northern half of the island remained free of Roman settlement, however, and its native tribes were insufficiently "pacified." By 84 A.D. Julius Agricola, perhaps the most highly regarded of Roman military governors in Britain's history, resolved to make all of the island's population bow to Rome's authority. Agricola's thrust into the wild heaths of what would one day be Scotland, crushing the immense army of Calgacus, chieftain of the Caledonii, marks the fullest extent of Rome's military triumph over the Celtic tribal world. At odds with the power of the state—Roman or otherwise—Celts down the ages can echo with feeling Calgacus' bitter reproach to Rome, "You make a wasteland, and call it peace!" But Rome's conquests would go no farther. Though Agricola set his sights on Ireland, his government would not finance more campaigns on that frontier. Even the garrisons already established in the northern third of Britain were abandoned, and never permanently re-taken. For all the power and glory it would yet enjoy for centuries, the Empire's economic tide had turned. The laws built into the very nature of the state would begin to erode its structure.

So Ireland—and, despite its scars, northernmost Britain—remained as pockets where the Celtic tradition survived intact. Though the Celts of those areas were constantly aware of the power of Rome, they never made it the center of their universe. Folk still lived scattered in family-groups over a land whose Goddess knew them because she had married their King. Bards and druids were still the sacred arbiters of society's needs—even if, with the loss of the British schools, they had shrunk to a more provincial, rustic level. Faith in the power of courage, beauty, and illumination continued to be the wellspring of art and poetry. To the Romans such unconquered tribesmen from the edge of the world were mere boorish *Scoti* devoid of civilized virtues; but they held the seeds from which Keltia would one day grow and blossom again.

Even in the conquered regions many of the old life-patterns survived, even if they were no longer held together by the same sense of cultural identity. Having disposed of the druids, the Roman authorities encouraged the local people to continue worshipping their gods within the limits of Roman understanding, identifying, wherever possible, each Celtic deity with a similar figure in the state-approved Graeco-Roman pantheon; but the two systems of belief were too different for such one-to-one identifications to work well on a deep level. For the Celts, the divine was too fluid a concept to be simply divided into intellectual categories; the gods were experienced as mysterious, not wholly comprehensible powers associated with certain places, times, and activities. Guardians of wells, of mountains, of sacred groves did not change their character, and continued to be held in awe. Rivers—the physical manifestation of the nourishing Goddess present in the Land—kept their old names, and with them something of their old ritual significance. Even as the language of the conquerors gradually replaced the language of tradition, many words—names of places, terms for various daily activities related to the Land, too familiar and necessary to be affected by Romanization— refused to be displaced, and so perpetuated a diffuse image of what had been before. In the countryside, outside the purely Roman order of the cities, there would linger for centuries, throughout Gaul and northern Spain, an echo of the Celtic version of reality, bound up with the appearance of the landscape, with a certain quality to life's patterns that the Land itself seemed to forever demand.

As we have already pointed out, the massive bureaucracy necessary to keep the Roman state functioning across its vast territories soon began to collapse under its own weight. Economic contradictions began to burden the system even while, outwardly, the Empire's commercial networks appeared to prosper. Three centuries after the conquest of Britain, an overextended, underpaid civil service struggled in vain to support and placate masses of unemployed laborers. The gap between rich and poor grew wider and more cruel in its manifestations. The military establishment, the state's real backbone, periodically expressed dissatisfaction, and with its defection would come about the final dissolution of the system.

However, over the same period, in the crowded cities of the Roman expansion there had arisen a spiritual power quite opposed to the principles by which the state operated. This new doctrine affirmed the spiritual equality of all people, and the unassailable dignity of each individual endowed with free will. It attacked the state's ability to bridle the individual with imposed ideals and obligations, foreign to the needs of the spirit. Understandably, the state tried to suppress these followers of the risen Christ, as it had earlier suppressed the druids. But the new movement's momentum carried it inexorably through some frightening persecutions and intimidations, until the state was forced to recognize its superior vitality. In 313 the Edict of Milan emancipated Christians within the Empire, and even gave them favored status. While this encouraged the invigorating tenets of the Christian faith to take root over a wider area, it also removed the opposition between Christianity and the state, and prepared the ground for the Church's co-optation by its old enemy.

But for the many small communities of converts scattered throughout the cities of the Empire, such concerns would remain nebulous for some time. The important thing was to spread the word, share the good news. So, from the Roman cities of Britain, a knowledge of Christianity began to trickle out into what was left of the Free Celtic world. This process was gradual and unspectacular: perhaps, here and there, a tribesman who had come south to sell his wares in a market town would be struck by the words of a preacher, and bring the new concepts back for discussion in his native territory. Ethnic Irishmen who had lived in Britain carried at least the basics of Christianity to Ireland. As early as the third century the Church father Tertullian could claim that Christian communities existed outside the borders of the Empire—surely a reference to Christians among the Free Celts.

In 410 Rome was sacked by Alaric and his Visigoths, who were actually disgruntled employees of the state. Although the Western Empire would continue to exist in name for several more decades, this event clearly marked its death as an institution: its credibility was gone, its power broken. Soon the intricate administrative channels that had sustained its cities collapsed as well, and hundreds of thousands of people were forced to leave, and died first from starvation and later from plague. A deep pessimism took hold of most thinking men. Where was God's Holy Spirit, who should have guided the Christian rulers of the Empire away from such catastrophe? Were people so utterly cut off from their spiritual roots in God, so depraved by their fleshly limitations, that it took a miracle of grace to make them attend to the voice of the Divine within themselves? With this emphasis on human sinfulness came, ironically, a hankering after the secure mechanisms of the state, and a greater identification of such mechanisms within the life of the Church. The Church began, in fact, to take upon itself the burden of the state, along with the habits of thought that implied.

But before Christendom in the West succumbed to that temptation the voice of a Celt was raised in warning. A celibate layman from Britain, Pelagius, appeared in Rome just before its fall and sought to counteract the fatalistic pessimism that had become prevalent. With his tall, corpulent barbarian's frame and his persuasive speech, he exerted upon the Roman world all the fascination of the brilliant foreigner. God's creation, he proclaimed, was good, and human nature, being part of that creation, was good also. Sin came from the imitation of bad example, and its effects could be reversed. He would have none of the dichotomies between humanity and nature, spirit and flesh, or the hierarchical oppositions of male and female, master and slave. All elements in creation were interconnected and coequal, and salvation came through the realization of kinship with one's fellows. But this sane, eminently orthodox voice was silenced by the Church's anathema, under pressure from the dying State.

"Pelagianism," a caricature of Pelagius's true teaching, was proclaimed a heresy, thus discouraging anyone from further investigating that teaching.

Fortunately for the Celtic world, the newly hardened bureaucracy of the Roman Church was prevented from imposing its authority over much of the West. Again, the German lands were in ferment; whole tribes poured into the tottering Empire to plunder its riches and stake out new territories. First the Christian Goths, who had lived within the Roman system, tried to twist it to their own profit, but only succeeded in tearing it apart; then the pagan tribes from the hinterlands, Franks, Burgundians, Suevi, and Alamans, to whom the southern cities were a legendary treasure-trove, were now rumored to be ready for plunder. Decayed from within and besieged from without, the structures of the Empire crumbled. German tribal kinglets found themselves sole rulers of the lands they had occupied, fighting over the broken pieces of a great, sophisticated mechanism that could no longer be repaired. Only the Church remained as a link with what had been, a survival from what many people remembered as a secure, comfortable time. Now completely identified with the spirit of the vanished state, the Church embarked on the arduous task of bringing the new rulers into its fold. It would be a long, drawn-out process, for the Church institution was weak and ineffectual.

So Christian communities among the Free Celts were allowed to develop with little meddling from Rome. At first the missionaries were Romanized British Celts, such as Ninian in Galloway and Patrick in Ulster. But Britain was not out of the reach of the destroying Germanic wave. As its protecting legions were called away to more urgent confrontations elsewhere, Angles, Saxons, and Jutes from the North Sea area established themselves on its eastern coast, and began the methodic conquest of the entire island. The English peril had materialized; the cities and the rich southeastern countryside were the first to fall. The urban-based Church hierarchy collapsed, along with all other state institutions. The Celts were on their own.

Perhaps what was left of their culture also would have been swept away by the new conquerors, but near the close of the fifth century something happened to check the English expansion. Did a military leader on the Celtic side inflict such crushing defeats on the invaders that their initial confidence was broken, and they were compelled to a truce? The chronicles of the period are too scanty to provide hard facts, but the later traditions of Wales, Cornwall, and Brittany are explicit in the answer: Arthur. Whether he was a Romano-British gentleman fighting to preserve something of the state's authority structure on the island, or a barely Romanized tribal chieftain aware of his duty to the Land, it was, in the end, the Celtic world he fought for. Later generations would make him into a High King, the ideal of all Land-rulers that have been or will be, as well as an eternal redeemer-hero, one who could, when no other hope remained, come back from the Otherworld to save his people from extinction.

Although the fertile plain of Logres, or Lloegr, was lost to them forever, the British Celts had indeed won a respite of almost a hundred years. When all vestiges of the state's power had faded away, the untamed tribesmen of the North began to look south and reclaim territories that had been under Roman rule for four or five centuries. Although Latin left its stamp on some aspects of the Brythonic languages, it receded before Celtic speech. Old values, old ways of looking at Land and people, regained their authority in everyday life. Conditions were ripe for the flowering of the Second Golden Age of the Celts, or, in Alan Stivell's words, "Keltia Two."

The Christian seeds that had been sown by the Roman presence grew vigorously even without further guidance from Rome. The Gospel message had become sufficiently assimilated into the Celtic view of things that it no longer felt like an import from a foreign culture. And the British Isles, though abandoned by Rome, were not cut off from the outside world. Maritime trade still linked them to the great cities of the East, which had not yet suffered the same calamities as the western Empire. Priests from Syria, monks from Egypt came to replenish the failing ranks of Roman-trained clergy. It was not a bureaucratic, hierarchical, purely exoteric church these newcomers emphasized; on the contrary, their accent on individual free will, contemplation, Divine blessing through Nature, and on faith lived in community awoke echoes at the most fundamental levels of the Celtic consciousness.

Monastic communities based on Egyptian prototypes, but fulfill-

ing an essentially Celtic impulse, popped up everywhere like mush-
rooms after rain. The origin of the spread can be traced to Saint
Illtud, who was, according to the author of the *Vita Sancti Samsonis*,
"by birth a good magician," a druid, whose many communities established in South Wales inspired his illustrious disciples—Saint
Samson, Saint Cadfan, and Saint Dewi, the future patron of Wales—
to go out and found new communities of their own. But it was in
Ireland, where the Free Celtic spirit had never been troubled by submission to Rome, that the monastic movement blossomed most
spectacularly. As the native guardians of religious tradition, the druids
and bards came to identify more and more with the Christian message and transferred something of the inspiration of their schools to
the new monasteries, a new dynamism took hold of society, which
focused on the ideal of monastic life. Clonard, Clonfert, Clonmac-
noise, Glendalough, Killeany—each one rose to be a center of intense spiritual activity, and then scattered its fertile seed to the four
quarters. Ireland, once on the margin of the Celtic world, had become, in all respects, its heartland.

It was easier for the Celts to relate to the principles of monasticism than to a hierarchical, institutionalized Church run by bishops.
A monastery was like a newly-formed tribe, held together by kinship. The abbot was the chieftain, and the monks were his adopted
children, who owed him respect and obedience as head of their kin
group. Bishops had to be invested so that new priests could be or-
dained—the celebration of the Eucharist was, after all, the sacred ritual focus of Christian life—but their authority was considerably less
than an abbot's. As spiritual master and guide, the abbot's influence
extended not only over his disciples but also across the countryside,
as far as people could walk to visit the community and partake of the
Holy Sacrament there. Thus, each monastery became the center of
Christian life for a whole territory, radiating its own specific aura
and its own style defined by the rules its abbot had set.

Young warrior-aristocrats felt drawn to the heroism of the spiritual life, to the feats of asceticism holy men could achieve—not from
hatred of the flesh, but from a passion to consciously control the entire body-mind organism. Endurance in the face of pain and fear in
battle they were already familiar with; endurance in the face of un-

conscious impulses seemed yet a greater dare. That so many apparently succeeded in meeting the challenge and became saints of evident spiritual power attracted other men and women to follow their example. Whether they lived in self-sufficient communities modeled after prosperous Celtic farmhouses, or chose to be alone to immerse themselves in the pristine beauty of the natural world, where the light of the Divine still shone undimmed by material ambitions, they renewed the excitement of purpose, adventurous courage, and creative desire in their society.

All of these elements were expressed with dazzling force in the life of Saint Colm Cille of Iona—Columba, the Dove of the Church, who in his youth had been Criomhthann, the beast of prey. A warrior-aristocrat who could have been High King, a bard fully aware of the resources of his pagan heritage, a fiery and incisive speaker, as well as a psychic gifted with second sight, he put all this in the service of his one transcendent vision. After establishing a number of communities in his native Ireland, usually on sites already sacred from pagan worship, he chose—in penance, some say—to turn his back on his beloved homeland, to become *Cúl ri hÉirinn*, as he is called in his poem, and sailed across the sea with twelve companions to an ancient place of power off the coast of Britain, there to contend with its spirit-guardians for the future distribution of its Otherworld resources. This settlement and re-consecration of the island of Iona would have profound consequences for the destiny of the Celtic world, and its effect can still be felt today.

In Colm Cille we find the true fusion of the two halves of the Celtic tradition: the fundamental druidic view of Tribe, Land, and Otherworld, and the Christian thrust towards salvation and the Kingdom of God embrace in conscious yearning for each other, as their energies mingle. When Colm's follower Odhran, at his abbot's suggestion, willingly had himself buried alive to secure the ancient spirit-forces of the place for his community's goals, it was a classic human sacrifice faithful to the pagan ideology governing such things; yet, what it gained from the Otherworld was entry into a higher plane than the old ceremonies had ever taken into account. The Old Way, smoothly and inexorably, came under the tutelage of the New Lord. Lugh, the champion-god of the Tribe, became Saint Michael and continued to watch over the Land from his sacred tors. The nurturing Goddess was mirrored in many a holy abbess, and ultimately in the Mother of God herself. The Celtic cross—the symbol of the Sun and seasons allied with the memory of Christ's passion—became the governing image of this Second Celtic Golden Age, and its familiar shape multiplied in blessing over every new community established by enthusiasts of the spirit along the coasts of the West. In his uncompromising integrity of vision, his openness to experiencing the Divine in the beauty of untamed nature, his concern for his followers, his tenderness towards animals, his intellectual grasp of all issues of faith, and his mystical conversations with angels, Colm Cille was the perfect master of that age, the embodiment of its spiritual ideal.

Colm died in 597. At the assembly of Druim Ceat in 580 he had argued successfully for the preservation of the bardic schools, thus ensuring once and for all that Christianization would not cut the Celtic tradition away from its roots, that the language of ancestral myth would remain vivid and accessible even to Christian seekers. After his death Iona was still a shining testimonial to that synthesis, a beacon that many saw and followed. But already storm clouds were on the horizon. The English, again, began to gnaw at Celtic territories. By the turn of the seventh century they had thrown their might against the northern British kingdoms in Strathclyde and Rheged. The *Gwyr y Gogledd*, the Men of the North, put up a heroic defense that fired the imagination of Welsh poets, but in the end, they failed. Taliesin's laments for Urien Rheged still echo through the ages, and scattered words and place-names in Cumbria remain to tell us that it was, not so long ago, a Celtic land.

Farther south, the English continued to push the British westward. In 577 they reached the mouth of the Severn, thus cutting the Celts of Devon and Cornwall off from the Celts of Wales. Hordes of refugees sought shelter farther and farther west and, in the end, across the sea. Already British Celts had begun to settle in Armorica, which had never recovered from Julius Caesar's genocide. Now the colony's population swelled with new arrivals from Cornwall, Devon, and South Wales. So predominant did their language and culture become in their new homeland that the whole territory would take on the name of Brittany, or Lesser Britain. For the first time in centuries, a vigorous Free Celtic presence had returned to the Continent.

Some of the refugees continued southward, and settled on the northwest coast of Spain, in the old territory of the Gallaeci, which the Suevi had claimed at the fall of the western Empire. This entity became known as Galicia, and for over a century it would bring the spirit of Celtic Christianity to the region. Unfortunately, surrounded as they were by Romance-speakers, and under growing pressure from the Roman Church, the Galicians gave up their language and fell out of the Celtic continuum. After the Council of Toledo in 633 the Roman hierarchy was again in control of the area's communities, and the assimilation of the Galicians had become irreversible. Yet they instilled a certain Celtic lyricism into the early Romance poetry of the region, and have retained an obscure sense of Celtic identity to this day.

Although Ireland was still beyond the reach of the English, some population shifts could be felt there, too. Irish colonists—in the same movement that brought Colm Cille and his disciples to Iona—established the kingdom of Dál Riada in northern Britain, thus creating the embryo of what would become Scotland. The monastic movement flourished there as it had in the old country: communities sprang up all along the coast, and deep in the wilds of Pictland.

Meanwhile, in the German-held lands of what had been the Empire, the Roman Church was struggling to reinstate itself as the central institution of the Western world. Pagan tribes like the Franks and Burgundians eventually consented to be baptized; but the Church's hold on them was insecure, and they had little of the political sophistication necessary to build a state. Much work needed to be done, including the re-evangelization of the countryside, the promotion of literacy, and the stabilization of society, which the Church, with its meager resources, was quite incapable of doing. So it was with a mixture of relief and alarm that it welcomed the steady stream of Celtic missionaries that began to explore the Continent late in the sixth century. The Celts celebrated Easter on a different date; their tonsure was a different style; they used the Gallican liturgy instead of the Roman one; and there was a host of minor ritual aberrations to which they remained stubbornly attached, despite any amount of censure. Yet—at least for a while, despite some initial clashes—Rome was willing to overlook their peculiarities, because it could not duplicate the work they did.

Still, for all the service it received from the Celts, the Church's attitude toward them remained exploitative rather than accepting. It needed more docile people, with no Christian tradition of their own, to groom as secular partners in the rebuilding of the state. Its choice fell on the Franks and, soon after, on the English. In the 590s Augustine of Canterbury began his mission in Kent, calling the English into the fold of Rome.

Although the British, who were fighting for their lives, felt little inclination to evangelize their enemies, the Irish did not suffer from such circumstances. They welcomed Englishmen into their monasteries, and went as missionaries into English territory. In 635 King Oswald of Northumbria, who had taken refuge on Iona when fleeing from a usurper at home, called Saint Aidan from that famous community to preach the Gospel among his people, and gave him the island of Lindisfarne for a monastic site. Modeled after Iona but inhabited by both English and Irish monks, Lindisfarne became a vital, uniquely creative center of Celtic spirituality. There, it seems, through a cross-fertilization of traditions, the Celtic school of manuscript illumination had its beginning. Basic Egyptian styles of knot work, enhanced by the Celtic fascination for complex forms and the Germanic love of color and contrast, developed into a powerful, abstract language of mystic vision, and spread back to Ireland through the monasteries of the Columban tradition, to culminate in that unequaled expression of Celtic genius, the Book of Kells. Collaboration between Celts and Englishmen did, indeed, have potential. We see a more modest instance of it in the Sutton Hoo burial, with its suggestion of easy cooperation between English rulers and Celtic craftsmen, as well as evidence of contacts with Egypt and the Levant.

It was not long before the Roman missionaries working in the English south entered into conflict with the northerners who had received their Christianity from the Celts. Despite the enlightened recommendations of Pope Gregory, an eventual repudiation of the Celtic side was inevitable; Rome could not, in the end, tolerate the existence of another tradition with its own separate authority. For the Celts, although they had never denied the spiritual primacy of Rome, would not recognize the right of the Roman Church to meddle in local affairs, or to impose conformity in matters of ritual; and they certainly felt no inclination to participate in the building of a state that contradicted everything in their own culture. The final confrontation came when the King of Northumbria married a Roman-educated Kentish princess. The differences in their religious practice, especially the celebration of Easter on different dates, caused tension at court, and eventually led to a need for official arbitration. At the Synod of Whitby in 664 Rome and Iona contended with each other, and Iona lost. The authority of Columba proved less formidable to the Northumbrian king than what the Romans claimed to be the authority of Peter. As a result, the break between England and Keltia widened, and could no longer be healed. The Irish monks left Lindisfarne. The English, now wholly in Rome's hands, could be perfected as the Roman Church's tool to affirm its authority throughout the British Isles.

Although Whitby and Iona's capitulation to its decisions circa 700 marks the beginning of Celtic Christianity's decline, after which many Celtic churchmen would devote themselves to spreading Roman values and concepts in their society, the spiritual fervor and artistic creativity of Celtic communities would remain strong for some centuries. What would bring the Second Golden Age of the Celts to an end would be not only pressure from Rome, but, once again, the explosion of the Germanic heartland.

Scandinavia had been far outside the scope of the Empire's conquering ambitions, and Christian missions had not reached it. Thus, in its culture and outlook, it had become quite alien to the rest of Europe. In the eighth century, by the operations of that cycle of climatic change and population growth which always seems to have affected the northlands, Scandinavian landholders unable to support themselves on the resources of their land organized expeditions to raid the fabled rich countries of the south. This was not only a repeat of the situation that had helped Julius Caesar's campaign, but also the last wave of barbarian scavengers who had come to pick over the bones of the Empire. Soon the sight of the Vikings's long ships at the mouth of a harbor, making for the walls of a monastery or one of the newly reestablished towns, became a familiar harbinger of panic, burning, and violent death.

But none suffered as much from these raids as the monastic communities of the Celts. Established during a time of peace on sites chosen for their isolation and freedom from secular interference, they were now out of help's reach and impossible to defend. The gold and jewels of the reliquaries and gospel-covers, the rich gifts from the East, were a powerful lure to Viking raiders, who knew they would find little effective opposition. Iona was sacked several times. Red martyrdom—giving up one's life in the steadfastness of one's faith—had, until then, been unknown in the Celtic Church; after the Vikings arrived, it became a test clerics might face any day.

Many, of course, could not meet that challenge. They left the insecurity of their monasteries for a less hazardous career of missionary work on the Continent, following in the footsteps of more adventurous predecessors like Columbanus, Gall, and Fursa. Celtic missionaries were still prized by the Roman Church, and would be for some centuries, for the brilliance and erudition of the Irish schools had nowhere been equaled. But as the work of the missionaries succeeded in re-Christianizing Europe and something of the old security returned to society, their influence with the Church hierarchy began to dwindle. Continental bishops overseeing a revitalized Church network no longer lacking for clergy had less need to import Celtic auxiliaries, and thus had less tolerance for theological idiosyncracies like the Celtic accent on free will and free conscience. These, essentially, were the aspects of John Scot Eriugena's theology that led to his condemnation, and perhaps to his murder, although he was surely the most brilliant thinker in ninth-century Europe. Nothing better exemplifies the clash between the Celtic spirit of adventure and the Roman spirit of legalism than the matters that, in the eighth century, pitted Saint Ferghil, the Irish-born bishop of Salzburg, a teacher fascinated by mathematics and scientific speculation, against Saint Boniface, a stolid Germanic prelate obsessed with doing things by the rules. Because Ferghil, in his time, was still irreplaceable, he did not suffer much in the conflict; other missionaries from across the sea were less fortunate.

The Roman Church had gone a long way toward reconstructing

the state. Using the Franks as an ethnic power base, it had proclaimed a Holy Roman Empire—hardly a good facsimile of the
Empire that had been, but a potent symbol of order and stability
nevertheless. The Franks, as the secular guarantors of that stability,
had the Church's tacit support as they extended their hegemony
over all the lands that had been Gaul. For a brief period they occupied Brittany—whose attachment to native Christian practices and
traditions caused constant friction with Rome—until the Breton
chieftain Nomenoe, at the battle of Ballon in 845, drove the invaders
out and secured a precarious independence for his land that would
last to the end of the Middle Ages. Still, over much of western Europe, a process of cultural uniformity was encouraged: Franks,
Burgundians, and Visigoths switched from their Germanic tongues
to the Vulgar Latin of the locals, and adopted a hierarchical system
of land-rulership—universally recognized, through the Church's ap-
proving influence—that gave social and political interactions a
dependable pattern. Thus feudalism was established, as a poor but
functional substitute for the intricacies of the old Empire's administration; and because, as a system, it included opportunities to concentrate power, it had the potential to develop into a more absolute,
centralized form of the state. The Celts, for as long as they remained
free, were outside that system.

   In Britain, the English played much the same role in imposing
uniformity and faithfulness to Rome's vision as the Franks did on
the Continent. For in the eyes of the Church administration Britain
and Ireland were a single province, which, ideally, should be a single
unit in terms of political rule as well; and the English were the perfect tool for bringing about such a simplification. After the gradual
coalescing of a united England, there would be a united Britain, and
then a united British Isles. By the close of the first millenium A.D.,
England had driven the Welsh west to the Severn, obtained the submission of the last Cumbrian holdouts in the north, and annexed
Cornwall. Scotland was a problem, since it had grown into a strong
kingdom itself, through the merging of the Gaels and the Picts. A
Celtic-speaking entity thus far opaque to English penetration, it
could not, as yet, be conquered by military means alone.

   The Vikings, too, remained a problem, but one more easily

solved. By and large they were not cultural colonists; when they established holdings on foreign soil, they were looking for material advancement and economic security, not seeking to impose their language and worldview on those they had conquered. They were only too happy, once they had discovered the rewards involved, to abandon their old ways and adopt the culture of their new homeland. The Church offered them political recognition in exchange for their allegiance, a bait they quickly took. Even the raiders whose homesteads were still in Scandinavia discovered that, as Europe's market-towns grew in sophistication and complexity (and in defensibility), they would gain more as Christian traders, within the system, than as heathen enemies, eternally on the outside, thieving for less and less profit. It was easy for the Church to exploit that vacillation. By the eleventh century Scandinavia was securely Christian, the final prize in Rome's sweep of the Germanic world.

Before long it became apparent that the Normans—the aristocracy of Viking settlers outside Scandinavia—were so well attuned to the Church's vision of an orderly, centralized feudalism that they were destined to become Rome's main political instrument, superseding earlier alliances when necessary. Norman dynasties gradually gained control of Frankish lands. In 1066 Norman rule was brought to England, and with it a foreign bishop, Lanfranc, who proceeded to administer the religious communities of Britain and Ireland from Canterbury with complete disregard for linguistic, cultural, and traditional differences. Norman bishops and abbots everywhere enforced uniformity of custom and practice. And Ireland, although it had not been invaded by a foreign army, bowed to Roman authority. At the Synod of Kells in 1152 all vestiges of Celtic Christian nonconformism were officially abolished. With this event the Second Golden Age of the Celts came to a formal close.

However, even as the last Free Celts were losing control of their political destiny, and their influence over European institutions was fading, new expressions of the Celtic tradition began, in an insidious, subterranean fashion, to pervade the thought of the Western world. For one thing, the adoption of Christianity, a religion based on the study of sacred writings, had weakened the Celtic taboo on writing down matters of spiritual importance. Though at first writing was done only in Latin, with all literature in native tongues still transmitted orally, as tradition dictated, there gradually came about reasons—the need to gloss difficult passages in the Scriptures, for instance—to put Celtic words down on parchment. From there, it was an easy step to recording brief passages of poetry; clever verses that were not destined to become part of larger compositions, but were too good to consign to oblivion. And at last, though the oral medium retained its primary importance in the tradition of the bards, the taboo was discarded altogether. Literacy in Celtic languages became a widespread reality just in time, for the Norman infiltration of all monastic communities promised to dilute their Celtic character, end their unofficial links with bardism, and cause a great number of oral traditions, formerly taken for granted, to disappear. It was surely, in part, anxiety over the fate of the native tradition that led so many of the old mythological tales from pre-Christian times to be committed to writing for the first time between the ninth and thirteenth centuries, although many of them were recomposed to conform to a new Christian reality. Thus the heroic deeds of the *Táin*, the magical transformations of Étaín, the cruel death of Conaire Mór, the twilight existence of the *fianna*, the wild imagery of Mael Dúin's voyage—and, a little later, the jeweled world of the Mabinogi—were preserved for posterity just as the memory of the people began to falter.

On the other hand, Breton bards familiar with Norman French discovered that their repertoire of stories could, in translation, have a mesmerizing effect on audiences in the great feudal courts of the Continent. Something in the Celtic material, it seems, spoke to a deep need in the soul of Europe at the time. For the Church had, by the twelfth century, succeeded brilliantly in its project: there was political stability, cities were growing, individuals could enjoy a level of comfort and independence unprecedented since the fall of the Empire. With this increase in comfort and independence came a craving for intellectual stimulation and new channels of self-realization, which the Church's rigid authority could not entirely satisfy. The first Crusade had opened the door to another world full of unreconciled cultural differences, a cornucopia of traditions that the intellectual elite of the West seized upon eagerly: Sufism, Persian esotericism, alchemy from Egypt, Qabalah from the Jews of Spain, the many faces of astrology—all these systems hinted at knowledge to be gained from human nature itself, available to any individual of good-will, whether the Church approved or disapproved. The rediscovery of Classical philosophy, including Aristotle, but also Plato and the Neo-Platonists, conferred a new dignity upon the strivings of the human intellect. There seemed to have been a wisdom of the ages, expressing itself through many symbols in different cultures, but ba-sically one, built into the fabric of Creation. And now the Celtic tales added their own array of suggestive symbolism, exotic yet from a source close to home: sacred kings and queens, castles of perilous testing, mysterious exchanges with the Otherworld, cauldrons of re-birth, shape-shifters, magicians, and fairies. It mattered little that the Breton, Cornish, and Welsh storytellers had woven their traditions around Arthur, their redeemer-hero, for political reasons; there was a deeper level of underlying ancient myth, which had a powerful im-pact on any sophisticated audience. So the Arthurian mythos entered the literature of most Western languages and, little by little, impreg-nated the Western mind with Celtic ideas about love, women, nature, and the sacred.

The Church, meanwhile, fought back against the pluralist, "heretical" tendencies that were appearing in society. ("Heresy," after all, means "choice.") The best way to affirm its authority seemed to be through a greater concentration of the powers of the state, work-ing in close harmony with the Church hierarchy. The Albigensian Crusade of 1209 steeped the south of France in an unforgetable blood-bath, cast a pall of fear over the rest of Europe, and sent all noncom-formist spiritual seekers underground. Although no one yet realized it, the stable spirit of feudalism had died; but the paranoia that comes with social change seemed to justify the Church's hounding of all those who in any way challenged the status quo. The great sover-eigns of Europe—the kings of England and France, the Holy Roman emperor of Germany—were acting to consolidate their personal power and enlarge the territories they ruled directly, often at the ex-pense of vassals and neighbors. So the relative peace of the twelfth century gave way to centuries of war that were wider in scope and more damaging.

The Celts, as ever, were the great losers in this process. Free Wales vanished in 1284 with the Statute of Rhuddlan, two years after Llywelyn the Last was beheaded in a field in Cilmeri. Scotland remained an unconquered kingdom, but already in the eleventh century, the Hungarian-raised, English-descended Queen Margaret had influenced it in favor of international, Norman-feudal practices, a process which her successors continued until, by the end of the Middle Ages, the country's original Celtic culture was ridiculed and marginalized in the wild, poor Highlands, while the wealthier classes in the Lowlands adopted a northern dialect of English and called it "Scots." Brittany managed to walk the political tightrope between England and France, though even there the upper class, pressured by powerful neighbors, was beginning to turn toward Norman-French culture. And, beginning in 1167, the Anglo-Normans were nibbling away at Ireland, displacing clans from their ancestral land.

Celtic culture, however, though attenuated and provincialized, continued to flower locally. For while the Norman overlords were rigid in matters of political and religious authority, they did not seek to change the language and customs of their subjects. Religious plays in Cornish were enacted on village fairgrounds. Generations of Uí Dálaigh poets illustrated the virtues of the bardic schools in Connacht. Welsh bards, the last guardians of a beleaguered tradition, developed a mythology around the sixth-century poet Taliesin, making him into a twice-born figure of enlightenment, and the focus of all that remained of the old way of the druids. In the tumultuous fourteenth century, from amidst the carnage of wars, heresy hunts, and the Black Death, the voice of the great Welsh poet Dafydd ap Gwilym sounds a clear and hopeful note with its praise of unspoiled nature, human vitality, and human wit.

Before the end of the Middle Ages the Welsh made a few valiant attempts to regain their independence, culminating at the turn of the fifteenth century with Owain Glyn Dwr's meteoric campaign—a campaign very nearly successful, cut short only by his mysterious decline and disappearance. And though, in popular belief, he went to join the Land's other redeemer-heroes in sleep under Eryri (and will perhaps awaken with them to save their people at the last) no leader emerged after him to speak for Wales on Europe's battlefields. The feudal kingdoms of the West turned into modern States, testing and defining their borders, bringing all their institutions under central control, and prescribing a standardized set of allegiances for their citizens; Wales had lost its chance to be counted among the states. The Welsh spent the last fire of their patriotism in backing Henry Tudor, trusting one of their own on the throne of England, and never recovered, as a nation, from the catastrophic results. The Tudors dedicated themselves entirely to the consolidation of the state they had inherited, on the cold, purely administrative terms the Church had already favored, with no regard or even tolerance for ethnic realities. English was the language of social and economic power; so they adopted English as the sole language of the state, and denied non-English communities within their borders the right to use their own languages. The Welsh language and traditions, in so far as they constituted an autonomous focus of concern within the state's borders, were to be actively opposed. Under Tudor rule the term "British" first appeared, meaning not, as it always had until then, the Celts native to the island, but all inhabitants of the kingdom ruled from London, and their standardized, *English* culture. Thus, an intentional confusion would occur between the terms *Britain* and *England*, with the part commonly being taken to mean the whole.

The first Celtic countermove to this process was the Cornish Rebellion of 1497, led by Thomas Flamank and Myghal an Gof in protest of Cornwall's forced support of the English military campaign against Scotland. A Cornish army set against the might of England was not, perhaps, likely to win, but the rebels got close enough to London to cause the government some concern. What was brought brutally home to Cornwall—and to all other parts of the English state's nascent empire—was that communities would live less and less to fulfill their own needs and purposes, but rather would serve the interests of an elite in a far-off, culturally alien capital.

The French state, beginning its own empire-building expansion, gained control of Brittany, first through military intimidation at the battle of Saint-Aubin-du-Cormier in 1488, then through the marriage of Anne, Duchess of Brittany, to King Charles VIII of France in 1491 and to his successor Louis XII in 1499. Duchess Anne, a strong-willed, patriotic sovereign, fought hard to prevent this union of the crowns from bringing about the complete curtailment of Brittany's autonomy. The Treaty of 1532, while formalizing France's annexation of Brittany, guaranteed the maintenance of Breton institutions, including a parliament, and exempted Bretons from military service outside their country. But in the centuries that followed, the French treated this document with contempt, violated its terms without qualm, and fought many of their wars with Breton blood.

The growth of the cities as centers of a non-feudal socioeconomic system had eroded the bases of the medieval order. Money rather than land became the primary factor of power and influence in society, through an emerging banking system that was in the hands of a strong and increasingly independent merchant class. The strain that the Church, by its greed, corruption, and institutionalized hypocrisy, put on society in its attempt to control these developments led to the final collapse of the West's spiritual unity. The cultural atmosphere changed in a profound way: in their newfound material security and their (material) hopes for a better future, people were no longer quite so troubled by the Pope's anathema; and some states, even, were beginning to find their close cooperation with Rome burdensome. Ignited in different places for different reasons, the spirit of the Reformation swept across Europe, placing millions of people beyond Rome's control and shattering forever the dream of a united, Church-ruled empire. But it took over two centuries for Europe to accept the permanence of the change; and whole generations were put to death savagely as Catholic states still loyal to Rome fought it out with Protestant states.

The Celts did not choose their sides in this conflict; sides were chosen for them by the states who had taken over their destinies. The Welsh, after some initial resistance, found themselves in the Protestant camp; the Irish, sustained by promises of political support from Catholic powers, remained faithful to Rome, and suffered for it. In Scotland, the Anglicized elite in the Lowlands embraced a particularly dour form of the teachings of Calvin and used it to attack the vestiges of Celtic culture in the Highlands. As Catholic France and Protestant England became enemies, the Celtic nations they ruled were pulled apart from each other. Brittany, once in close contact with Cornwall and Wales, found itself cut off from the rest of the

Celtic world. And Ireland's Catholicism caused a rift to open between it and the Celtic nations where Protestantism triumphed. This deep wound to Celtic unity has never been healed.

One great good, however unintentional, was done to Wales in this context. Although they were, in theory, committed to imposing English as a standard everywhere, the rulers of Britain thought spreading Protestantism was a more urgent task, and could not go about it realistically in Wales without using Welsh, since most of the population spoke no English at all. So in 1588 a Welsh Bible appeared, and a Welsh liturgy, and the language's position at the center of social life found itself strengthened. The Cornish, however, despite their second, religious-based rebellion in 1542 and their forceful refusal of an English-language liturgy, were not so fortunate. Dismissed as too small a nation to be a political threat, they were never granted a Bible and a service in their tongue; as a result, their cultural identity eroded rapidly until, at the turn of the eighteenth century, with the birth of its last generation of speakers in the extreme west of the country, the Cornish language was moribund.

Since they resisted the state with so much more determination, the Irish were not treated as considerately as the Welsh. The Uí Néill and the Uí Dhomhnaill, descendants of High Kings, organized a military venture against the English, which failed and forced the Irish aristocracy to flee to the Continent in 1602, thus leaving the nation without its traditional leaders. Unwilling to trust a gradual missionizing process in Irish, the English resorted to a more radical method: plantation, the deliberate flooding of at least one part of the country—Ulster, the traditional hotbed of native rebellion—with Protestant, English-speaking colonists who dispossessed the local population and established a two-tier, racist social order based on fear and contempt for the conquered. The Cromwellian purges, which left deep scars on all English-ruled lands, further weakened the vestiges of the Celtic system in Ireland; and the Penal Laws, making pariahs of all Catholics, condemned most native Irish to the lowest, poorest strata of the state hierarchy.

So the last of the Irish bards, deprived of their aristocratic patrons, and prisoners of a society increasingly blind to their tradition, found themselves facing the death of all they held most dear. The great Aogán O Raithille and his contemporaries put their poetic gift in the service of their *aisling*, or vision: their experience of a beautiful woman, archetypally lovable but ill-used, crying for redress but with little assurance of obtaining it. This was the Land-goddess, bidding a final farewell to those who still implicitly believed in her. O Raithille could still hope for the success of the Jacobite cause; a generation later, Art Mac Cumhaigh would see no solution but to have the Goddess take him away with her to the Otherworld.

It is easy, today, to see the flimsiness and hopelessness of the Jacobite cause, to dismiss the inefficiency of its leaders, and to understand that the Protestant merchant class who ran the English state would never again grant power to a Catholic monarch. The Scottish-descended, French-influenced Stewarts, rulers of both England and Scotland since the union of the crowns in 1603, had been driven from the realm for their Catholic tendencies and unambiguously defeated at the Battle of the Boyne in 1690. But to the native Irish and Highland Scots the image of the rightful ruler in exile easily acquired a mythic aura, and became the promise of a redeemer-hero who would restore ancestral rights and bring peace at last. The Pretender took on the traits of the tribal God, the true consort of the Land-goddess. Countless songs, *aislingí,* bear witness to the almost religious fervor the cause inspired in both Scotland and Ireland. When in 1707 the wealthy Anglicized ruling classes of the Lowlands engineered the abolition of the Scottish Parliament, despite opposition of much of the people, thus binding Scotland's destiny to that of "Britain" (that is, England), the alienation of the Gaelic-speaking Highlands reached an extreme point and concentrated all hopes on a Jacobite victory. But those hopes were dashed with brutal finality on Culloden field in 1746: Celtic tribal warriors armed with weapons from their heroic prehistory were thrown helter-skelter by inept foreign strategists at the state-of-the-art firepower of the English state's army. Swords and individual bravery were nothing in the face of cannon and bayonets. The most proudly held values of Celtic culture were ground into the dust, and never rose up again from the gore of that battle and from the genocidal fury that followed. In its last stand, the Celtic tribal world had its back broken. The language, dress, and customs of the Highlanders that survived were proscribed. Their allegiance to Roman Catholicism was shaken, and collapsed in most places. A numb despair settled over all the Gaelic communities of Ireland and Scotland. Although Ireland would flare up briefly again in 1798, led by English-speaking Protestant intellectuals, this was not a Celtic development; it had its roots in the political aspirations of the international merchant classes, and—unintentionally, perhaps—exploited the vestigial hopes of the Gaelic peasantry to prod them into a conflict they did not understand. Far from gaining a greater autonomy, Ireland lost its colonial parliament in 1800 and, in turn, became a part of "Britain."

For the world order continued to change, inexorably, in favor of the merchant-classes. The opening up of the New World and its incredible wealth of resources brought in an unprecedented increase in capital—and with it, power—to those who had gained control over them. Freed from the Church's long-standing prohibition of usury, businessmen in Protestant countries built, on the foundations of interest banking, the first manifestation of the modern capitalist system. The system proved to be such an efficient means of concentrating power that soon even Catholic areas, held by rigid Counter Reformation bureaucracy, found themselves obliged to compromise their principles in order to keep abreast of the shifts in the world balance. But to the rising bourgeoisie—whatever their private religious affiliations—the political confrontation between Catholic and Protestant nations was irrelevant and bad for business; everywhere the merchant classes worked at stripping away the last remnants of feudal privilege and taking over the machinery of the state for their own use. With the explosion of France in 1789—the fall of the monarchy and break of the Church's authority—the world's Catholic-Protestant alignments lost their meaning; Reason—the analytic intellect unhampered by subjective participation—was enthroned as culture's guiding principle, and the stage was set for capital to rule unchecked by spiritual considerations. Though in its earliest phases the French Revolution stressed the rights of the individual and showed a populist concern for the aspirations of local communities, it was rapidly seduced by the coercive possibilities of the French state, and created an administrative model far more centralized and intrusive than that which had preceded it. And Brittany, after siding

with the revolutionaries in the hope of achieving national liberation, found its last autonomous institutions abolished, its existence as
an entity denied, its language proscribed, and its deep sense of the sacred trampled upon by the atheist state. Small wonder that the
Bretons began a counter-revolutionary insurgency, which the French
crushed. For the two centuries that followed, the French state has
unrelentingly reviled and persecuted all manifestations of Breton national identity.

Throughout the Western world, then, the spirit of capitalism won
over the hearts of the social elite. Money, rather than land or lineage,
became the absolute indicator of status. A single-minded preoccupation with material concerns led to a view of the natural world as an
inert, unconscious continuum—devoid of spiritual, subjective elements—to be shaped by human whims; which in turn encouraged
the emergence of the scientific method, allowing—with the help of
new accumulations of capital—the development of sophisticated,
vastly productive technologies, bringing in yet more wealth. Materialism, made arrogant by success, denounced as "superstition" any
challenges to its philosophical authority, and depreciated the experience of past generations. Only the quantifiable was accepted as
"real." Human beings, encouraged to disbelieve in spiritual transcendence of the material state and in the interconnectedness of all
things in spiritual destiny, became alienated from their environment,
their fellow living creatures, and, increasingly, from each other. In the
Protestant countries, freed from the Church's normative influence,
this worldview and its economic consequences progressed most
rapidly, and left their mark on Celtic communities. Though the
Welsh, with both Bible and worship in their tongue, kept a strong
and dynamic link between faith and community, and Though the
development of Quakerism and especially Methodism returned to a
deeply felt, transforming spirituality, as witnessed by the quiet mysti-
cism of Ann Griffiths and the sincerity of the hymns William Williams
Pantycelyn, still they could not avoid, in the very heat of their "reformation," a turning-away not only from their personal past but also from
their past as a nation, and thus from some of the richest aspects of their
tradition. Even the little Isle of Man, which was stubbornly sure of
its national identity despite centuries of Norse, Scottish, and English

rule, and which in 1775 obtained—as Cornwall had never been able to—a Bible in its own language, fell prey to the spirit of the age. Even as he sowed the seeds of a renewed spiritual life in the souls of those who came to listen, John Wesley, in his mission to the Isle of Man, denounced the existence of the Manx language as an obstacle to progress. The social elite of the island believed him: in less than two generations, the language was in decline, neglected in all spheres of public life (except for ceremonial occasions) in favor of English, and with it the unique and ancient traditions of the land—Norse subverted by Celtic—began to wither away as well.

With the secularization of France and the eclipse of Spain, Catholicism ceased to be a political threat to the English state, so by 1820 it was judged safe to restore basic rights to Catholics living in English-occupied territories, and the native Irish thus found themselves emancipated from the Penal Laws. This could have signaled a period of prosperity and self-assurance for Ireland, but actual events took a quite different turn. Anti-Irish racism continued unabated. The Roman Church, eager to occupy the mainstream of "British" society, attacked the Irish language and pressured Irish-speakers to teach only English to their children—a process in which the English state gladly cooperated. Then, in the 1840s, when Irish cultural confusion was at its height, the Famine struck. As the potato crop—the sole food permitted to small tenant farmers—blackened and rotted away, a million Irishmen starved to death under the cold eye of the English government, and a million more fled to survival in America, never to return. Although private charities attempted to help, the authorities were content to shake their heads and accuse the Irish of improvidence and pointed to the Famine as one more consequence of the backwardness of the Irish temperament and the negative influence of the Irish language. (For all that, the tenant farmers had little choice in the disposal of their crops, which, with the exception of the potatoes, were slated by their Protestant landlords for the export market.) And, in their agony, the Irish believed them; "Irishness" was the cause of their downfall, and had made them incapable of standing up to the successful English. Almost overnight, Irish-speakers blocked the language from their minds, and forced broken English upon themselves and their children. The links with the past, with

tradition, with the Land were broken, violently. The despairing
flight to America went on and on, generation after generation.
Sadly, the only element of their identity the Irish still clung to was
their allegiance to the Roman Church, which by the latter half of
the nineteenth century impressed them with a narrow, authoritarian, life-denying Jansenist ideology that could no longer be miti-
gated by the life-affirming Celtic tradition. The magnitude of this
cultural suicide left Ireland with a trauma that has not been healed to
this day. Only in the shrinking Gaeltachtaí of Connemara, Tír
Chonaill, and West Munster did natural Irish-speaking communities
survive; but even there, many lived only with the dream of the boat
to America, the hope of escaping the stagnation of a land with no
future.

   In Scotland, although open persecution of the Gaels by the state
ceased in 1784, the failure of the Jacobite cause robbed Gaelic society of any clear vision of the future. The chieftains of the Highland
clans, opting for Anglicization and the capitalist order, betrayed their
kin by giving over their land to large-scale business exploitation.
During the first half of the nineteenth century the infamous Highland Clearances, in which thousands of Gaelic-speaking crofters
were forced out of their homes and sent (those who did not die on
the roads) to exile in Canada, bled Gaelic Scotland dry as efficiently
as the Famine killed Ireland. Everywhere the centralized economy,
stressing heavy industry and the needs of the cities, drove marginal
rural areas into depression, and Celtic populations into emigration.
The Cornish, by and large, went to Michigan, and to Australia; the
Manx to Ohio; the Bretons to Quebec. After generations of Welshmen had settled in Pennsylvania and parts of the Midwest, an effort
was made, beginning in 1865, to establish a full-scale Welsh-speaking
colony in Patagonia; but even this *Gwladfa*, after a brilliant start, was
forced to assimilate by the cultural centralism of the expanding
Argentine state. Deprived of both economic and cultural resources
by their conquerors, the Celts seemed, at last, to be facing extinction.

   However, beneath the pall of hopeless gloom, the embers of renewal were glowing. Celtic culture, threatened with final dissolution, mustered its deepest transforming resources, the mythic power

at the root of its tradition and the magic of the Cauldron of Cerridwen. The process began as a trickle, coming to life in small circles
of people and sometimes in the most unlikely places, and only gradually came to affect large sectors of the population. Because at first it
seemed no more than a harmless concern of antiquarians, it was, for
a long time, allowed to develop unmolested by the watchdogs of the
state.

Around the year 1700 the Welsh scholar Edward Lhuyd published evidence that the six modern Celtic languages were closely
related to each other, as well as to the language spoken by the Celts
of antiquity. This fact had been forgotten—a consequence of the divisions imposed by colonization, of the loss of tribal memory due to
social disruption and the decline of the bards, and of a general lack
of interest in the Celts on the part of Europe's intellectual establishment. Lhuyd's findings would begin to reverse those trends. The
term "Celt," previously used only to designate the ancient people,
became applied to the modern survivors, and thereafter stressed
what they had in common, beyond late historical differences in religion, second language, and state allegiance. And through the channel
of their native languages, the tradition of the modern Celts was seen
to stretch back into the remote past, to the mysterious wisdom of
the druids, the earliest sources of Europe. Non-Celtic intellectuals
seeking a philosophical tradition that would distance them both
from the church and the established Greco-Roman humanism
thought they might find it among the Celts, and made Celtic studies a respectable pursuit. The manuscripts of ancient tales compiled
during the Middle Ages, unread for generations, were now avidly
collected, translated, and interpreted. Slowly this international enthusiasm began to rekindle the Celts' self-respect. If their heritage
had a true worth of its own, and was not just a farrago of supersti-
tions unsuited to the rationalist present, then did they not have a
right to their identity, a right to dialogue as equals with the other
cultures of the world, whatever the state authorities might say?

An odd figure—a wizened gnome clad in outlandish fantasy
garb—appeared at the end of the eighteenth century with a frac-
tured, disconcerting message, a package of lies that conveyed, however improbably, an important truth. A south Welsh stonecutter,

Edward Williams (to be known forever after by his bardic name, Iolo
Morganwg), was driven by his passion for the old Welsh literary tradition to compose a long series of imaginative "additions" to it,
which he thought would elucidate its links with the teachings of the
bards and druids. If he had published those compositions under his
own name, they would have been considered no more than an interesting development of Welsh literature; but since he chose to present them as genuinely old documents he had found, they at once
took on the authority of antiquity, and had an extraordinary impact.
Though much of his work expresses the humanist-progressive ideals
of his generation, so keen was his imaginative intuition that he developed the imagery and diction of the old literature into a mythology not inappropriate to the spirit of the Celtic tradition, so that it
implanted itself with relative ease among Welsh-speaking intellectuals. Claiming to be a druidic initiate, Iolo devised a liturgy for his
philosophy, and organized a "church" of bards, the Gorsedd, which
engaged in ceremonies and sought to maintain the spiritual standards of Welsh culture. This body came to be the focus of the National Eisteddfod, still the main cultural institution of Welsh-speakers
to this day; and Iolo's forgeries continue to determine to a large extent what the average person anywhere in the Western world thinks
about druids. Although Celticists long ago discredited his work as a
scholar, Iolo's lesson—that myth and ritual can play a fundamental
role in reviving a culture—should not be forgotten.

Iolo was not the only one at the time to forge Celtic material;
Macpherson's *Ossian*, a period-style reworking of Scottish and Irish
Fenian mythology, reached a far wider audience and influenced the
international artistic community, especially the Romantic movement,
which sought to counteract the spread of materialism with an emphasis on subjective participation in nature, and found a ready ally in
the Celtic spirit. If *Ossian* reads like a pale fakery today, one must remember that it favorably disposed the European avant-garde toward
the idea of Celtic civilization, and led many to explore the genuine
Celtic heritage. Charlotte Brooke, an Irish Protestant fascinated by
the native tradition, collected and translated genuine Fenian lays.
Eoghan O'Curry, one of the first generation of Irish-speakers to
profit from Catholic emancipation, published the great literary monu-

ments of the Irish Middle Ages. Lady Charlotte Guest introduced the world to the *Mabinogion*. J. F. Campbell and Alexander Carmichael investigated the wealth of oral tradition that survived—though in a moribund state—in the Scottish Highlands. And Hersart de la Ville-marqué, a Breton admirer of Iolo's mythology, emulated his predecessor by forging a collection of "ancient" epic ballads for Brittany, the *Barzaz-Breiz*, which directly inspired Luzel's studies of the true Breton folk tradition, and also provided a basis for modern writing in Breton. Gradually universities—even, grudgingly, in England and France—came to recognize "Celtic" as a field worthy of serious study.

Heartened by such widespread admiration for their past achievements, living Celtic communities began to organize for survival. In the 1830s the event subsequently referred to as *Brad y Llyfrau Gleision*, The Betrayal of the Blue Books (condescending, racist documents on Wales published by the English government), led a substantial sector of the Welsh population to cultivate the Welsh national consciousness. Despite the catastrophic aftermath of the Famine, small cells of activists worked to restore interest in the Irish language, an activity which led to the founding, in 1893, of Conradh na Gaeilge. Impelled by the vision and enthusiasm of Douglas Hyde, another Protestant devoted to the Irish language, the new organization aimed to promote the use of Irish at all levels of society, and thus to re-create a self-sufficient Irish identity. During its first two decades of existence the effort met with considerable success. In 1894, An Comunn Gaidhealach was established, along the same pattern, in Scotland. Breton-speaking intellectuals came together in the *Feiz ha Breiz* movement; and, a generation later, Mona Douglas almost single-handedly steered the Manx-language tradition into a sense of its worth and need to endure.

But the most successful—and mythically charged—episode of this period was raising the Cornish language from the dead. By the turn of the nineteenth century the last generation of fluent Cornish-speakers was gone; the merchant classes of Cornwall, pressured by the development of English capitalism and buoyed by a flourishing tin industry, had succumbed to assimilation, and the rest of the population eventually followed them. Then, as cheap tin from Malaysia appeared on the market, profits from Cornish tin evaporated, the industry came close to collapse, and the country lost its primary route to economic prosperity. Cornwall was again a remote, depressed area, its people pushed into emigration or into serving the interests of outside entrepreneurs, with no more than broken fragments of tradition to shore up its ethnic identity. But their language, though now forgotten in speech, had, in happier centuries, been recorded; manuscripts survived, mostly of religious plays from the end of the Middle Ages. Only scholars, of course, could still read them; yet was it so unlikely that at last some scholars—especially those of Cornish birth—should come to view the language not as a dead museum specimen for objective study, but as a living, beloved link with the Land? One such scholar was Henry Jenner, who, from his study of the written evidence, taught himself to use the language in everyday speech, and by 1903 was able to present an oration in living Cornish before the recently-founded Celtic Congress. Jenner's revolutionary move had a galvanizing effect on many who loved Cornwall but had had no way of fully expressing their identity. As others followed his example, a Cornish-speaking community was born. A generation later, Morton Nance combined the grammar and lexicon found in the medieval texts with evidence from the last stages of the language to produce a rich "Unified Cornish" that became the new standard. Stories, poems, and essays appeared, fleshing out the language's imaginative field. Eventually children grew up with Cornish as their mother tongue. Although it has suffered rifts along linguistic and ideological lines, the Cornish movement survives, and is slowly but steadily gaining ground.

To an era of seemingly irreversible decline, loss, and despair, the miracle of Cornish brings an unprecedented message of hope. Small wonder that state-identified academics have sought to disparage and discredit it. It shows, with exhilarating definitiveness, that no thing of the spirit that has died cannot, by will and imagination, be brought back to life.

It was to be expected that wherever the Celtic cultural revival had achieved a solid base of self-confidence, it would translate itself into a political struggle. Representatives of the Celtic nations set themselves openly against the power of the state, seeking freedom through negotiation or, if that route was closed to them, through armed insurrection. The English government had made certain that the Celts could never have enough representation in Parliament to seriously influence policy (and the French, of course, did not recognize the existence of Brittany at all). The Welsh and the Scots, who in recent generations had suffered only an indirect, insidious form of persecution, by and large opted for parliamentarian nationalist movements; but in Ireland, where the fruits of ethnic hatred remained glaringly obvious, there was more widespread disillusion with what could be obtained through the "British" system. It was, to a great extent, the cultural ferment of rediscovered identity initiated by Conradh na Gaeilge that led to Patrick Pearse's mythology of blood sacrifice and the Easter 1916 rising. Though doomed from the start in purely military terms, the romantic flavor of that very Celtic gesture conveyed a mythic, archetypal message to the imagination of the Irish people. The possibility of independence was realized; the momentum was there; and—with a bloody, divisive war in between—the Irish achieved Home Rule in 1921, and a Republic in 1949. For the first time in centuries a Celtic nation had regained political sovereignty. But it was, in many respects, a Pyrrhic victory: the Irish government was taken over quickly by Anglicized bureaucrats who were implicitly hostile to the country's Celtic heritage, and did not wish to cut themselves away from the English capitalist network; the country was partitioned, six of its northern counties remaining in England's grasp, with profound social and political implications still unresolved; and the Roman Church was left with a stranglehold on government policy, making enlightened development of social relations unlikely. Though lip service was paid to the language revival, and several generations had Irish as a compulsory subject in school, it was taught badly and repressively, and failed to recrystallize the national consciousness. The social stigma attached to native Irish-speakers was not reversed, and only recently has begun to fade. The Gaeltachtaí continued to erode under the pressure of assimilation and emigration. The *spiritual* liberation of Ireland, at least, is a long way from being achieved.

The twentieth century's two world wars took a heavy toll on Celtic communities. Highland Scots and Bretons especially were

decimated in the carnage of World War I. In the 1930s, as the
French state developed an even more arrogant attitude toward its
colonial dependents, Breton reaction took a militant turn, experi-
menting with bombs and armed commandoes. During World War II
this developed into an organized resistance against both the French
and Nazi invaders. The French maquis responded with assassinations
of Breton resistants and cultural leaders, culminating with the murder of Father Yann Perrot, a revered patriot and language activist, on
the way to his church in Skrignag in 1943. Enraged by the crime,
the Breton resistance redoubled its actions against France, and a few
of its members went so far as to seek collaboration with the Germans. This was what allowed the French, after the defeat of the Nazis
in 1944, to blacken the entire Breton movement and indulge in an
unprecedented purge of the Breton leadership—military, political,
cultural, and spiritual. Beginning with those who had in fact partic-
ipated in the armed operations, the persecution soon extended itself
to virtually all educated Breton-speakers, and the long series of gaol-
ings and executions came to an end only when sympathetic Welsh
journalists exposed the attempted genocide in the world press. Even
so, the Land had almost been dealt a killing blow. The teaching of
the Breton language and of any aspect of Celtic civilization was forbidden by law in 1947, and the ban was not lifted until 1959.
Terrified by the scope of persecution and the venom of the accusa-
tions, the population of Brittany found itself compelled to feel
ashamed of its own culture, to reject its own language in favor of
that of its conquerors (as Ireland had done a hundred years earlier).
The largest surviving community of Celtic-speakers was neutralized, made unwilling to pass its heritage on to future generations.

The postwar boom in technology posed a further challenge to
the survival of traditional cultures everywhere. Previously the state
had imposed its culture through the schools, but traditions could live
on at home; the new phenomenon of television invaded the privacy
of every family, allowing the infiltration, in the guise of entertainment, of state propaganda that shaped the most intimate values, fan-
tasies, and aspirations of large segments of the population. Bespelled
by the hypnotic nature of the medium, children turned to "the box"
as a higher source of authority than their parents, who were them-

selves defeated by its charm and unwilling to contest its influence. Television—the quintessential realm of the artificial, studiously avoiding any mention of the true needs and aspirations of the human condition—became the supreme arbiter of reality. Anything that— by the choice of the state or the capitalist network that held the states in place—was *not* depicted on the screen could be assumed not to exist, or to be beneath notice. So undesirable minorities like the Celts, deprived of representation in the media, were excluded from the consciousness of the masses and remained the concern of only a marginal, dwindling elite.

Yet the media revolution had an unexpected side effect. By downplaying the cold, objective approach that had been the foundation of materialism, and appealing instead to feelings, visceral impulsions and symbolically charged images, the media masters unintentionally gave the Age of Reason its death-blow, and made humanity more susceptible to the power of myth in all its forms. It was, of course, an entirely pernicious myth they sought to impose, one that would encourage dependence on the mechanisms of the capitalist order and settle people into a happy, unconscious slavery; but the depths of the unconscious, open as they are to the Otherworld, are a perilous, shifting realm, where unexpected forces can come into play. The human psyche, when sensitized by shoddy myths, also is made susceptible to deeper, life-giving ones. The 1960s, in their rejection of all establishments and their chaotic search for meaning, were a natural development in the process. Although that mass movement dissipated for lack of a true focus, the craving for ultimate meaning remained, along with the sense that it would be found in a reactivation of the mythic dimension. The environmental movement discovered it in a subjective participation with the Earth. This had always been an essential element of the Celtic tradition; and the Celts had been the oldest and strongest guardians of the mythic realities of the West. Could they, despite centuries of humiliation and weakness, resume such a role? Certainly the final war for Celtic survival would be, and still is, a war of the media and of myth.

Several events strengthened the Celtic will to fight back. In 1965 the valley of Tryweryn, a stronghold of Welsh traditional culture, was drowned to provide water for the city of Liverpool, in contemptuous disregard for years of passionate Welsh protest. This vivid new demonstration of Welsh colonial status led to a brief experiment in armed resistance (the Free Wales Army), and more importantly to the formation of Cymdeithas yr Iaith Gymraeg (The Welsh Language Society) which, through legal and illegal actions, won greater degrees of official status for the Welsh language and its tradition. In Ireland the accumulated injustices of the colonial presence in the North caused a military explosion of far more damaging proportions, but also forced the entire island—even the complacent rulers of the Republic—to confront the issues of Irish sovereignty and Irish culture. And in between, the communications-hungry 1960s had begun to disseminate some vital images provided by Celtic civilization. Ecologically-inspired neo-pagan movements claimed (however spuriously) Celtic antecedents. Celtic music, which can provide a glimpse of the Celtic soul across the language barrier, worked its magic on millions as the Chieftains, De Danann, Planxty, and Alan Stivell's harp sent their message around the world on vinyl and the airwaves. A new awareness began to spread of the ancient, life-giving wellsprings of meaning to be found in the Celtic heritage.

To overcome the weakness of their isolation and dwindling numbers, the six separate Celtic nations were gradually faced with the necessity of pooling their resources. Ever since Edward Lhuyd had revealed the original unity of the Celtic tradition, Pan-Celticism had been seen as a desirable goal by some. From the founding of the Celtic Congress in the 1890s to that of the Celtic League in 1961, a number of organizations have been promoting Pan-Celtic exchanges in the domains of economics, politics, and culture. Given the extraordinary influence of music in the Celtic movement, Pan-Celtic music festivals like those at Lorient and Killarney have been particularly effective in promoting a deep sense of Celtic identity in the face of media opposition. Harp and bagpipes have become potent mythic symbols of Celtic vitality throughout the Celtic world. Slowly, those who are fighting for Celtic survival are discovering that the resources which will give strength and impact to their movement will have to be drawn from the amassed wealth of the First and Second Golden Ages of the Celts—ages of myth, faith, and wonder.

So, the battle goes on. Can it be won? Contrasting images come out of the struggle. Ten young Irishmen fast to death under the cold gaze of a state no longer capable of realizing that it is being dishonored by their action. Mass protests in Brittany force the French state to back down, to dismantle the nuclear power plant they had arrogantly imposed on the people of Plogoff. Gwynfor Evans fasts against the English state to obtain a Welsh BBC channel, and his demand is fulfilled, thus gaining the Welsh language entry into the continuum of televised "reality"; but even as the battle of the media begins to be won, an influx of outsiders indifferent or hostile to the native culture is breaking up Welsh-speaking communities by pricing houses out of the natives' reach. In the face of this *mewnlifiad* ("inflooding," as it is referred to by native Welsh-speakers), which is encouraged by the indifference of the state, the natives have at times turned to burning the holiday homes of the invaders. Are the odds not overwhelmingly against Celtic survival? Is not the steady wasting away of Celtic communities an irreversible trend, the result of an economic process too vast to be affected by the actions of any minority, however determined?

Or, will the old dream become reality? Will the Celts survive the current crisis to emerge united and self-confident in a Third Golden Age of their civilization, a "Keltia Three?"

The battle is not yet over. The six Celtic languages are still alive, if not well. In them is stored, as on a disk, several millennia of a people's unique experience, waiting to be given a new dynamic expression by that generation who will dare to break the colonial shackles of fear and self-doubt. Now more than ever do we need the devil-may-care valor of the Celtic warrior. Now more than ever do we need the druidic clarity of vision, the bardic ability to draw resources from the unlimited potential of the Otherworld. We must, as they did, have the imagination to give flesh to life-giving myth, and the will to work its pattern upon our existence. Indeed, time is short. Everyone of us who has felt the beauty of the Celtic world-vision must act, each in our individual ways, NOW, before it is too late. GWNEWCH RYWBETH! DO SOMETHING!

The above is an unabashedly romantic, partisan account of Celtic history. As such, it is no less valid than any other approach—say, one that would have ordered the facts around the concept of economic determinism, or one that would have highlighted, as a positive trend, the development of the state. All history is an attempt to impose meaning on the stochastic plethora of events. In all historical narrative, certain events must be emphasized more than others in order to reveal patterns that will suggest a direction to the infinitely varied field of human experience. But the pattern we seek is chosen in advance; it is chosen in function of the meaning we wish to see in the flow of time; and that meaning is the expression of our own moral nature. The values that guide our actions in the present also allow us to perceive sequences of events that relate to those values, and compel us to integrate our own lives into the significant patterns that are thus brought out. So each cultural ideal creates its own history out of the chaos of fact.

Why, then, choose to see a special significance in the survival of Celtic civilization? After all, even the most positive interpretation of the facts makes the story of the Celts one of relentless decline and powerlessness. Why imply that it would be a good thing to struggle against that trend and reverse it? Or even imply that it is possible to do? Is not the far-reaching, homogenizing effect of modern industrial civilization a natural process that cannot be opposed, and rather should be welcomed? It has succeeded, current majority opinion states, because it offers humans the best adaptation to life on this planet. Lesser cultures cannot compete with it, and die out of their own accord. And with each vanishing language one more barrier to human communication is removed, and we are brought closer to our long-sought unity.

But today it is becoming harder and harder for thinking people to take such a view for granted. It now takes a singular lack of awareness not to perceive that the Earth is dying, that the systems that have maintained life over the aeons since its emergence are crumbling under pressure, that the foundation of our own lives is threatened. It is also difficult not to understand, with a minimum of reflection, that so extreme a situation has been brought about by the behavior that the Western capitalist establishment encourages: the treatment of all external reality as something objective, quantifiable, and to be manipulated. There is nothing that cannot be converted to money, that is, to a means of accumulating power; and as each individual needs such power to survive, nobody is left with much leeway to question the philosophy on which the whole system is based. So complete is the hold of that worldview over our lives that, even when we become aware of the suicidal course the culture is on, we are powerless to do anything to alter it, because the realization of our doom, dulled as it is by the everyday tension of economic competition, cannot rise very far in the hierarchy of our concerns. As our imagined future grows grimmer, we simply cease to think about it.

If Western intellectuals are running out of resources to deal with the problem and have tacitly yielded to despair, much worse is the case of people in general, manipulated as they are by the media. The profoundly dystonic patterns of television have by now shaped the mental processes of at least two generations, abolishing memory and discouraging reflection. Conditioned to passively receive an endless stream of disjointed information, most people no longer have the leisure to develop the mind skills that would allow them to process that information, question its value and intent, and arrive at an original viewpoint motivated by their own needs and experience. Wherever television becomes implanted, local cultures vanish, as though dissolved by strong acid. In their place the guiding images of Anglo-American mercantile capitalism establish themselves. There are some who welcome this emergence, through television, of a "world culture." But a folklore of shared commercial slogans is not enough to make a viable civilization. For necessary growth to occur, there must be a powerfully motivated, life-affirming rationale for action that focuses on the real world in all its complexity, not on a shallow, fantasized world of entertainment. And we must not forget that, even if it achieves greater depth, the "world culture" is not growing out of the pooled resources of humanity's individual cultures: it is itself but one culture, very limited in viewpoint, that has managed to silence all its rivals.

If the dominant culture seems to lack the resources to tackle a crucial problem, the solution will have to be sought in another cultural tradition with a different worldview. It is here that we come to realize the absolute survival value of cultural diversity. But just as our capitalist greed has, through wholesale destruction of ecosystems, lowered the genetic diversity of the biosphere to the point where it may be endangered, so has it reduced cultural diversity and left humanity with a serious shortage of true alternatives, even though our lives will depend upon them. Where, today, could we find a cultural viewpoint compelling enough to replace our destructive guiding images with wholesome ones? The much-vaunted "socialism" of the Eastern bloc is not only largely discredited, but was never a real contender in the first place: it was always no more than a hypertrophied version of Western capitalism, with even greater accumulation of power at the center, and an even more rigid ideological adherence to the Western greed-rationale of materialism. Thus, it completely lacks the flexibility necessary to the discovery of new survival strategies. Such strategies will, then, have to be sought among small, powerless groups—those scattered survivors from a time when humans felt a subjective kinship with the Earth.

In the European context, the Celts represent such a tradition. During its First and Second Golden Ages, as we have seen, Celtic civilization achieved a creative balance between Tribe and Land, between the activities of the human community and the imperatives of its natural environment. The balance was maintained by a guiding mythology that personalized all relationships, whether among humans or between humans and the rest of nature. Right and wrong attitudes towards the non-human world were not determined by an analytical evaluation of their consequences, but by a visceral sense of appropriateness or inappropriateness, imbibed from early childhood. The Land was a mother, alive, aware, constantly nurturing; so one felt for her, spontaneously, what one feels for a mother. Stories and images reinforced this relationship at every level. And the human community itself was organized to discourage too great concentrations of power, which would do violence to its traditional structure and give it an illusory independance from natural cycles.

Of course, the Celts are but one of many traditional cultures around the globe who held such a worldview, and the revitalization of other such cultures is a no less praiseworthy enterprise. But by virtue of being a European culture, they have a special link with Western history, and the myths and archetypes in their tradition have resonances in mainstream Western culture. They are best placed, then, to be agents of the transformation of the Western outlook. A vigorous Celtic world seeking to fully realize the potential of its First and Second Golden Ages could become a powerful source of inspiration for the disoriented West.

This is not to suggest that the Celts should develop imperialist ambitions, striving to replace other cultures with their own, or that they should cultivate a racist sense of superiority. Disparagement of other national and ethnic groups only leads to further imbalance. Rather, the Celts ought to cultivate a healthy pride in the unique, irreplaceable value of their heritage. Such solid, unapologetic self-assurance would lessen the Celts's vulnerability to the judgment of their neighbors, without necessarily leading to an institutionalized hostility. And the lessons learned through the Celtic struggle could eventually be of great profit to other Land-focused minority cultures that are faced with essentially the same problems as they confront the mechanisms of the state.

But how can that self-assurance be regained? As we see them today, Celtic-speaking communities are surviving precariously in a situation of great economic uncertainty, and retain only the most tenuous hold on their own tradition, which they are under constant pressure to give up entirely. Two (admittedly difficult) goals must be worked toward simultaneously: enlargement of the Celtic-speaking communities themselves, by persuading assimilated Celts to relearn the speech of their ancestors; and encouragement of pluralism within those communities, so that Celtic languages do not become associated with a limited range of interests and activities, excluding much that is essential to the society's functioning. A culture must be able to make use of all existing personality-types, and to apply to its needs, on its own terms, all the knowledge available in all fields at a given time. What we are not after is some fantastic "recreationism": we are not trying to bring back the Iron Age, or the dawn of the Middle Ages. Few people, after all, would seriously argue for the revival of head-hunting and human sacrifice; although they are indeed part of Celtic tradition, their enactment is not necessary to its survival. And things like computers, long-distance communication, printing presses, and the like are desirable assets that are not in contradiction with Celtic values. So the Celtic tradition must be envisaged as something dynamic and adaptable to changing circumstances, though rooted in the certainty of its unchanging essence.

The successful revival of Keltia will be achieved through a fierce struggle on a broad range of fronts. On the political front, measures must be taken to subvert the power of the state over Celtic communities, and to develop strategies and institutions that will give those communities enough power to control their own destiny, without endangering the principles on which Celtic society is based. On the pedagogical front, efforts to promote the teaching of Celtic languages must be coordinated and constantly refined for greater efficiency, ensuring that those who have reacquired their traditional language are fluent and comfortable in it, and will use it as a community tongue. On the economic front, the exploitation of resources will have to be arranged to provide the maximum self-sufficiency and stability to Celtic communities—which implies some opposition to the patterns imposed by the capitalist world-order. On the cultural front, a creative exploration of all arts and sciences should be taking place at all times in Celtic-language milieus, without the usual reliance on external (imperial-culture) sources. And on the spiritual front, a compelling articulation of myth and ritual must be devised to capture the imagination of people at a deep level and root the values and aspirations of the culture in a base of certainty and empowerment.

Having spelled out this grandiose plan of action, we will now lower our sights considerably and devote the rest of this book to one specific aspect—perhaps the most neglected one—of the revival process. This is the largely spiritual realm of myth-expression, the patterning of a culture's existence upon life-giving metaphors. We have seen how, at various turning points in its history, the Celtic tradition has drawn on its Otherworld connection to revitalize itself, allowing certain powerful images from its store of myth to emerge with particular clarity and give meaning to the community's identity. Precisely the same rerooting is necessary today: most Celtic-speakers are alienated from their culture's mythology, and more influenced by colonial philosophies, so that the empowering base of their identity is crumbling. If the mythic images were once again given life through imagination, a great many other things would fall into place.

The materialist, objectivist worldview of our age has encouraged a sense of powerlessness, the idea that people are absolutely separate from one another, that an individual's communication with any other is doomed by imperfection, and that his/her influence on the world is extremely limited, entirely dependent on his/her accumulated physical and social power. Traditional worldviews, on the other hand, recognize the interconnectedness of all beings, their origin in and continuing relation to the Otherworld, and the power of thought-forms to influence events along those connections. Rituals, as they repeat certain associations of thoughts, archetypal images and actions in relation to specific times and places, can determine the way reality is perceived, and what, in the end, reality *is*. Even in the West certain marginal groups—ceremonial magicians, Qabalists, Neo-Pagans of all stripes—are aware of the potential in this approach and are actively engaged in implementing it. The same approach should be systematically made a part of the Celtic movement—a *part*, because it cannot, at this stage, appeal to all Celtic revivalists (even very dedicated and sincere ones), and would no doubt arouse hostility in some, who identify rigidly with Roman Catholicism, Protestantism, or some form of modern secularism. Yet a minority group of this sort should definitely exist, as the soul or conscience of the Celtic movement as a whole, in an attempt to express Celtic authenticity at the fullest, and as a last-resort focus for Celtic identity. Activists taking this approach would, through their ritualized observance of Celtic holidays and their profound understanding of the symbolic language behind the rituals, create a living sacred pattern to underlie events unfolding in the Celtic world today. They should offer their support to all aspects of the movement, and should never seek to gain control of the movement as a whole. Their activity should speak for itself, without supplementary politics.

In the course of this book I will present some possible guidelines for the establishment and running of Celtic-ritual circles in organic solidarity with the revival of Celtic civilization. Such circles could function independently, or in an eventual network. Their primary focus should be the six Celtic nations, but they should attract people from the lands of the Celtic diaspora, and in ex-Celtic lands. Much of the material in subsequent chapters has been inspired by the activities of Céli Dé Circle between 1982 and 1988. Thus, it can be said to have shown its worth, but it must not be taken as a rigid formula. Aspects of it could be improved, or adapted to meet the needs of individual circles, provided that the entreprise is rooted in a genuine knowledge and love of Celtic tradition.

In Celtic tales of initiatory voyages to the Otherworld, the chosen hero was visited by a Goddess bearing an apple branch. With its blossoms and leaves of jewel-like perfection, that branch spoke of another, larger reality, a place beyond time and entropy, where winter did not mean the loss of flowers, where the source of all the world's beauty endured eternally. Entranced by the fragrance of the blossoms and the wild melody of his visitor's song, the hero, Connla, or Bran Mac Feabhail, understood that he was being called to find his heart's desire. But the way there was perilous, and could not be traveled without effort. There would be pitfalls, temptations, illusions to turn him from his path into destruction. And the land to which he traveled was in many respects the opposite of everything he had known: a land of sharp clarity, where before he had known comfortable, non-committal greyness; a land of women, where direct intuition was more important than analysis; a sea-country, constantly shifting yet never losing any of itself. Still the hero would persevere, and arrive at last in the Land of the Ever-Young, the Plain of Honey, the Place of Life. There, on the four-footed island of bronze behind the rampart of fire, under the spell of never-ending song, he would find the Otherworld feast, the ultimate center of peace, community, and happiness, presided over by Manannán Mac Lir. And then, if it was not yet time to part with his earthly life, he would return strengthened by the memory of the Land of Apples to a fuller participation in the world of his tribe.

We offer you the apple branch. Returning to the roots of your Celtic heritage will be a journey of transformation, of recovery, of joy. It will also be perilous, with ample opportunities for discouragement; but clear-eyed and courageous seekers will come at last to Eamhain Abhlach, to Afallon.

CHAPTER TWO

Drawing the Circle

et us say that you have taken the offer of the apple branch, that the cultivation of the Celtic consciousness has become one of your important life-goals. The Celtic worldview—however imperfectly glimpsed—has captured your imagination; you wish to explore its guiding symbols, give them flesh in the patterns of everyday life; and you hope to do so within a community of people who share the same ideal. People sensitive to the dimension of myth and ritual are not too difficult to find; with the widespread revival of astrology, Qabalah, alchemy, tarot, and other ancient methods of knowledge, there has been a blossoming of various neo-pagan, Rosicrucian, and New Age groups dedicated to the communal experience of such levels of being. More than likely, if you are at all interested in these matters, you already have had some contact (whether direct or indirect) with groups of that type. You probably have discovered that many of them have a very positive response to the term "Celtic," which they associate with ancient wisdom, and some of them even claim "Celtic" antecedents for their group's traditions. So it will not be difficult to draw people to a range of activities self-described as "Celtic." Of course, the label alone is not enough. What is *Celtic,* from the point of view of a ritual-oriented group forming today? What are the boundaries of the concept?

What are the guidelines that will prevent one from straying out of Celtic tradition into ungrounded fantasy?

In the previous chapter, we have seen the unfolding of Celtic tradition through the ages as a process of growth, the adaptation of a single cultural organism to many different circumstances, with each stage remaining inscribed in the total heritage of the culture. The Celtic tradition endures as long as Celtic-speaking communities remain. It is still here, in the present. Any Celtic-oriented movements that ignore its contemporary existence and limit their interest to past stages in its development have turned their backs on reality and cut themselves off from the very life-giving sources they profess to seek. While it is true that the wellsprings that will revitalize the Celtic world are to be found in the First and Second Golden Ages of Celtic civilization—the periods in which it was most self-assured, most spiritually aware, and most creative—we must remember that their life-giving symbols are of primary value for *that* tradition, that they have their greatest meaning in relation to its survival. Let us then rule out, right from the start, any merely private fantasizing about Rhiannon or Cerridwen or Cúchulainn that blinds itself to the Celtic reality of today.

But we all realize, *especially* if we have been brought up or live in a modern Celtic-speaking community, that the present-day Celtic milieu has, in many respects, distanced itself immensely from its spiritual roots in the two Golden Ages. Although the continuity of Celtic tradition is still evident, centuries of colonization, self-doubt, and yielding in the face of alien domination at many levels have left their mark on the culture. Many of the attitudes modern Celts share and take for granted vary with those their ancestors displayed, and in some cases are in direct contradiction to the ethos of Celtic civilization at its highest. Are we to simply accept such developments, even if they imply a diminution, a falling-away from the ideal, a compromise with potentially harmful influences? Surely not. How, then, are we to discriminate among various aspects of Celtic reality? What are we to reject, and what are we to retain?

We will have to proceed cautiously in this, since anything that loosens our contact with the living Celtic world is destructive, and there are some philosophies that are fundamentally anti-Celtic in their cultural impact (the more extreme expressions of Calvinism, for instance) that many Celtic-speakers consider to be essential to their identity and heritage. To openly challenge too many such assumptions would be to alienate the very communities we are trying to support. In many domains we will have to show tolerance and respect for attitudes that we must disagree with, and would not encourage within our own circle. Yet, there are some broad areas where our response should be clear and certain.

First, the question of race. When dealing with Celtic-interested groups, especially among the Celtic diaspora, one often encounters an obsessive preoccupation with ancestry. Honoring one's ancestors is indeed part of the Celtic ethos; but in most cases, flaunting of ancestry is intended as a self-sufficient badge of Celtic identity. It is enough to have a surname beginning with "Mac" or "O'" to declare oneself a "Celt" and the inheritor of the Celtic tradition, even if one has no community experience whatsoever of that tradition, and no intention of acquiring any further knowledge of it. Sometimes, if one's parents or grandparents don't have recognizably Celtic surnames, one will hunt further back in one's genealogy for proof of a "Celtic" ancestry that will justify using the label for oneself. Although the worst forms of this silliness are to be found in the diaspora, Celtic countries are not immune to it. Sometimes new arrivals in Celtic communities, even if they have gone so far as to learn the language, are branded "foreigners" and discouraged from identifying with the community's mainstream, often by "natives" who no longer speak the language of tradition and have no claim on it save their ancestry. It must be understood and stressed that the Celtic tradition is a *cultural* continuum, a way of thinking and imagining the world. It has to do with language, symbolism, and action, not with genes and physical appearance. Anyone who will freely and wholeheartedly embrace it can become a part of it. Ancestry is indeed one of the most powerful motivations for adhering to a particular culture, and should not be discounted; but there are many other, less tangible reasons for identifying with a tradition; and no sincere newcomer to the Celtic world should ever be turned away because of racial considerations.

Then there is the question of national allegiance. If you identify yourself primarily as "Celtic," chances are you come from an ex-Celtic land, or do not actually have a Celtic background. If you live in a Celtic country or in the Celtic diaspora, you are most likely to think of yourself as "Irish," "Welsh," "Scottish," and so forth, and it would take some effort for you to identify with the term "Celtic" as a further definition of who you are. This simply reflects historical reality; today there are six Celtic nations, each with a distinct cultural identity. Under the influence of colonization they have drifted farther and farther apart from one another, to the point of developing hostile oppositions: English-dominated versus French-dominated, Catholic versus Protestant. The colonizing states have engineered these oppositions to their advantage—encouraging, for instance, the Welsh and Scots to despise the Catholic Irish, settling Ulster with Scottish colonists, and using Scottish troops to quell Irish nationalism. Our circle, Pan-Celtic in its principles, must combat any such ethnic prejudice. It should be clearly understood that the Celtic nations are most likely to survive if they are united, and that the vigor they need to survive will be drawn from their common heritage, which dates back to their ancient unity. The modern Celtic nations are like six branches growing from a common trunk. Each of the branches bears foliage, flowers, and fruit that are uniquely its own, yet all six of them draw their nourishment from the same source, and would eventually wither and die if cut away from it. So we must cultivate our awareness of this unity-in-diversity. If we found a circle in Ireland, for instance, we must resist the temptation of making it a purely *Irish* circle; although Ireland, of course, will be the focus of most of our concerns, we still must endeavor, through the shape and content of our rituals, to maintain a consciousness of the five other nations, and of the Celtic continuum as a whole. It will be an exercise in true unity, as opposed to the enforced uniformity of technocracy and mass culture.

A group dedicated to the *spiritual* renewal of a cultural tradition will of necessity have to face questions of religion. Ultimately, because it relates to the deepest levels of every individual's self-definition, religion can be a far more divisive factor in such a group than ancestry and nationality. Most Celtic-speakers today are either Catholic or Protestant (unless, repudiating their Celtic background, they have turned to some form of secular materialism). Yet, a majority of the people who would take a spontaneous interest in an endeavor based on myth and ritual identify to some degree with neo-paganism, and share most of the attitudes encouraged by that movement, notably a militant hatred of Christianity. They would tend to approach the Celtic heritage only in terms of its First Golden Age, completely ignoring the Second Golden Age and attempting to "purify" the medieval texts of Christian "admixtures." There is nothing wrong with a sincere espousal of neo-paganism, which surely can claim a place in the Pan-Celtic movement. But any attempt to deny the Christian element in the Celtic consciousness does a disservice to Celtic revival; it reflects a neo-pagan agenda, not a Celtic one. The Celts have been Christian for fifteen hundred years. Their latest period of self-assured independence and creativity was to a large extent motivated by their experience of Christianity, and owed its success to the absorption and rechanneling of all the energies that had sustained their culture in the pagan period. What remains of that energy after its final flowering is all that, consciously or unconsciously, sustains the Celtic community today; and to block it for any reason would greatly reduce the culture's chances of survival. To tap into the true richness of the Celtic consciousness, one must accept the dual nature of its heritage, pagan *and* Christian.

Yet, in identifying with the Celtic world, both sides will have to modify their positions; they will have to become *Celtic* Pagans and *Celtic* Christians. Neo-Pagans who have been used to various Gardnerian-inspired "Wiccan" traditions—often under the mistaken assumption that they are "Celtic"—will have to come to terms with the imagery and values of the true Celtic tradition, which may in some cases contradict what they had hitherto taken for granted. Christians will have to put aside their denominational distinctions, which are mostly a facet of the colonial legacy, and concentrate on the Celtic experience of Christianity (this in no way rejects their faith's message of universal brotherhood; it is only a decision to live it day-by-day according to the terms of their own culture, not somebody else's). It means accepting a form of Christianity that is sacramental, mystical, certain of the fundamental goodness of the Creation and of the absolute value of individual free will, respectful of hierarchy without taking it too seriously, and sensitive to the beauty of nature, with an open, unfrightened interest in the pre-Christian aspects of its heritage.

So, just as the six ethnic identities of the modern Celts are to be treated as equal members of a single unit, distinct but co-inhering, Neo-Pagans and Christians will have the opportunity to cooperate in a spiritual enterprise that transcends their differences, without denying or belittling those differences. Once mutual rejection ceases, there should be few obstacles to such cooperation. Neo-Pagans can, without becoming Christians, recognize that the religious life of Christianity comes from the same well of symbolic material as their own, and respect the image of Christ as a source of illumination. Conversely, Christians must admit that the symbolic patterns set by paganism continue—despite the change of viewpoint caused by the Incarnation—to be operative even in their own faith, and that, where the relation to the Land is concerned, there is no good reason to discard the pagan model, which remains valid even by Christian standards. It is by their mutual adherence to the *Celtic* worldview that the two groups will find the most common ground; the proper interaction of Tribe and Land will be a primary concern for both, whatever their attitude to salvation through Christ.

Tribe and Land, then, will be the spiritual parameters of our circle, whatever our supplementary beliefs may be. But how must we define Tribe and Land and our relationship to them today? How do we integrate ourselves with the socio-cultural reality of the Tribe, and the physico-spiritual reality of the Land? Let us begin with the Tribe.

A Tribe is a community defined by a common experience of the world, both synchronically and diachronically. All the individuals in the Tribe feel that they participate in a group identity of shared presuppositions about the nature of things, and that this identity extends into the past and (one hopes) into the future. The cement that gives cohesion to such a group identity is language. This is true of group-allegiance at all levels, from the most superficial and ephemeral trends to the deepest forms of self-definition. We note that the many subcultures within the larger framework of a culture, be they motorcycle gangs or stamp collectors, use a more or less extended vocabulary peculiar to themselves to express the range of experience that distinguishes them from other groups. An outsider will not immediately understand this vocabulary, but will adopt it if he comes to identify with the subculture. The extent and complexity of such a specialized language and the number of elements it shares with the language of the parent culture will define the degree of autonomy and self-sufficiency a subculture enjoys. A single system of symbolic communication that is designed to express *all* the facets of a group's experience, without extended reference to language shared with outsiders, marks that group as a fully autonomous culture, not a subculture. It is a unit of this sort that we will call the Tribe: a historical entity defined by a shared language, changing slowly over time but maintaining a continuous identity, exactly like a human individual. The language of the Tribe contains—in its structure, vocabulary, word-associations, and sound symbolism—all of the Tribe's past experience, which is available to all of its members at any given time, and helps define their own contemporary experience, and the shared values they need for cooperation. Sometimes a number of well-defined cultures share so many recognizable similarities in their languages that they feel linked; although the languages are quite distinct and autonomous, the similarities between them suggest a shared experience in the remote past which, if explored, becomes a part of contemporary consciousness. This is the case with the Romance languages and Slavic languages, for instance, (and, of course, the Celtic languages). With the right motivation at a particular point in history, it can lead to the formation of a functional "overtribe."

So the Tribe is defined by its language. Celtic culture, it follows, is defined by Celtic language. It will hold together only through the continued use of the Celtic languages to express the full range of the community's activities. A circle affirming its link to the Celtic continuum, therefore, cannot evade the language issue. Within the context of the Celtic lands themselves, this will seem obvious. Especially in Wales and Brittany, any group that claims to identify with the national culture without adopting the national language has very little solid ground to stand on. In Scotland the linguistic situation is a bit more complicated; and in Ireland, the trauma of cultural suicide continues to manifest as a subconscious hostility toward Irish, but there, too, the conceptual linkage of "Celtic" to language will be understood with a minimum of discussion. Yet in the Celtic diaspora and in ex-Celtic lands, the issue can become divisive. Many people who feel strongly attracted to the imagery and values of Celtic civilization, as they have experienced it in translation, see no need to turn to the original languages to explore that realm in more depth. Speakers of imperial languages like English and French, who have never been forced to use a second language and have never experienced linguistic relativism firsthand, often find it difficult to accept that other languages really do present a different view of the world, that they are not simple mirror-translations of the language they already know. Such people argue that if the Celtic heritage can come across as so powerful and inspiring in translation, why not continue to explore it through the medium of their imperial language, instead of expending the time and effort to learn Celtic languages? Would anything essential be lost?

First, it must be stressed that linguistic relativism *is* a reality. Languages are *not* interchangeable; deep symbolic correspondences that are self-evident within the context of one language may be absent, or substantially different, in another. Patterns of derivation, generating new words and channels of meaning, can vary enormously from one language to another. Even at a fairly surface level, Irish and Welsh exhibit a pattern for organizing concepts quite unlike that used in English. Paradoxically, it is just this indisputable difference that often makes "Celtic" enthusiasts reluctant to undertake the study of Celtic languages.

Second, we must realize that a culture is an extremely intricate construct, which cannot be reduced to just a few of its more salient features. Those aspects of Celtic culture which have been judged sufficiently striking to be discussed in the context of other cultures cannot—beautiful and enriching as they are—represent the full scope of the Celtic consciousness. When placed back into their original linguistic context, they resonate with centuries of experience, and display a rich, many-layered array of associations that could not have been perceived otherwise. As such, focusing the full historical resources of their culture, they become truly dynamic rather than merely decorative. English-speakers who identify with Celtic images and ideals while refusing to adopt Celtic languages are not relating to Celtic culture at all, but creating a pseudo-Celtic subculture within Anglo culture. They may have strong affinities for Celtic culture, but remain separated from it by a major conceptual barrier; and they remain vulnerable to unconscious influence from profoundly "anti-Celtic" elements in the structure of the Anglo heritage. Unable to "think Celtic" spontaneously as Celtic-speakers do, they will rely more and more on external props to affirm their identity: visual motifs, clothing and jewelry, specific literary themes, and so forth. Instances of this also can be found in the Native American movement, which has much in common with the Celtic revival; younger people who no longer speak the language of their grandparents and thus have no direct access to the culture of their ancestors, but who still want to affirm their Indian identity, often stress non-linguistic externals like dress, ornaments, and dance. Yet when they speak about their heritage they often present a diluted, New Age-like "Pan-Indian" version of it directly derived from romantic Anglo conceptions of Indian culture—quite unlike the many very distinct traditions characteristic of the various tribes, each defined by its linguistic field.

So, if our circle is to have a true relation to the Celtic world and a perceptible impact on its heritage, there can be no compromise on the language issue. The circle should see itself as a part of the Celtic-language continuum, and strive to conduct as many of its activities as possible through the medium of Celtic languages. If most members of the circle are not Celtic-speakers, it should be a mark of their commitment that they make the effort to become reasonably acquainted with a Celtic language. There is likely to be some resistance to this, of course. Such resistance can usually be traced to two sources:

- Intellectual laziness. Unflattering as this sounds, it must be recognized that for most people this is the main reason for balking at anything that involves true mental discipline, although they usually provide some other rationale for their reluctance. As we have mentioned before, speakers of imperial languages often let their language-acquisition skills atrophy, and their cultural envi-

ronment makes it hard for them to understand the need to expend so much effort. Then there is the entertainment-hungry,
thrill-seeking component in many people who are attracted to
ritual work, especially in some neo-pagan milieus: they are
open to passive enjoyment, the reception of vivid images, participation in simple and pleasurable communal exercises, all of it
given an ego-boosting importance by its relationship to some
poorly-articulated "mystery" or "tradition" that involves mis-
pronounced exotic names of "ancient" provenance; but they are
quickly bored by anything that steers them toward the active
mental effort and discipline necessary for real spiritual progress.
We are back in the realm of sterile playacting. It must be realized from the start that every spiritual tradition, whatever its
scope and impact, deals with transformation, and that true
transformation, whether of the self or of the world, involves the
perfection of cognitive skills as well as of contemplative and
imaginative ones. To balk at effort is to give up the hope of success.

• Unconscious colonial prejudice. This is a far more insidious obstacle, much more difficult to pinpoint and neutralize. Many
people who claim to be drawn to the Celtic heritage have in
fact internalized the colonizing culture's attitude toward Celtic
civilization. They feel "safe" dealing with aspects of the Celtic
world that a certain elite in the colonizing culture has judged
acceptably interesting—Celtic mythology (in translation), Celtic
art, traditional music—but exclude elements that are disapproved of by the state, like language and the separate identity of
living Celtic communities. English and French symbolize material and social success; Celtic languages symbolize backwardness
and powerlessness. To shift one's primary allegiance from an imperial language to a Celtic one is to transfer oneself from the
world of the colonizer to the world of the colonized, a move
understandably fraught with anxiety. That this is in most cases a
completely unconscious attitude makes it no less far-reaching in
its consequences. People brought up in Ireland who are interested in Celtic matters are often willing to talk *about* Irish at
great length and in the most favorable terms, but are oddly re-

luctant to say anything *in* Irish. In the Celtic diaspora the sources of such attitudes are buried even farther below everyday consciousness, yet they still operate. If you feel a spontaneous reluctance to face the language issue, honestly examine your inner motives to discover whether your attitude might have such an origin. There *are* fundamental differences between the culture of the colonizer and that of the colonized, or there would be no opposition between them; both can be known separately, but they cannot be "combined" without adulterating one or the other. To affirm the integrity of Celtic culture, one must cease to see it from the viewpoint of the conquerors. There is no other way. (This is not, of course, meant to discourage the use of English and French as *linguae francae* for international communications. Bilingualism or multilingualism is always healthy.)

This book is written in English because, as a result of the historical process outlined in the previous chapter, the Celtic languages are too weakened to mobilize all the resources necessary for a Pan-Celtic revival at a deep level. Many of the people who would have the most to contribute to the movement cannot, at present, be reached through Celtic languages alone. Yet one must never forget that the Celtic languages are to be the ultimate beneficiaries—and, before long, the primary medium—of the revitalization. When Bran Mac Feabhail received his invitation to visit the Otherworld, the apple branch, for all its magic beauty, was not itself the Otherworld experience. Bran then had to expend considerable effort, facing perils and hardship, before he could attain the state of being hinted at by the branch. So the mysterious glamour of Celtic art and music, the symbols of the mythology glimpsed in translation, are the equivalent of the apple branch to an outsider who is approaching the Celtic heritage as a sacred tradition with transformative power. There is much work to be done and much knowledge to be gained, before the beautiful images can be returned to their proper, dynamic context, and one can come to the Land where the wondrous apple trees grow.

We must realize, of course, that not everyone has the same linguistic skills. Some people pick up any number of languages with ease, others make little headway even with concentrated study. As we have said, speakers of imperial languages grow up in unilingual situations and fail to develop their innate ability to learn other languages. As long as an effort is made, one must make allowances for such discrepancies. We are not suggesting that everyone in the circle should be as fluent as a native speaker. But every circle member should cultivate an interested, accepting attitude toward the languages and assimilate the basics of at least one; and each circle must have at least one person who is reasonably fluent in one or more of the languages and can serve as the focus for the circle's Celtic connection, ensuring that its ritual activities remain attached to the living Celtic continuum.

Finally, we must stress that learning the Celtic languages is, despite all the effort involved, an exciting, pleasurable, and rewarding enterprise. They are rich, flexible mediums with an immensely engaging literary heritage. And if one's espousal of Celtic tradition is truly motivated by a desire for transformation, for the return to a worldview more in tune with the needs of Tribe and Land, there is no more dramatic sign of such transformation than a complete shift in language. When one becomes able to use a Celtic language instead of the dominant imperial language, one has crossed a barrier into a different world. It is as effective a way of establishing a new continuum, a new set of presuppositions about the universe, as any amount of ritual gesturing. It can, indeed, be exhilarating.

Now that it has been established that the circle must be committed to the use of a Celtic language, the question remains: *which* Celtic language? There are six living ones to choose from. If your circle is operating in one of the six Celtic countries, you should use the language of that country. In the Celtic diaspora and in formerly Celtic lands, there are other factors involved. One can choose the language of one's ancestors, a language one is particularly interested in, or simply a language that a member of the circle happens to know. It must be stressed, however, that circles in ex-Celtic lands should not, in circle context, use regional minority languages of non-Celtic origin, like Galician and Occitan. Such languages have fascinating and beautiful traditions of their own, and should be cultivated in the proper contexts, but they are not a part of the Celtic continuum, and their inclusion in Celtic-revival activities can only confuse and hinder the movement.

Language has placed us within the Tribe. Now we must become familiar with the Tribe's structure, the internal functions in which we are to participate, and which our circle must reflect. Celtic tradition, as we have seen, defines three functions essential to the Tribe's survival: the sovereign function, which guides the Tribe by reminding it of its ideals, conserving its lore, arbitrating its disputes, and providing a link with the source of all values in the Otherworld; the warrior function, which develops the qualities necessary to defend the Tribe against all threats from outside; and the fertility function, which provides for the Tribe's physical sustenance. In addition to these three essential functions, there is a floating "fourth function" of craftsmen and artists, individuals possessed of unusual talents, of gifts direct from the Otherworld. Each function has its own ethos, its own guiding symbols, its own ritual language, although all of it goes to make up the larger construct that is the Tribe. Individual circle members may identify with some particular functions more than with others. There will not be many "pure" first- or second- or third-function people, involved with one function in exclusion of the others; and such compartmentalization is hardly to be encouraged, given our age's need for individual flexibility. Still, many people are likely to find that one or another function predominates in their concerns. First-function people are intellectuals, scholars, educators, ritualists, and anyone dealing with the culture as a concept, value system, or symbolic organism. Second-function people are not only those in military or law-enforcement careers, but also those with the personal daring and strategic acumen to protect the Tribe's heritage from its enemies. The third function includes, farmers, of course, but also all people who are involved with the ups and downs of material wealth, like economists and traders, as well as all people in a nurturing role, such as nurses, midwives, and full-time mothers, and the like. Creative artists and craftsmen make up the fourth function.

We must always remember that our participation in the Tribe cannot be limited to our representing it in ritual. Though ritual work does indeed, by itself, have an impact on reality (or it would

not be worth undertaking), it gives better results when it is combined with more exoteric forms of activism. As the saying goes,
"God helps those who help themselves." Ritual work initiates contact with specific Otherworld influences that are to pattern the
course of events in our world; but those influences are more likely to
root themselves deeply and permanently if the right conditions have
already been created to receive them—if they are, so to speak, met
halfway. So circle members should complement their in-circle focus
on Celtic consciousness with more mundane activities that further
the Celtic cause. A member of a circle in Wales, for instance, could
be active in *Cymdeithas yr Iaith Gymraeg*, or in *Mudiad Ysgolion
Meithrin* (the Welsh-language nursery-school movement). Irish circles could be involved with Gaeilscoileanna, or cooperative farms or
economic ventures in the Gaeltacht. One also should provide support for the political forces that are favorable to the cause at a given
time, but this must not turn into unconditional allegiance to any political party, since such entities are notoriously fickle, and in the end
cannot help but seek the power of the state for themselves. Circles
outside the Celtic countries can do irreplaceable work educating the
public about the achievements and continuing value of Celtic civilization, and can campaign to win support for the struggles of the
Celtic nations—perhaps through an organization like the Celtic
League. And, of course, given the tight bond between Tribe and
Land, all circles should stay in touch with environmental issues.

Such activism will entail cooperation with people who will have
little understanding or sympathy for the path you have chosen. It is
important to respect those people, who may be sincerely dedicated
to the Celtic cause from their own point of view, and whose contri-
bution may be very great. A passionately sectarian Roman Catholic
or Methodist, viscerally repelled by anything that smacks of paganism and suspicious of "Celtic" approaches to Christianity, may be far
more solidly grounded in Irish or Welsh reality than the most enthu-
siastic newcomer full of images from the *Mabinogion*. A Welsh-speaking
rock fan is likely to have far greater insight into the Celtic consciousness than an English-speaking Irish American with an encyclopedic
knowledge of traditional fiddle music. Circle members who are new
to the Celtic continuum, only beginning their acquaintance with

the languages, should listen and learn in such milieus, and avoid any ideological confrontation, especially all aggressive, divisive proselytism. The path advocated by this book can never appeal to more than a minority of highly individualistic people, and will succeed best if it keeps a low profile, free from the distortions of media publicity. This is not to suggest that contemporary Celtic society should be immune from challenge and criticism. As already stated, many attitudes common in Celtic communities today contradict the highest ideals attained during the First and Second Golden Ages, and we have a duty to oppose them, not only in the social sphere, but also in their potential influence on ourselves. Anything that encourages racism, sexism or homophobia, anything that promotes an anti-communal, imperialistic, or authoritarian approach to society should have no place in Celtic tradition.

In the end, every activity of the Tribe involves an interaction with the Land. Indeed, it is this awareness of the indissoluble link between Tribe and Land that distinguishes the Celtic worldview from the mainstream Western worldview today. Most of us are brought up to think of physical nature as no more than a backdrop and support system for human activity. We pay attention to natural phenomena in so far as they abet or hinder specific human projects; processes that are not directly relevant to such human activity are judged unimportant, and we are reluctant to be conscious of them. But there is nothing superfluous in nature: every element in it, whether or not humans know of it, participates in balancing the whole—and eventually has an impact on the whole, including human life. We need not recapitulate the many instances of this which environmental groups have been urgently publicizing over at least the past twenty years: the importance of tropical forests as reservoirs of genetic diversity, and as oxygenators for the entire globe; and the importance of marshes as a vital link in the food chain between land and sea. While the narrow anthropocentrism of the industrial-capitalist establishment is evidently a destructive lie, the truth is that human beings are caught in the midst of natural process, participating in it whether or not they choose to, constantly giving or receiving influence as the balance shifts. The most productive next step would be to *consciously* participate, fully aware of—and full of respect for—the

larger structure one belongs to. The Celtic tradition, as it was articu-
lated in its Golden Ages, offers a time-proven pattern for such participation.

As representatives of the Tribe, the circle should cultivate a permanent subjective link with the Land. The first step toward this requires a growth in knowledge and awareness. Just as in traditional
Western thought, an individual can be envisaged as either a body or
a soul, though both are linked, so does the Land, in its living, personal aspect, have a dual nature, physical and spiritual, and we must
be fully acquainted with both. The physical Land is at once apparent
to the senses, yet we must learn to see it not only where it interacts
with our cultural concerns, but also as an organism in its own right—
a node of processes intent first and foremost upon fulfilling its own
needs, and ours incidentally. The bones of the Land, on which the
rest of its features depend, are its mineral topography, its expanses of
sediment and igneous rock, its "hard" and "soft" zones, which will
determine its relationship to the water cycle and its eventual fertility.
Mountains, hills and valleys will affect the flow of water and air, and
mean temperature will change with altitude. Rivers, the most powerfully evident nurturing presences in the Land, run where the
bones of the earth let them, carrying and dispensing the water that is
necessary for the survival of living organisms. Subtle variations in the
combinations of mineral nutrients, permeability to water, and temperature will determine which organisms survive where, as individual ecosystems of interdependent plant and animal life. Exposure and
poor, acid soil give rise to heath and moorland. Where conditions are
more favorable we get forests, in which a great many species interact. In low places with the right amount of water retention marshes
form, where dead organic matter is dissolved back into nutrients.
And, of course, rivers eventually flow to the sea, the original cradle
of life and still an indispensable source of the Land's sustenance, with
the borderland between them a rich habitat for many creatures, including humans. Each ecosystem contains its own roster of species,
all of them contributing something essential to the functioning of
the Land as a whole, whether or not they are of immediate use to
humans.

This, then, is the body of the Land-goddess, from which the

Tribe may deduce something about her spirit. If the Tribe is truly to become her kin, she must be accepted in all her aspects, not just the immediately attractive and "useful" ones. Spiders, adders, and wasps, thistles, gorse, and nettles, are as much the Land's children as domestic animals and crops or the showier birds, butterflies, and wildflowers. Rain is as important to the cycle of life as sunshine. Storm must balance calm. Winter alternates with summer. Niall of the Nine Hostages, ancestor of the Irish High Kings, attained the High Kingship only when he recognized the Land-goddess in the guise of a repulsive crone. The Loathly Damsel stands on the path to the grail of fertility and well-being. While the Tribe's economic needs will necessarily have an impact on the appearance of the Land, care must always be taken that the changes not lessen its variety, that no aspect of its being—however unattractive or irrelevant to the Tribe's everyday life—be lost as a result. If the Tribe comes to dismiss such concerns and places its need above that of the Land, the balance is broken, the Land's blessing is withdrawn, and before long the forces that sustain life cease to serve humankind, as we see today.

From the subjective interaction of the Tribe with the personalized Land, a spiritual topography emerges. Striking features of the landscape—mountains, rivers, caves, forests, and so forth—become, because of deep-seated archetypal associations, points of contact between human experience and that which is wholly outside it, still flavored with the boundless potential of the Otherworld. Such points become the focus of rituals, and the accumulated energies of centuries of ritual activity eventually make them reservoirs of power in their own right. The Land is dotted with these power-centers, some more prominent than others. The Tribe's continued use reinforces them, even as it draws power from them for magical applications. The mythological traditions of the Celtic world provide an explication and a mnemonic pattern for the full extent of this spiritual personality of the Land, which constitutes the Tribe's link to its Land-goddess.

A circle established in one of the six Celtic countries will find it fairly easy to enter into a relationship with the Land. Tradition has set the patterns for it, which remain quite vigorous, despite more or less long disuse. Records both oral and written, both national and local, will tell you where the greater and lesser power-centers are, what is the nature of the powers that inhabit them, and what images, names, and contexts unlock those powers. Although you may not be able to physically conduct rituals at all of these power-centers, you can and must use them as conceptual referents within rituals, in order to become a part of the spiritual and magical continuum they represent. Again, language will play a primary role in breaking you away from the alien concepts of the imperial culture and restoring you to the intimacy between Tribe and Land that occurred at such spots in times gone by. Once the circle has gained some self-assurance in its structure and functioning and has been operating for a year or more, you may be astonished at the promptness and definiteness of the Land's response.

For circles in ex-Celtic lands, the task will be only a little harder. Although here the cultural continuity has been broken, local tradition can be remarkably tenacious, and, unless rural settlement patterns have been completely uprooted, one usually can, from a variety of historical, toponymic, and folklore sources, discern a great deal of the heritage of the Celtic tribe that once occupied the territory. You will know the names of mountains and rivers, the location of significant power-centers, even, perhaps, the attributes of divinities associated with them. You will find certain folk customs to be remnants of Celtic practices, still usable when seen again from a Celtic perspective. But you will have to go to the six Celtic countries to get most of the linguistic and symbolic material you will need to renew the ritual link between Tribe and Land.

It is in the Celtic diaspora that we may run into a problem, since there will be an obvious discrepancy between the Land as conceived in mythological terms—the Land historically settled by the Celtic Tribe, Keltia-in-Europe—and the land on which the circle actually lives. One could, theoretically, try to relate to the new land using Celtic vocabulary, defining its power-centers and other functional features with imagery taken from Celtic tradition; but in most cases, a spiritual barrier will stand in the way. Celtic immigrants in, for example, the Americas and Australasia are living on a Land that has already enjoyed long ages of ritual communication with its own

Tribes, now displaced. The astral structures resulting from this activity are still in place, and constitute the most direct path to spiritual knowledge of that Land; foreign ritual concepts will—at least for a long while—"fall on deaf ears." Yet, this does not mean that the immigrants should blithely seek to step into the Tribe's role and adopt the former culture's ritual language; if they have a strong imaginative affinity for their own ancestral culture and its symbolism, the likelihood that they will successfully assimilate completely alien cultural systems is rather small. Besides, it is inappropriate for Europeans to usurp the spiritual destiny of the aboriginal peoples. What is called for here is a kind of dual vision. Commitment to Celtic identity should not be lessened, and the symbolic language that goes with it should be learned thoroughly, in addition to cultivating an attachment for the ancestral homelands where the culture evolved. But at all times one should also be aware of the Land one experiences from day-to-day, of its specific nature and needs, its character and moods, and love it in all its aspects, as is the Land's due. In the context of seasonal rituals, even though the main focus will be on forms drawn from Celtic tradition, an effort should be made at some point to speak to the Land in its own language—humbly, simply, and succinctly (the less elaborate the attempt, the less likely it is to fail). Different circles will devise different strategies for doing this. There are signs that the Land, in such cases, may be more responsive to respectful communication from self-declared foreigners who admit that their sacred homeland is overseas.

Our circles must, then, wherever they happen to be, feel bound to the Land that gives them sustenance by unbreakable ties of caring. All circle members should try to gain some knowledge of the intricacies of its structure, and be concerned for the survival of the many nonhuman organisms with which they share its body.

We are now secure in our perspective on Tribe and Land, and on the relationship between them. We can therefore begin to express and enhance that relationship by means of the ritual activity for which our circle is designed. Although the content of the rituals will vary according to the festivals they commemorate, a certain basic framework—and a common symbolic vocabulary—should be formulated in accordance with Celtic tradition, and adhered to by all circles working in the same cause.

The precise number of members in a circle is unimportant. The interaction between only two people can be enough to produce a very effective ritual. As a general rule, five is about the minimum number a circle should contain to be truly effective over a period of time. When a circle has gained much over twenty members, its inner dynamics tend to become confused or unbalanced, and it will often split of its own accord. The stage at which this critical threshold is crossed will vary from one circle to another, but it is always best to anticipate it and perform the division in a peaceable way, before unresolved psychic conflicts manage to weaken the circle as a functional whole.

The circle should have a leader, normally the person most experienced in both ritual work and Celtic lore. Those who come from "Wiccan" neo-pagan milieus will expect the dual leadership of a High Priest and Priestess, expressing the polarity of the God and Goddess and the polarity which gives rise to magical force, but (taking it for granted that there will be both men and women in a circle) a formal arrangement of this sort is not necessary in our tradition. The circle leader, aside from presiding at circle functions, serves as the circle's supreme decision maker, approves or disapproves suggested rituals, and trains neophytes (unless there are others equipped to do this). All circle members defer to his/her decisions in a spirit of unity and co-operation, but there should be no hint of autocratic leadership. Any decision that concerns the group as a whole must be the result of a discussion among all circle members—ensuring that every side of the argument is thoroughly expressed—and must be at least minimally acceptable to all. As they grow in experience, circle members should avoid being passive followers, and take more initiative and responsibility. The one area in which the circle leader has an absolute, unassailable power of decision is where matters of principle are concerned, matters that have to do with the integrity of the tradition itself.

Besides the symbolic imagery from which ceremonial work is constructed (and with which this book will be largely concerned), ritual work entails certain psychodynamic techniques that help open the consciousness to Otherworld contact. These techniques, relating as they do to the universal structure of the human psyche, are not culture-specific, and can be learned interchangeably from many different religious or magical traditions. If you have engaged in any form of ritual work before, it is likely that you already have some experience of such techniques. They usually involve exercises with breathing, concentration, and visualization. We will not dwell on this preparatory material here, but refer you either to an individual teacher or to the many excellent books on ceremonial magic, Tantra, Tai Qi, and other disciplines that will give you the basic starting points. (Each circle should have at least one member—preferably the leader—capable of providing such training.)

Now our circle is fully constituted, and is ready for its first meeting. Any such meeting will occur within a specific context of space and time. From the Celtic point of view (indeed, from that of any traditional culture) all correlations of space and time have *meaning*, which cannot be ignored. When we establish a ritual context, time and space become sacred, and their meaning is experienced firsthand. Our orientation in space will express a specific attitude toward the Otherworld influences that shape our reality, since the structure of sacred space is reflected in the structure of the Tribe. Time progresses according to a perennial cycle, determining the combined transformations of Tribe and Land at all levels, assuring that all the processes necessary for the maintenance of both have been gone through. Thus, each ritual will relate the energies inherent in a particular period of sacred time to the constant matrix of sacred space. We must, in order to do ritual work that is relevant to the Celtic continuum, become thoroughly conversant with the symbolic language that describes sacred space and time in the Celtic tradition.

The primary guiding concept in the Celtic worldview is that of universal polarity. Although before the stage at which events manifest there is primordial unity, all phenomena emerge from the interplay of polar opposites. The original polarized duality is variously expressed as Day and Night, Summer and Winter, God and Goddess, Tribe and Land, this world and Otherworld. Neven Henaff, a Breton nationalist thinker of the early twentieth century, referred to it as the

"Sam-Giam" opposition, from the Old Celtic *samos* and *giamos*, "summer" and "winter." It is the fundamental difference between these two principles that allows change to occur, and individual entities to exist. Every unit of existence, great or small, whether in space or in time, is made up of the two principles in interaction. Space, taken as a whole, contains a primary contrast between South, which is Night, and North, which is Day. The yearly cycle of time also divides into two halves: *giamos*, from November 1 to May 1, the "Night," or Winter, half; and *samos*, from May 1 to November 1, the "Day," or Summer, half. These primary divisions also can be halved, revealing the Day-Night duality within their own structure, to produce quarters; and the splitting can go on *ad infinitum*, until the smallest perceptible unit of space or time can be shown to contain the same inherent duality as the largest. The Coligny Calendar gives us a good example of this, dividing the year first into six-month *giamos* and *samos* halves, then identifying each month as either *matos* (good, Day-governed) or *anmatos* (not-good, Night-governed), and finally extending the same distinction to every single day in each month, so that the overall pattern of the year comes to resemble a giant chessboard (itself a symbolically charged image in Celtic tradition). At this stage we need not concern ourselves with the finer aspects of the division, but only become familiar with the primary sections that are constantly referred to in ritual. Let us begin with the symbolism of sacred space.

When creating a ritual space, we must first establish a center. This center is identified with the invisible presence of the World Tree—the *Bilios*—at the heart of reality, which spans all the planes of existence with its height, allowing access from this world to the Otherworld. It is at the foot of this Tree, resplendent in gold leaves, that Conn of the Hundred Battles met the Land-goddess and received the Sovereignty of Ireland from her in a wedding-cup. It is also the same Tree that Peredur saw, burning on one side, healthy and green on the other, on the edge of the river that is the boundary between the worlds. The two sides of the Tree, then, will define the two halves of our ritual space. The northern half will represent Day, Summer, the God, the Tribe, the living, all conscious activity, which can be summarized as the *samos*-mode. The southern half, conversely, will stand for Night, Winter, the Goddess, the Land, the dead, all unconscious processes, and all nonhuman agencies that impact on our lives, the *giamos*-mode. We are, thus, in the presence of the two first principles that shape our experience.

For most ritual purposes, sacred space is further divided into quarters, corresponding to the four cardinal directions. The text called *Suidigud Tellaig Temra,* "The Settling of the Manor at Tara," gives us the Celtic tradition concerning the meaning of the quarters. This differs considerably from the Qabalistically-derived attributions used in ceremonial magic, and adopted by most neo-pagans. If you have become used to invoking the quarters in some such tradition, you will have to unlearn all the attributions before becoming able to function in this type of Celtic ritual context. The quarters, in Celtic tradition, correspond to the functions within the Tribe. The first function, *fios* (knowledge) is placed in the West; the second function, *cath* (battle) in the North; the third function, *bláth* (plenty), in the East; and the "fourth" function, comprising all that which is left over from the trifunctional scheme, and which is referred to as *séis* (song), the mysterious inborn gift of artistic talent), is in the South, the direction of the Goddess. The center, where the High King traditionally resides, holds all these functions together in balance (through the exercise of *flaith* or sovereignty). As we will see throughout Celtic tradition, the same symbolic construct can be analyzed and interpreted in several different ways simultaneously. On the one hand, West and North are seen as divisions of the Northern, "God" half, while East and South both belong to the Southern, "Goddess" half, pointing up the link between the food-producing function and the Land. But on the other hand, the three essential tribal functions can appropriately be placed in the Northern half that belongs to the Tribe, so that the "different" symbolic quality of the South can be highlighted, giving it the entire "Goddess" half of sacred space to itself. This last view is well expressed in the figure of the Celtic Cross: the bottom (Southern) arm extends itself to become the shaft that supports the whole structure with its three other arms, just as the Land is the base that sustains the existence of the trifunctional Tribe.

From the *Lebor Gabála Érenn* and related texts we get further information on the attributes of the quarters. The gods of the Tribe, called the Tuatha Dé Danann in this context, obtained the powers governing the tribal functions from four Otherworld "cities," which can be made to correspond to the symbolism of the cardinal directions as we have seen it in *Suidigud Tellaig Temra*. From Goirias, the "burning fort," came the Spear of Lugh, who is Lord of Light and Sovereign of the gods, as well as supreme bard and patron of all scholars; so the lightning-spear dispels darkness, a symbol of the mind and of the first function, and is placed in the West. From Findias (modern Finnias), the "bright-white fort," was brought the Sword of Nuadu Airgetlam, the king of the Danann-folk before Lugh's accession, representing battle-valor and championship, the second function in the North. From Muirias, "fort of the sea," the "undry" Cauldron of the Dagda, which leaves no one unsated, is clearly a gift of fertility, an instrument of the Eastern third function. And the Stone of Fál, from its eponymous city of Fáilias, is the most important of the four "Treasures" (*séta*), since it was placed in Tara—the sacred center of Ireland—to cry out at the coming of a rightful High King. Since only the Land-goddess can confer Sovereignty on anyone, the Stone is obviously her attribute, and represents the Southern quarter. We are also told of *físidh*, or seers, now given pseudo-Biblical names, who dwell in the four cities and who once instructed the Danann-folk in their arts. These are, of course, comparatively late traditions, not always spelled out consistently, and not necessarily a faithful reflection of any pre-Christian situation; but they do conform to the Celtic model of sacred space we have just outlined.

The four Treasures will appear familiar to many people who have no background in Celtic lore. They are directly related to the "Grail Hallows" that are brought out in procession before the questing hero in the Grail romances. But they are also very reminiscent of the four instruments—wand, sword, cup, and pentacle—of the magician in the ceremonial magic tradition, which serve as the basis for the four suits of the Tarot. These last represent the Classical Greco-Roman period elements of Fire, Air, Water, and Earth, and the human faculties that correspond to each. There is little evidence to suggest that the theory of the elements was a part of the Celtic consciousness before the medieval period; yet it *is* possible to find elemental correspondences for the cities and their Treasures: the names of Goirias and Muirias clearly associate them with fire and water respectively, and *Fáilias* (the enclosure), the place of the Stone, easily stands for earth, which leaves Findias to represent air. That these correspondences agree by and large with the ceremonial-magic ones can be both a help and a hindrance to circle members who have previous experience of such traditions. On the one hand, the images of the Treasures and their basic significance will have a familiar feel about them from the start, allowing immediate identification with their functions; on the other hand, their quarter-attributions are completely different, and the symbolic system they articulate is based ultimately not on elemental theory, but on the Tribe-Land ideology we outlined earlier.

From the names of the cardinal points in the Celtic languages it is clear that the East—the place of the Sun's rising, the source of all Light—was the privileged direction to face in prayer and ritual; the Welsh *gogledd*, "North," literally means "under the left hand," while *deheu, de* mean both "South" and "right hand;" and the Irish *iar*, "West," originally meant "after," corresponding to *oir* meaning both "East" and "before" (*are-* in Old Celtic). Solar images constitute a seminal model for ritual activities, in general. As in many Indo-European ritual traditions (especially in India), only sunwise movement (i.e., toward the right) is considered auspicious in ritual space; Irish tradition calls this *cor deiseil*, the "auspicious" right-hand turn which collaborates with the Sun's creative energy, and differentiates it from *cor tuathal* (the "profane" or "mundane" left-hand turn), which is never used except in destructive operations like cursing and black magic, where something is "unmade." It also appears evident that the distinctive characteristics of the quarters are in some measure "reflections" of the Sun's influence; thus, the birth of quickening Fire in the East is "reflected" in the West's association with illumination, and the Sun's final resting place in the vast ocean of the West (where the dead go) is "reflected" in the East's association with Water and fertility.

It will be useful to memorize the following correspondences:

Spear	=	West	=	First Function
Sword	=	North	=	Second Function
Cauldron	=	East	=	Third Function
Stone	=	South	=	"Fourth" Function, Land

Each of the Treasures must be wielded by a divine agent in order
to be effective, so we will, in ritual, put them in the care of the God
of the corresponding function. The Spear belongs to the Many-
Gifted Lord (or Lord of Illumination), the trickster-god who wins
by magic and guile rather than by brute strength, but who also, because of his superior knowledge of all things, serves as champion and
arbiter of society as a whole (this, of course, is Lugus/Lugh in Celtic
tradition). The Sword belongs to the Lord of Battles, the defender of
the Tribe, skilled in fighting but also in healing, the guardian of the
borders of the settled world. The Cauldron (although it is, originally,
an attribute of the Land-goddess) belongs to the Lord of Riches, the
fat God of material comfort, who is the direct recipient of the Land's
fertility, and can share it with the Tribe and translate it into wealth.
And the Stone, which draws to itself and grounds the powers of the
three functions, belongs, of course, to the Land-goddess herself, the
Great Mother on whom all creatures depend for sustenance, the
supreme reality of life on this plane.

It is a good idea for the circle to obtain a set of Treasures of its
own, talismans that will serve as a ritual focus for the quarters and
the functions associated with them. They also will dramatize the circle's role as microcosm of the Tribe, with all the Tribe-Land functions in its keeping. There is no need to make major expenditures on
realistic weaponry! Anything that satisfies the circle as a good symbolic representation of Spear or Sword will do the job very well.
And the Cauldron need not be a facsimile of the Gundestrup Cauldron; any large vessel can have the right connotations. The Stone
should be a chance-found stone that a fourth-function circle member finds to be of significant interest.

There are many other less well-marked attributions for the quarters in Celtic tradition, which you may or may not want to explore
at this stage. Any mythological or folkloric elements that come in
pairs or in groups of four or eight tend to have sacred-space asso-

ciations. The one important quaternity that we do need to introduce before we go further is that comprised by the four animals that Fintan Mac Bóchra, and later Tuan Mac Cairill, transformed into after their first deaths: Boar, Stag, Eagle, and Salmon. The same animals—which independently play important roles throughout Celtic mythology—reappear in combination in the *Culhwch ac Olwen* story, in which three of the five "oldest animals" are the Stag of Rhedynfre, the Eagle of Gwern Abwy, and the Salmon of Llyn Llyw, and the Boar Trwyth is, of course, one of the main protagonists of the plot. They are also the only animals mentioned in that cryptic and powerful incantation, the first Song of Aimhirgin. The Eagle (or Hawk; the Old Irish term *séig* often used in this context seems to have denoted raptors generically) should be placed in the North; the Salmon in the East (though as *bradán feasa* it is also linked with knowledge and poetry, and can have western and southern associations); while the Stag and Boar share the symbolic representation of South and West, a situation occasioned by the mobility of the Boar in the Cosmic Boar Hunt, which we will discuss later in the context of sacred time, so that the Boar is in the South (as a chthonic, Goddess-owned being) during the *giamos* half of the year, and in the West (as a solar teacher) during the *samos* half, with the Stag occupying the complementary positions—a practice Céli Dé Circle introduced and followed profitably.

This last ambiguity highlights the peculiar significance of the Southwest in Celtic sacred space, as the direction most intimately associated with the Goddess and most immediately open to Otherworld influence. It also reminds us that, besides the model of sacred space that depicts it as a quartered circle (the Tara model), there is another one (the Uisneach model) which draws it as a pentagram, making Southeast and Southwest cardinal directions, South-east being symbolically linked with "fourth function" activities (i.e., oriented toward the Tribe), and Southwest with the image of the Goddess (i.e., oriented toward the Land, the nonhuman environment, the Otherworld). There are ritual occasions on which use of this alternate cosmology is appropriate, but within the framework of this book we will use the Tara model as a basic reference throughout.

Besides the twofold and fourfold divisions of the expanse of Land on which we stand, ordered around the center defined by the *Bilios*, it is traditional also to see a threefold division of the world vertically along the axis of the World Tree. Above us is Sky (*nemos*), whence comes our light and everything that promotes clarity and understanding, and where we place the original home of the gods of the Tribe: this is the realm of order and permanence, of everything that promotes and sustains cultural values. Below us, encircling the Earth and supporting it, is the realm of Sea (*mori*), which merges with the watery Underworld: the realm of darkness and chaos, but also of all fertility; the home of the "antigods" who own the mysteries of Death and Life, and the home of the ancestors. Where we ourselves stand is the four-sided Earth (*terrês, talamu*), the meeting-place of Above and Below, and where it is our task to balance out the contradictory influences of the two other realms so that we may survive and prosper.

From the archaeological record it is evident that the appearance of Celtic sanctuaries varied quite a bit over time. The earliest ritual sites were probably forest clearings or groves that were cut off from the mundane world by their intrinsic sacredness, with no permanent structures marking them. Eventually forms of religious architecture developed: the rectangular enclosures known to archaeologists as *Viereckschanzen* seem to have been meeting-places where certain community matters could be solemnized in the presence of the gods. (The second century B.C. inscription from Vercelli in northern Italy apparently commemorates the dedication of such a space: the sanctuary itself is referred to as an *antos* or "precinct," and it is given over to the use of the *deuogdonioi*, or "gods and mortals together.") Often sites of this type had a ritual shaft dug near them for offerings to the powers of the Underworld. By the later Iron Age more elaborate temples appeared: the so-called "Belgic" shrines, like the one at Gournay near the river Oise. In sanctuaries of this type, the *nemeton* (or "place made heavenly") was cut off from the mundane world by a deep ditch. Inside, the center of ritual space was usually marked by a post representing the *Bilios* or World Tree (or several posts representing the quarters), and there would be spaces for communication with the powers Above and Below, by means of the primal elements of Fire and Water: a shaft for offerings directed at the watery Underworld, and a place for bonfires whose flames reached upward toward the celestial realm. When Christianity came to the Celtic world, many of the ideas about sacred space remained unchanged, and it was still customary to cut the *nemeton* (now round rather than square, symbolizing the cosmos rather than just the earthly plane) away from the world by digging a ditch around it.

With the symbolic structure of the sacred space about us clear in our minds, we can begin our ritual. Whether we decide to hold it indoors or outdoors, at a historically significant location, or anywhere convenient is not very important. Most rituals should begin after sunset, since it belongs to the realm of activity that is symbolically ruled by the "Night" side of time (although some rituals, like the one for Bealtaine/Calan Mai, are specifically intended to be performed at dawn). At our designated sacred center we will establish an altar area, where whatever ritual implements we will need must be placed. This need not be a raised altar, as in ceremonial magic and some neo-pagan traditions; it is best to place the altar furnishings directly on the ground, perhaps on a tablecloth of the appropriate seasonal color. The furnishings can be as elaborate or as simple as the circle prefers. Among the essentials are: a means of designating the World Tree at the center (a tall pole, if space permits; one can also use a living tree, if outdoors; or if indoors, something as simple as a potted shrub!); a bowl of water for lustrations; a bowl or cauldron to receive the offerings for the powers Below, which then can be given to the soil outside (an outdoor shrine could, of course, have an offering pit); a corresponding means of manifesting the presence of Fire (a bonfire outdoors, or, if indoors, something as simple as a candle); effigies of the four Treasures to mark the quarters (the circle's actual talismans need not be used this way except on special occasions, to be described later; for most rituals, mere pictures of them will do); and, since our sacred space—in the novel way we conceive of it today—is also to be a microcosmic Celtic World, Pan-Celtic in the consciousness it will promote, there should be some symbolic representation of all the Celtic countries, arranged around the center in more or less geographic order. Since there are six countries and four quarters, the arrangement will have to be a symmetry of compromise. The suggested positions are: Scotland in the North; the Isle of Man and Ireland to the north and south of West; Wales and Cornwall to the north and south of East; and Brittany in the South. The tokens themselves can be very simple—perhaps colored tiles bearing images that have had widespread use and much resonance, such as thistle, trinacria (the three-legged symbol on the Manx flag), harp, dragon, chough, and ermine.

Fire and Water are of primary ritual importance in Celtic tradition, representing the polarity of *samos* and *giamos*, expansion and contraction. People who have assimilated the constant use of the four elements as points of reference in ceremonial magic may feel more comfortable if the other two elements are also present on the altar, in the shape of incense and salt. There is nothing inherently wrong with this. Incense did not play a demonstrable part in early Celtic tradition, but it can be very effective in ritual of any kind, and there are a number of scents derived from symbolically-charged herbs that function perfectly in a Celtic context. Early Celts rarely had access to the aromatic gums from the Middle East that were used in Mediterranean ritual, and whose usage spread with Judaism and Christianity; if they used fragrances at all, it was most likely through the means of steam.

The only personal implement each circle member may want to have in a public ritual is a wand, which serves to focus and extend the energy concentrated in a ritualist's own person. The wand should be made from the wood of one of the ritually consecrated types of trees: oak, holly, rowan, hazel, ash, apple, alder, birch, willow, or yew.

Before the ritual, if one isn't in a permanently consecrated shrine, one must separate the ritual space from mundane space. This can be done by the circle leader with his/her wand, helped in his/her visualization by the rest of the circle members. The cutting-away from the mundane either can be done either with the participants already inside, or, in more elaborate and dramatic rituals, the participants can come in *after* sacred space has been established, through a "doorway" opened by the ritual leader. This, of course, is a borrowing from modern magical traditions. In early Celtic practice, sacred space—whether it was a temple building, or a grove outdoors—existed in and of itself, and, once it had been cut away, needed no further ritual to separate it from mundane space; but a circle today may not always have the luxury of a permanent and private meeting-place it can definitively sacralize.

Each ritual will consist of some events in unvarying sequence. First, we must establish an awareness of sacred space through the invocation of the Quarters, in which the original energies behind the tribal functions are called from the Otherworld into the ritual area; and we must visualize the three realms of existence. Once our space is open to contact with the Otherworld, the ritual can proceed "in the presence of the Divine." The simplest and most basic expression of Celtic ritual is a communal feast "of gods and mortals together," since in Celtic tradition a feast presided over by the local ruler or family head is the prime means of solemnly formalizing decisions that affect a particular community. There will, however, usually be a mythic pattern for the ritual to follow according to the nature of the occasion or its place in the seasonal cycle, and this will be presented through some poetic or dramatic means. Then the rite can be enacted, in which the appropriate ritual gestures accomplish the exchange with the Otherworld that is called for at that time; and the Feast, which serves to balance and sort out the energy raised, and is also meant to recall the Otherworld Feast, the Celtic equivalent of "Paradise;" and, finally, the dismissal of the powers must achieve the restoration of mundane space. This sequence will seem familiar to most people, and not without reason: it follows the logic of the dynamics of ritual, which is expressed almost identically in all cultures.

The invocation of the Quarters, performed by the ritual leader with the concentrated backing of the other members, will combine visualization with sonics, and will serve here as an example of how one may eventually approach other parts of the ritual. Magical traditions from around the world agree in defining all material existence as vibration in many frequencies, each frequency resulting in a different observable phenomenon, and all frequencies impacting on each other. Ritual uses this great "Oneness" on the vibratory level to encourage changes in external and internal phenomena by a simultaneous application of mental images (thought, too, is vibration) and actual sound. For our invocation, we will concentrate on certain commonly agreed-upon visual cues to represent each of the Quarters, while the ritual leader calls them up with an appropriate chant.

This last aspect again raises the question of language. While ritually effective chants can be devised in any tongue, a chant that has spectacular power in one language cannot be simply "translated" into another: the sonics involved will be too different to yield the same results, whatever else may happen. Thus, one must not glibly provide English or French texts for chants originally composed in Celtic languages. Although in parts of ritual that are merely spoken the choice of language is not very important (even here, however, there will be subtle differences in effect), where chanting is concerned the combination of measured pitch, rhythmic stress and pauses, and the specific field of sonic vibration that corresponds to a certain language's phonetic range produces a structure so intricate and multifaceted that no major element of it can be changed without grossly adulterating the whole. So there can be no substitute for Celtic languages in a Celtic ritual context. Their use, in any case, should be a continuing sign of the circle's commitment to the heritage of the Tribe.

During the invocation the primary chant should be a *cantlon* recited by the ritual leader at each of the quarters, while the other circle members concentrate on visualizing the features that are symbolic of the influence of that quarter. The *cantlon*, in this case, is a rapid chant on three or four tones, identical in style to the type of "Ossianic Chant" used in the southern part of the Outer Hebrides for epic recitations. At its culmination the entire circle intones the induction, a short formula which actually draws the power of the quarter into the circle. Every sound of this phrase must be vibrated separately and fully. (In circles whose members still have only a beginner's familiarity with Celtic languages, a spoken summary of the *cantlon* in an imperial language may be inserted between it and the induction.)

Which language, and which texts, should we be using? This will depend very much on an individual circle's abilities, knowledge, and inclinations at a given time. Here, we suggest one format that has the advantage of being tried-and-true. There is no need for other circles to try to reproduce it exactly, but it will provide a good enunciation of the basic principles that all circles should hold in common. Taking the four larger Celtic countries to represent the quarters (keeping our original altar pattern, but giving the West to Ireland and the East to Wales), we will use Scots Gaelic as the language for the invocation to the North, Welsh for the East, Breton for the South, and Irish for the West. You may, after following this procedure a few times, be struck by how effective it is and how perfectly the sonic contours of the individual languages correspond to their quarter-associations.

The ritual leader first faces the East in salutation; then, pivoting in the direction of his/her outstretched left arm, turns toward the North, and begins the invocation.

NORTH

CANTLON

Tha mi tionndaidh mu thuath, gu Finnias, an Chathair Glé Gheal,
 Dùn nan Treun,
 Dùn nan Gaisceach,
 Dùn nam Misneach,
 Dùn as an tig gach dion is fearalachd,
 Dachaidh do Thighearna nam Blàr,
 Tighearna nan Cath,
 Tighearna nam Buadh,
 Tighearna nan Cogaidhean,
Tighearna aig a bheil cumhachd air gach neart is làidireachd,
 Ar leis an Claidheamh,
 An Claidheamh nach fuiling ruaig,
 An Claidheamh nach giùlain call,
 An Claidheamh a tha freagarrach don Righ Mòr,
 Agus ar leis an t-Iolair,
 An t-Iolair geurshùileach,
 An t-Iolair tromsporach,
 An t-Iolair cruaidhghobach,
 An t-Iolair leathann-sgiathach air Gaothan an Neimh,
 A Churaidh,
 A Laoich,
 A Ghaiscich,
 A Threunlaoich . . .

Spoken: *I turn to the North, to Finnias, the shining-white fort, home of the Lord of Battles, Keeper of the Sword, Master of the Eagle and of All the Winds of Heaven!*

INDUCTION: *Thig Anochd!*

Visualization: A mountaintop environment, with much bare rock, steep escarpments, and snow on peaks. Sensation of cold, of violent wind. The Fort, at the summit of a high and steep tor, has a diamond-like consistency, charged with cold, bright light. The Lord of Battles comes from the Fort toward us: he is, in physical attributes, bearing, and adornment, the divine epitome of the Celtic warrior-aristocrat (see the many descriptions in the *Táin Bó Cualnge*, among other sources, for helpful reference). The Lord is best seen as tall, slender, muscular, and fair-haired; he may be visualized more specifically as Nuadu with his silver hand. He holds a great, shining sword, which he places in our midst. We may see the image of the Eagle superimposed upon it; or some aspect of its decoration may contain the figure of the Eagle.

The circle leader then turns to the East, and goes on through the remaining quarters in a deosil or clockwise direction.

EAST

CANTLON:

Trof i at y Dwyrain, at Morwys, Dinas y Môr,
Dinas y Rhai Ffrwythlon,
Dinas y Rhai Hardd,
Dinas y Rhai Maethlon.
Dinas y Rhai sy'n gweithio am fwydo'r ddaear,
Cartref i Arglwydd y Goludon,
Arglwydd genedigaeth,
Arglwydd tyfiant,

Arglwydd y blodeuo a'r medi,
Arglwydd y casglu a'r rhannu,
Yr Arglwydd tew o bob daioni,
Yr hwn y mae ganddo'r Pair,
Y Pair a rhoes fywyd,
Y Pair llawn,
Y Pair na fydd byth yn wag,
Lloches i'r Eog,
Yr Eog cigrudd,
Yr Eog corffgrwn,
Yr Eog o'r Dwr Dwfn,
Yr Eog o'r Ffynnon lle mae'r Dduwies yn esgor,
O Toreithiog,
O Cnydfawr,
O Maethol . . .

Spoken: *I turn to the East, to Muirias, the Fort of the Sea, Home of the Lord of Riches, Keeper of the Cauldron, Master of the Salmon and of All Fountains and Springs!*

INDUCTION: *Tyrd Heno!*

Visualization: At the seashore, sunlight on the waves, a sense of teeming marine life, fish, colonies of seabirds, shellfish, kelp, and seaweed of many kinds washed up on the rocks. A rich, organic smell in the air. The Fort, a vast, low, round structure covered with seaweed and barnacles, rises directly out of the water, with foaming waves beating upon its ramparts. The Lord of Riches, a very fat, smiling, good-natured figure (the Dagda in *Cath Maige Tuireadh* may be used as a model), brings the Cauldron to us. This is an immense vessel, steaming and full of boiling liquid, from which come the most mouth-watering smells of nourishing food. An image of the Salmon may be superimposed on the Cauldron.

SOUTH

CANTLON

Treiñ 'ran betek ar C'hreisteiz, betek Gwaloues, Kêr an Tonkad,
     Kêr ar Re Fur,
     Kêr ar Re Guzh,
     Kêr ar Re Gevrinus,
     Kêr a zo tost ouzh gwrizioù an Douar,
     Kêr d'an Itron Veur,
     Itron an Noz,
     Itron ar Galloud,
     Itron ar Beli,
     Itron ar Goañv hag an Hañv,
     Hag a vez ganti ar Maen,
     Maen an Diougan,
     Maen an Awen,
     Maen an Dibab Sur,
giamos: Tarzhiad d'an Torc'h,
     An Torc'h gouez,
     An Torc'h pounner,
     An Torc'h deus an Torgennoù Kleuz,
     An Torc'h a zo Kannad an Donder,
samos: Tarzhiad d'ar C'harv,
     Karv ar Serr-Noz,
     Karv an Henchoù Kuzh,
     Karv er C'hoad Neved,
     Karv a stur betek Bed an Anaon,
     O Kevrin,
     O Skoazell,
     O Kaerder . . .

Spoken: *I turn to the South, to Failias, the Great Enclosure, the Fort of Fate, Home of the Great Mother, Keeper of the Stone, Mistress of the Boar (Stag) and of All Deep Things.*

INDUCTION: *Deus Hennozh!*

Visualization: Twilight at the edge of a forest. Atmosphere of mystery, secrecy. The Fort is underground, marked by what appears to be a tumulus grave, and its door in the side of the mound opens on pitch darkness. The Great Mother, a tall woman of powerful aspect, clad in outer garments of muted earth colors under which flame-colored inner garments can be glimpsed, reveals the Stone, a table sized, oblong object covered with intricate carved interlace. The image of the Boar, or of the Stag (depending on the season), may be superimposed on this.

WEST

CANTLON:

> Iompaím siar go dtí Goirias, an Chathair Tintrí,
> Dún an tSolais,
> Dún Teasa,
> Dún Feasa,
> Dún Lúfaireachta na h-Intinne,
> Baile don Tiarna Ioldánach,
> Tiarna na nÉagas 's na bhFile,
> Tiarna na nDraoithe 's na Naomh,
> Tiarna na gCeardaithe 's na Saor,
> Ar leis an tSleá,
> An tSleá a pholann na scamaill,
> An tSleá a mhileann an dorchadas,
> An tSleá a bheireann bua ar an damhna,

giamos: > 'S ar leis an Carria,
> An Damh-Allaidh maorga,
> An Fia nach bhfuil eagal air,
> An Carria a chuir solas na Gréine 'na bheanna,

samos: > 'S ar leis an Torc,
> Torc na Gréine,
> Torc na Saíochta,

Torc a aiséiríonn as a fhuil féin,
A Fhionnghil,
A Lonraigh,
A Fheasaigh . . .

Spoken: *I Turn to the West, to Goirias, the Burning Fort, Home of the Many-Gifted Lord, Keeper of the Spear, Master of the Stag (Boar) and of All Illumination!*

INDUCTION: *Tar Anocht!*

Visualization: On a fertile plain at sunset, with the sky colorful and still bright. The Fort looks incandescent with red and golden flame. Harp music in the air. The Many-Gifted Lord—Lúgh, who is widely mentioned throughout Celtic tradition—appears, surrounded by solar radiance, carrying the Spear with its point of blinding light. The image of the Stag, or of the Boar (depending on the season), may be seen within the aura of light.

After invoking the Quarters the entire circle focuses on the center, visualizing the four Treasures in their Otherworld aspect coming together in the altar area, establishing the sovereignty of the Tribe. Then the Realm Above and the Realm Below must be invited to communicate with our Middle Realm. We become aware of existing on three levels, with the source of mind-awakening Light above us and the chaotic, creative, and fertile Darkness below us, and our consciousness the middle ground on which they can interact. We call the respective powers "from above" and "from below," so that the Tribal concept of the settled Land becomes impregnated with the primal energies of the universe.

Once sacred space is established and the powers of the Quarters and the three levels of existence are activated inside the circle, we can begin the ritual presentation of the symbolic material associated with the feast we are celebrating. Of course this material will vary with each occasion, and will determine the content of the Rite and even, to some extent, that of the Feasting which ends the ritual. Such specific elements are conditioned by sacred time, the evolution of energies (and of this world/Otherworld exchanges) during the seasonal cycle, and we will explore them later.

If we are working in a temporarily consecrated space, when the ritual has been completed the powers of the Quarters must be dismissed and the visualized entrances to the Quarters sealed back into the Otherworld. Again the ritual leader proceeds to each Quarter in turn, tracing a Celtic cross with his/her wand across the Quarter, seeing the two bars of the cross closing off the visualized scene from the circle space, and the tracing of the ring banishing the visualization itself. After the dismissal of each Quarter the entire circle intones a valedictory formula, preferably something short and ordinary, such as "*Slán libh*" (particularly easy and effective to vibrate) or "*Henffych well.*" Then all participants must take a moment to make sure that whatever energy is left over from the ritual is properly grounded, and will not remain as a psychic overcharge in everyday life. Once this has been accomplished and a sense of quiet and balance prevails, the leader announces the end of the ritual, and we are back in the mundane world. But not quite, for Otherworld forces have been invited to influence processes in our everyday reality, and their effect will continue to be felt in subtle ways.

We now come to the subject of sacred time, the cyclic continuum within which sacred space exists. We have already mentioned that in the Celtic worldview the structure of time is, like that of space, dependent on the fundamental "Day-Night" dualism that gives rise to all phenomena. The primary cycle, the Year (*bleidni*), is divided into a *giamos*-half beginning on November first and a *samos*-half beginning on May first. The *giamos*-half comes first because the unconscious precedes consciousness, an unseen gestation in the dark of the womb precedes birth, and so Winter is felt to be the gestation of the Summer (in Celtic reckoning a "day" period begins at sunset, the daylight "growing out" of the night). Thus Samhain, the feast that opens the *giamos* season, is also the New Year. If each half is further divided into quarters, we get two new seasons: Spring (*vesrâ*), beginning on February 1, within the *giamos*-half; and Harvest (*methâ*), beginning on August 1, within the *samos*-half. Spring is thus the "light," *samos*-oriented half of the *giamos* season, and Harvest is the "dark," *giamos*-oriented half of the *samos* season. Each of the four seasons is inaugurated by a feast day: Samhain, Imbolc (or Oímealg), Bealtaine, and Lúghnasadh (or Lúnasa), to give their better-known Irish names (these are familiar to many outside the Celtic world, since they have been adopted as holidays by a wide variety of neo-pagan groups—usually, though not always, with some of their original connotations).

The passage from one God- or Goddess-dominated unit to another constitutes a "hinge" that belongs to neither. In such an area one is exempt from normal conditions of space and time, and more immediately within reach of the infinite potential that the Otherworld provides. Where, in the context of color-symbolism, the *samos* and *giamos*, God and Goddess, principles are represented by white and black, the element that comes between them and causes change from one to the other is signified by the color red—perhaps because it can be associated with sunrise and sunset, the passage between day and night. So the quarterly feasts can be seen as "red" factors within the black and white halves of the year. Red, the color of life and creativity, thus also becomes an indicator of Otherworld influence. The larger the units that are joined by such a feast, the more powerful is that influence during the feast. Samhain, as the passage from one year to another, is the most important and magically powerful of the four; Bealtaine, the hinge between the year's *giamos*-half and *samos*-half, is second in importance; and Imbolc and Lúghnasadh are in third place.

The four seasons may be seen as the quarters of the circle within the Celtic cross, while the feasts appear as the dividing arms, with Samhain at the longest, "Southern" position. Each feast, representing a different change and a specific form of exposure to the Otherworld, is celebrated with its own rituals suited to its symbolic function. The four quarterly feasts will serve as the primary focus of the circle's ritual year, but they are not the only milestones to be commemorated in sacred time; and, in fact, there are three different cycles running concurrently through the year that are of direct concern to the circle. They are:

1. The Cycles of Earth and Sun.
2. The Cycle of the Moon.
3. The Cycle of Events, or the Cycle of the Tribe.

The Cycles of Earth and Sun, as its name suggests, is itself a combination of two different cycles, one them astronomically precise, following the solstices and equinoxes of the solar year, and the other consisting of the aforementioned quarterly feasts, which have no traditional astronomical basis, and were originally celebrated in relation to natural events affecting the agricultural cycle (probably guided in some measure by a lunar calendar), for which reason they may be appropriately called "earth feasts." However, since in practice the solar feasts always occurred approximately midway between the quarterly "earth feasts," it has become usual to treat all of them as a single cycle of eight consecutive festivals. Each solar feast functions as the ritual fulfillment, or "closure," of some important element in the quarterly feast preceding it. Although the Celts, at the time their civilization began to spread across Europe, showed, to the best of our knowledge, no strong consciousness of astronomical phenomena, the megalith-builders who had occupied the land before them clearly were experienced stargazers, and must have created a vigorous tradition around the solar feasts, with which their Celtic successors surely had become familiar by the time of their own First Golden Age. So, whether or not the cycle of the Sun was ever a part of "druidical" lore remains a controversial question, there is a certain amount of early precedent (possibly confirmed by the Coligny Calendar) for giving the solar feasts some prominence in the Celtic year—and they certainly have come to play an important role in more recent Celtic tradition. It must be remembered, however, that the "earth feasts" rank higher in ritual importance than the cycle of the Sun, and no attempt must be made to locate them as astronomically precise midpoints between solstices and equinoxes, treating them as "cross-quarter days" secondary to the solar feasts themselves, as is commonly done in many non-Celtic traditions.

While the Cycles of Earth and Sun reflect vast seasonal changes that have obvious impact on Tribe and Land alike, the Cycle of the Moon has a more intimate significance, relating to the life of the circle itself, and even to the psycho-spiritual development of each individual member within it. The Moon, closer to Earth and the world of mortals than the Sun, and visible mostly at night, the Goddess-ruled time of the unconscious, serves as a mirror for the self, presenting back to it, enlarged and clarified, its sensations, its conscious desires and unconscious impulses. By ritually following the Moon in her phases throughout the changing year, circle members will become sensitized to the subtle influence of the environment on their psychic functions, and will discover a new ability to use such influence to further their long-term projects. This ritual activity need not involve formal meetings of the entire circle; it can be conducted just as effectively by individuals singly or in small, intimately associated groups. There are different ways of recognizing the thirteen months of the lunar year; we will discuss them in a later chapter.

Finally, the Cycle of Events or Cycle of the Tribe consists of rituals that have their roots in historical accident, in past events that have helped to consolidate tribal identity. They are not spread evenly throughout the year, but occur at the points where chance and tradition have placed them. The precise number of them that the circle will deem important enough to commemorate will vary, though there are a few that are essential parts of the ritual year. Foremost among them are the festivals that have long served to crystallize the historical identities of each of the six Celtic nations. These usually coincide with the feast-days of saints with strong national associations. Some will object that this puts too much focus on specifically Christian elements; the point, however, is that it taps the considerable energy that is already directed at tribal symbols on those days. The rituals constructed by the circle for celebrating such occasions can draw upon the power of the symbols without necessarily referring to the feast's modern religious background (though there is nothing wrong about ritually commemorating particular saints, should one feel so inclined!). Since Saint Patrick is the patron of both the Irish and the Manx, we can choose to celebrate Tynwald Day—the day on which the Manx laws are publicly promulgated every year—as a date to focus on the distinctive identity of the Isle of Man. And because of the powerful Pan-Celtic influence of Iona, we can add Colm Cille's Day to the cycle as a feast to enhance Pan-Celtic perceptions. This gives us the following cycle of seven feasts: *Là Fèill-Anndrais* (Saint Andrew's Day) for Scotland, November 30; *Gwyl Dewi* (Saint David's Day) for Wales, March 1; *Goel Pyran* (Saint Piran's Day) for Cornwall, March 5; *Féile Pádraig* (Saint Patrick's Day) for

Ireland, March 17; *Gouel Erwan* (Saint Ives' Day) for Brittany, May 19; *Lá Cholm Cille* (Saint Columba's Day) for all Celts, June 9; and *Laa Tynvaal* (Tynwald Day) for the Isle of Man, July 5. The accidental concentration of festivals in the month of March (with the addition of the Spring Equinox) can be a welcome source of enthusiasm and purpose in what is, over much of the world, a rather dreary month! Of course, a circle in one of the six countries may wish to celebrate its own national feast in a particularly lavish fashion, but the other feasts in the cycle should not be forgotten, as they help maintain a consciousness of the full scope of the Celtic Tribe.

While the feasts listed above would be held by all circles in common, individual circles might wish to have one or more holidays of their own, expressing something of their specific identity or history. This would be entirely at the discretion of the circles themselves; they could choose a date with some regional resonance (a circle in Galicia, for instance, might like to celebrate the feast of Santiago), or one with an entirely private meaning, significant only for members of the group. It would strengthen the circle's sense of its life as a separate, individual entity within the Tribe.

Our journey through the festivals of the sacred Year will take us into a forest of primeval images, a place of powers stored, undiminished, for millennia, and ever ready to spring to life at the call or touch of the right person. The ancient drama of Day and Night, of growth and harvest, is played out by great divine figures, familiar yet full of glamour, whose deeds are the living pulse of our Tribe's heritage.

CHAPTER THREE

The Cycles of Earth and Sun

The essence of Time is, of course, change. Not one of us is, in all particulars, quite the same person he was yesterday, or indeed an hour ago. All around us the processes of growth and decay are evident at every level of earthly existence. Even symbols of permanence such as rocks and mountains are eaten away at last by their exposure to events in Time. Coastlines advance and recede; lands like Is and Cantre'r Gwaelod are now at the bottom of the sea, with submerged houses between Cornwall and Scilly to show us that there is a basis of fact to such legends. The careers of nations, languages, aesthetic perceptions, and belief systems undergo similar alternations of vigor and eclipse. Truly, as Heraclitus observed, *panta rrhei*, everything flows, nothing stands still, nothing keeps its shape for long. And yet, for all that we acknowledge the changes each day brings to our experience of the world, we still see ourselves as having a single, continuous identity. The tree that stood bare and lifeless through the snows of winter breaks out in buds with the spring thaw and before long is as green as it was the year before. Last year's herbs are dead, but their seeds grow into faithful replicas of them. Each yearly cycle is different, yet also much the same.

The Celtic heritage has always been fascinated by this tension between change and permanence, between the temporal and the eternal. It is an expression of the fundamental duality which, as we have seen, gives rise to manifest existence. All things are possible in the Otherworld; yet they will not impact our reality unless they come under the laws of Time. For, even though Time opens the way to entropy and loss, without Time there can be no action. So, if we take the imagery of the God-Goddess pair for our root symbolism, the God represents the active will applying itself through the dimension of Time, while the Goddess is that which guarantees the endurance and continuity of experience—ultimately, the Otherworld, beyond the laws of Space and Time, irreducible in its eternity. All beings exist at the contact-point of these two principles.

What is involved in change, as a linear sequence of events, is easy for us to grasp, since our perceptions are conditioned by the experience of Time. But how do we understand the principle behind continuity? What is it that resists the enforced change of Time? If we observe instances of permanence and continuity in our environment, we will come to the conclusion that what endures is a certain recognizable structure. The cells of our bodies die and are replaced, yet they remain organized in the same fashion. As forests are cut down, deserts appear, and the climatic map changes, but the functional relationship between different elements in the environment remains the same, the "laws of Nature" we have always known. This permanence of structure which exists in Time, but is somehow independent of it, is one of the main characteristics of the Goddess-realm. We could, in general terms, relate it to Space, but the principle implied, while it can be expressed through both Space and Time, ultimately precedes either, and is best simply called Form. Form, in this sense, is the Otherworld blueprint from which events originate. The Time-oriented, change-inducing will of the God is applied within the structures that the Goddess maintains.

We have seen that, in the Celtic perception of sacred time, units dominated by the God-principle alternate with units dominated by the Goddess-principle. The primary division is that of the Dark and Light halves of the year, *giamos* and *samos*, but the *giamos*-mode and the *samos*-mode are both operative within any process. In the *samos*-mode action is encouraged, linear causality in Time is dominant, and things are allowed to happen rapidly and in full view. In the *giamos*-mode, by contrast, the experience of changing Time is minimized, the will is muted, and what is needed is contemplation of the ever-present Form out of which new events will grow. Yet, what is it that causes the shift in dominance from one mode to the other; why do the two principles—equal in importance—never achieve a static balance? Here, as we have mentioned earlier, the Celtic heritage introduces the triad, the fundamental imparity which keeps balance ever-shifting, which makes change speed up or slow down. From the Otherworld comes—or, in mythological terms, the Goddess "chooses"—an element that alters the course of the active God-principle, leading it toward either the *giamos-* or the *samos*-pole. Since in both cases the agent in Time is still understood to be the God, the mythological response is to portray two gods—specific variants of the God—upon whom the Goddess alternately bestows her favor. And here we encounter God-figures like Cernunnos and Maponos.

We have already become familiar with the expression of God and Goddess as Tribe and Land, which is the one we experience most directly in everyday life. Human activities are an ever-changing continuum of causal events, for which the Land is a permanent supporting structure. In the mythology of this dimension, the Goddess of the Land is the eternal Queen, bestower of sovereignty upon the tribal King, while the God of the Tribe is, in his highest manifestation, a figure like Lugh, who represents the entire range of human activity with idealized perfection. But it is obvious that the yearly cycle—the winter dormancy of the earth, the return of green things—occurs independently of any human presence, that it represents an interaction between God and Goddess within the realm of the Land itself, preceding and overshadowing the relationship between Tribe and Land. It is the God's role at this primordial level that the Cernunnos and Maponos God-types represent.

The image of Cernunnos is now well-known to all people with an experience of neo-paganism; yet, perhaps because of certain choices made by the founders of Wicca, that image has been twisted away from its role in the original Celtic context. The tendency is to think of him as a priapic Pan-figure—surely a possible component of his nature, but far from the essence of his symbolic role. He is not, as modern non-Celtic imagination has made him, simply a "horned god." He is the god *with antlers*. The main characteristic of antlers, which distinguishes them from horns in general, is that they are cyclic, they fall off and grow back again. Thus, they mark Cernunnos as a God-form specifically related to the natural changes that make up the year. Whether his antlers are on or off will determine which half, *giamos* or *samos*, he is going through. Several traditional representations of Cernunnos show this alternation of states. On the Gundestrup Cauldron, we see the familiar depiction of him with antlers, holding a torc and a ram-headed serpent, and surrounded by wild beasts, on an inner panel; and another depiction without antlers, but identified by accompanying stags, on an outer panel. The Cernunnos altar from Saintes shows him antlered on one side, flanked by a stag and a bull, and with a smaller pair of figures, male and female, in the background; while on the other side, still holding out a torc, he sits beside his Goddess-consort, now the same size as himself (his head is now missing, but most likely he no longer had his antlers). Many items of Gallo-Roman statuary, identifiable as depictions of Cernunnos by the presence of determining attributes like the serpent, exhibit no antlers or budding antlers, or suggest the possibility that removable antlers were attached to them.

Mythological stories about a love-triangle in which two men compete for the favors of a woman are, of course, one of the most conspicuous elements in Celtic literary tradition. In some instances the motif is applied specifically to beings with supernatural associations, so that we are presented with fairly explicit renditions of the Cernunnos-Maponos theme. In the first Branch of the Mabinogi, for instance, Arawn Lord of Annwn (the Otherworld), who first appears in pursuit of a stag, is the rival of Hafgan (Summer-White); and Pwyll, Arawn's champion and successor, must compete for the favors of Rhiannon (Great Queen) with the Otherworld being Gwawl (Light, Shining). Even more explicitly, in *Culhwch ac Olwen* we are told of the rivalry between Gwyn ap Nudd—traditionally the leader of the Wild Hunt, who has his seat under the Tor of Glastonbury—and Gwythyr ap Greidawl, whose name again suggests shining and heat—for the hand of the goddess-figure Creiddylad, and the cyclic, ever-recurring nature of their confrontation (*hyt dyd brawt,* until the day of doom) is clearly pointed out. Here, too, we meet with Maponos by name, as Mabon ap Modron, "Great Son of the Great Mother," the prisoner who must be freed before Olwen, the Giant's daughter, can become a bride. And of course the entire story of the wooing of Olwen is, as we shall see, an expression of the divine "changing of the guard" as the year passes from *giamos* to *samos*. The same motif is represented in several folklore traditions by the image of the Black Man and the Green Man as seasonal rulers.

The most complete mythological rendition of the Cernunnos-type, however, is given in the story of Myrddin Wyllt (and, to a lesser extent, in its Irish imitation, *Buile Shuibhne*). There is no full extant version of the story in the original Welsh, but Geoffrey of Monmouth's Latin *Vita Merlini* seems likely to have followed native tradition quite closely. Driven to madness by the slaughter he has witnessed at the battle of Arderydd, in which kinsmen of his were slain on both sides, Myrddin (or Lailoken, or Llallwgan, as he is called in parallel sources) flees into the forest where he lives like an animal, cut away from the concerns and values of human society. His wife, left behind, takes another husband. Yet even as he bewails his solitude and physical discomfort, Myrddin begins to reap the benefits of his return to primal nature: a wolf becomes his companion and teacher, and he identifies with all wild things and becomes their master. Freed, by his abandonment of cultural norms, from a linear Time-perspective, he gains the power of prophecy. Eventually he resumes communication with the human world, aided by interaction with his sister Gwenddydd (or Ganieda) and his brother-in-law, the king Rhydderch Hael. Most significant from the point of view of mythological correspondences is the episode in which he defeats his rival, his wife's second husband. Riding on a stag, and accompanied by a herd of stags, he challenges the other man in front of his own former home (which the other has occupied); when his rival appears at an upper window, he slays him by pulling off the antlers of the stag he is riding and throwing them like knives. We have here an icon no doubt charged by centuries of druidic ritual, an echo of the various representations of Cernunnos with budding or absent antlers. Surely, at an earlier, more ritually conscious stage of the story's development, it was his own antlers—the symbol and consequence of his exile—that Cernunnos would throw at the young God of Summer, when the latter's period of influence in the cycle had come to an end.

One point of teaching that the figure of Cernunnos dramatizes is that the *giamos* and *samos* principles, although their dominance alternates, are never, on the level of human experience, manifested in an unmixed fashion. Even when the general circumstances of a situation suggest that the *samos*-mode is operative, some aspect of it is experiencing the *giamos*-mode, and vice versa. Thus, it is during the Light half of the year, when the entire natural world is given to the active exuberance of the *samos*-mode, that Cernunnos, deprived of his consort and of the ability to direct his creative energy outward, undergoes his own *giamos* phase, in which contemplation replaces action, the Otherworld can be perceived without the barriers of Space and Time, and the internalized energy produces illumination, symbolized by the growth of antlers. Then, during the year's Dark half, when the Land is dormant and immobile, Cernunnos is reunited with the Goddess and thus becomes capable of the *samos*-mode of active exchange, which will result in the Land's renewal. Always, when one of the two principles is evident at the surface level, its opposite is also at work on the deep level.

What of the Goddess' other choice, the God of Summer, the Maponos or Divine Boy? We have seen him as Mabon in Welsh tradition, but the best-rounded depiction of him in Celtic lore is surely to be found in the Irish tales of Aonghus an Mac Og, the archetypal young lover, vulnerable in his openness to passion yet immensely powerful in the determination of his love, and the protector of all young mortal lovers who pay homage to his archetype, especially if they rebel against the rigid values of their elders. His vitality and seductive nature win over the Goddess and lead her to choose him over her older consort, the Cernunnos-type. In the early Welsh versions of the Arthurian mythos we see him also as Melwas, who visits Gwenhwyfar secretly and elopes with her on his green horse to his Otherworld court, where she remains of her own free will until Arthur comes to win her back by force or by ruse. There is always, in portrayals of the Maponos-type, this suggestion of secretiveness, of hidden persuasion, highlighting perhaps the privacy of love, its uniqueness in every individual's experience. But, of course, the freshness and youthfulness are transitory: their blossoming is the expression of the *samos* season, and they end with it. The Maponos goes into *giamos*-mode by suffering death, or perhaps "imprisonment," like Mabon. According to various branches of the tradition, he will resurrect in the spring, or more often he will be reborn at the Winter Solstice, be stolen away, recovered, grow to manhood, and reclaim the Goddess at Bealtaine. Cernunnos, meanwhile, is the permanent witness of all the events in the year, capable of existing in both seasons, and of passing from one into the other; it is this ability to cross boundaries, to straddle not only winter and summer but concepts such as wilderness and cultivation, This-World and Otherworld, that led some of the ancient Celts to use his image as a symbol of material well-being and success, fostered by easy exchange of resources: the Lord of Riches.

If, as we have said, the Samhain-Bealtaine division of the year corresponds to changes in the Land itself, independent of human activity, Imbolc and Lúghnasadh are—on the contrary—reflections of the relationship between Tribe and Land. Imbolc marks the inception of the agricultural year, the beginning of an actual physical working of the Tribe upon the Land which will yield its fruit on Lúghnasadh, the official opening of the Harvest. Both feasts have as their symbolic rulers figures strongly linked with the Tribe-Land concept. The celebration of Imbolc centers on the figure of Brigantia (early Irish *Brigit*, modern Irish *Bríd*), later Christianized as Saint Bridget; she appears to be the Celtic "Minerva" noted by Roman observers like Caesar, patroness of arts and crafts, consort not only of the King but also of every creative individual—Muse of all creative endeavor. Yet she is also the Land, or more accurately the life-giving principle within the Land, which is revealed, through her influence, as having the same effect on both physical nature and the human spirit. As for Lúghnasadh, it is of course the feast of Lugh, the High God, the idealized model for any activity a member of the Tribe might undertake, but also, through his very nature, the great unifier of the spirits of the Tribe (the Tuatha Dé Danann who, in Irish tradition, represent specific areas of cultural activity) and the spirits of the Land (the *Fomhoraigh* or Fomorians, who are not necessarily friendly or accessible to humans, but are necessary to the continued fertility of the environment). Therefore, the celebration of these two feasts will focus on the linking of human labor with Otherworld patterns.

A reader used to the compartmentalized divinities of late Classical mythology may well wonder what the relationship is between Lugh and the Cernunnos–Maponos scheme. Is Lugh the same as one of the two? Or an expression of both? Is he superior to them? Or do they transcend him? To the Celtic mind, such questions have little meaning. In an Otherworld–centered context, many versions of one story can be true simultaneously. Looked at from one angle, a specific pattern will emerge; from another angle, the pattern will be different. All the patterns are interwoven, all are related, yet each one can stand on its own. Thus the figure of Lugh exhibits some strong Maponos elements, so that on some levels the two can be identified with each other; yet, like Cernunnos, he can also represent inner illumination, and he is adept at crossing boundaries, linking unrelated concepts, and ensuring the transfer of goods and ideas, making him, among many other things, a patron of commerce; and, as High God of the Tribe, he specifically transcends the opposition between the seasonal gods. All is determined by the ritually appropriate viewpoint: whether one wishes to stress his transcendence and his eternal marriage to the Land; or whether one wishes to stress his cyclic nature, as an eternally returning champion of the Tribe, with a life-history patterned after—but ritually distinct from—that of the Maponos.

We thus have, in the context of the Celtic Year, two different mythological cycles that provide imagery and narrative content to the rituals: one based on the alternation of Summer and Winter, focusing on the Land; and one focusing on the relation of Tribe to Land in agricultural activity, dramatized as the interplay between the spirits of the Tribe and those of the Land, culminating in the triumph of Lugh, who finally grants victory to the Tribe. The two cycles have separate "plots," but are linked together ritually, as we shall see.

The solar feasts—the solstices and equinoxes—may appear in the Coligny Calendar (which is perhaps, as we have seen, a late synthesis of ideas from various sources), but in tradition they are clearly secondary to the earth feasts, and may not be an ancient part of Celtic heritage at all. Some purists maintain that only the earth feasts should be commemorated in a Celtic context, since the rituals associated with the solar feasts are almost always made up of material related to the nearest earth feast, usually carried forward in time. But the fact remains that most Celtic-language communities have given the solar feasts a place in their ritual Year; so that, whatever their historical origin may be, they have become a part of Celtic tradition. They are best viewed as days on which the forces put in motion by the ritual of the earth feast immediately preceding them are grounded and made to bear fruit. The practices occurring around the Autumn Equinox, for instance, constitute the closing of the harvest rituals initiated on Lúghnasadh, and the celebration of Midsummer is in many ways a completion of ritual themes already presented during Bealtaine.

This garland of eight feasts encircling the year is, when celebrated communally, a powerful source of bonding between a group of people and the Land they live on, and just as powerful a means of strengthening the identity of such a group. Although the ritual core of each feast will require dedication, concentration and hard work, it also should be an occasion for fun and good cheer—something children can enjoy, remember with fondness, and anticipate with excitement. Ideally, if you are in a Celtic country, at least some aspects of the celebration should extend to the community at large, outside the bounds of the circle, although this may be difficult to manage at first. In all rituals dedicated to the link between Tribe and Land, there should be an element that reaches out to the entire Celtic world.

As we examine the themes associated with each feast, we must bear in mind the basic ritual framework outlined in the preceding chapter.

Samhain/Calan Gaeaf

Kala-Goañv, Calan Gwaf, Oie Houney—NOVEMBER 1

> *Scél lemm duíb:*
> *dordaid dam,*
> *snigid gaim,*
> *ró-fáith sam.*
> > —Eighth century Irish poem

(I have news for you: the stag bells, winter snows, summer is ended.)

Even with their astronomical bias, the compilers of the Coligny Calendar could not ignore the most solemn high feast of the Celtic Year: it is, in fact, the only one of the earth feasts listed there. They refer to it as *Trinouxtion Samonii*, which implies that the celebration extended over three days (or, more accurately, nights), reflecting the Celtic predilection for triadic structures. It occurs in the month *Samonios*, first month of the Coligny Calendar yet traditionally interpreted as "end of Summer." Thus, the old name of the feast can be translated as "Three Nights of the End of Summer." It marks the end of the *samos*-half of the year, and the abandonment of the activities and attitudes that characterize that half.

More importantly, however, it marks the beginning of an entire new cycle. With the return of Darkness the Year itself returns to the Otherworld womb from which it will grow to blossom again. All true growth takes place in darkness; the source of vitality is in the unconscious, before consciousness discovers the limiting forms of rationality. Seeds sprout underground, away from the Sun. A child takes shape secretly in the lightless world of the womb, and is fully-formed when born. The impulse to create a poem or any other work of art does not, in essence, come from the realm of logic or conscious purpose, but from unconceptualized elements below the level of consciousness. We have here the Womb/Cauldron image so dear to Celtic tradition, which made of gestation one of its great central metaphors. The Cauldron is first filled with unpalatable raw things, but after applying the magic of Fire and Water, it yields the same things transformed into an appetizing and nourishing meal. What enters the womb is a combination of sperm and egg, tiny wads of genetic material, life reduced to its simplest expression; what comes out is an individual human being with a unique spiritual destiny. Transformation, then, never ceases to be possible, there is always hope for rebirth, no matter how shrunken and devitalized anything is it can grow to a new wholeness if it submits to the processes of the Otherworld womb, the Cauldron of the Goddess. This is a truth we must bear in mind constantly, especially when the weakening of our tradition and the sheer power of the forces against it make us inclined to despair. It is not statistics and "scientifically" projected trends that should serve as the principal basis for our cultural activism, but an unapologetic, completely trusting passion, with its roots in the pre-rational Otherworld. As surely as last year's green things will survive the frost of winter and bloom vigorously after an apparent death, so will the Celtic soul emerge newly empowered from the Cauldron when the time is ripe. It is the very essence of Celtic tradition to believe this.

So the beginning of a new cycle, a new year, is a chance to return into the Cauldron and receive the blessing of the Goddess's transforming power. This involves, for the Land as well as for a human individual, entering the *giamos*-mode of experience. There will be rest, passive attentiveness to the unconscious influence of the Otherworld, an openness to growth that is slow and unforced. But we must also stress the theme of *renewal*; on Samhain the agricultural year ritually comes to a close, all work must be finished—or if unfinished, must be abandoned—to give way to new things. The Tribe's contract with the Land, in so far as reaping benefits from her is concerned, has expired, as it were, and the relationship will not resume, in its first stages, until Imbolc. In many regions this idea is expressed by the folk belief that any berries left on bushes after Samhain must not be picked, because they have come under the influence of the "devil," that is, the spirits of the Land, who, with the end of the ritual Harvest period, are no longer being compelled to cooperate with humanity by the spirits of the Tribe. Ending, of course, only serves to dramatize new beginnings; much of the Samhain celebration focuses on a symbolic rekindling of the home fire, a summoning of energy for new tasks in the future, even if they are not to be undertaken for as long as Darkness reigns and is welcome.

Another aspect of the new beginning is that, as the year changes, there is a break in the continuity of Time. In order for the new year to emerge from its Otherworld source, the God's power over the linear progression of Time is held in abeyance (this is visualized as Cernunnos and Maponos trading places, with neither properly enthroned as the God for the duration of the feast), and the Otherworld can appear unmasked, free of the space-time barriers that normally hide it. Instead of being perceived only in imagination and dream, the Otherworld can, for the duration of the break, be experienced directly within our world. Celtic narrative tradition is full of examples of such contact: either of incomprehensible monsters suddenly invading the lands of mortals; or of heroes entering the otherwise impervious *síd*, the fairy-mounds, and discovering a hidden world of supernatural beauty, opulence, and excitement. It was on Samhain that, for twenty-three consecutive years, the Otherworld creature Ailléan Mac Míodhna would charm the denizens of Tara to sleep with his music and then burn the fortress to the ground with his fiery breath, until Fionn Mac Cumhail, in the crowning achievement of his boyhood, slew him; and, earlier than that, Fionn had undertaken an adventure that led him to confront the dwellers of the *síd* under the Cíocha Anann, when they too were being made accessible by the Samhain change. It was on Samhain that strange birds invaded Ulster, tricking Cúchulainn into falling under the love-spell of the goddess Fand; and on Samhain that the Connacht hero Nera was taken on his nightmarish journey beyond the laws of Time. The imagery that continues to be associated with Halloween today reinforces this tradition.

Also counted among the denizens of the Otherworld are the dead, those of our people whose presence can no longer be experienced in everyday life. The Samhain break removes the barriers that separate them from the living, so that during the ritual period all the members of the Tribe, both seen and unseen, can commune together. The importance of this aspect of the feast is underlined by the fact that the Church calendar has made its own commemoration of the dead coincide with Samhain, thus mobilizing the thought-energies that were already associated with this season throughout western Europe.

Finally, the suspension of the laws that maintain the space-time continuum could be extended symbolically to the suspension of the laws of the Tribe itself. This would not, in practice, apply to laws that are essential to the Tribe's cohesion and survival; one could not, for instance, commit murder and get away with it simply because the Samhain break had put in abeyance the concept of law. But there are many elements of social custom—such as the deference accorded wealth or age, or the forms of behavior assigned to the sexes—that can easily be dispensed with over a brief period of time, in such a way that their arbitrariness, their origin in the world of culture (not nature), in the pure sphere of the Tribe, is pointed up. This realization offers a significant release from social tensions, even if the structure of society does not change as a result. It adds a characteristic dimension of boisterousness to the Samhain festivities.

All in all, the traditional celebration of Samhain in the Celtic world may best be analyzed by classifying its elements according to the ritual themes they are meant to express. Five main themes, related to the material we have just discussed, are immediately apparent:

1. The Theme of Renewal, which focuses primarily on the bonfire ritual.
2. The Theme of Hospitality for the Dead.
3. The Theme of Dissolution, which includes disguises, trickery, etc.
4. The Theme of Timelessness. The momentary escape from the linear progression of Time encourages the practice of divination.
5. The Theme of Sacrifice. The Harvest must be paid for, so the spirits of the Land receive tribute.

To these we must add the overarching mythic theme of the transition from *samos* to *giamos*, in which the figure of Cernunnos plays a leading part.

The bonfire ritual was clearly the main religious focus of the festival in pre-Christian times. It is from Ireland that we have the best traditional evidence and the best mythological substructure for the practice. Although Samhain was surely celebrated at the ritual centers of tribal lands throughout Ireland, it was above all the "Feast of Tara," focusing on the residence of the High King as the still point of stability at the heart of the entire Land (Tara is traditionally visualized as a *square* structure, denoting completion and stasis), in which the renewal of the year would take seed, and from which it would then spread to the Land's secondary divisions. All household fires, on the eve of Samhain, were to be extinguished. Then the sacred bonfire would be lit, not at Tara, but at Tlachtga, a dozen miles away to the northwest. This is the burial-place of the eponymous Tlachtga, the daughter of that Mogh Ruith whom Irish tradition remembers as an archetypal druid of immense power; and she herself is primarily recalled as a sorceress. According to the seventeenth-century Irish poet and antiquarian Geoffrey Keating's interpretation of sacred space within Ireland's central province, the site of Tlachtga symbolizes the kingdom of Munster, which itself represents all the traits associated with the Southern quarter, as we have outlined them in the previous chapter: pre-human nature, intuition, innate qualities, the unconscious, the realm of the Goddess unaccompanied by the God. Thus, the fire of the New Year is—most appropriately—seen as the gift of the Goddess to the Tribe assembled at the Land's sacred center. Although we have no concrete documentary evidence of this, it is both possible and ritually fitting that the fire of Tlachtga was kindled by women, since in most other contexts it is women who appear as symbolic representatives of Munster. Offerings—perhaps objects intended to depict the wishes of supplicants, or ailments to be healed—were cast into the bonfire, and then brands would be lit from it to rekindle all the home fires of the Tribe: the fire of Tara first, to be sure, but also all the farmhouse hearths that had been left dark for the turning of the year. Upon receiving the flame of the new cycle's beginning, one's mind could focus on new projects and hopes.

Bonfires remain a part of the seasonal celebration even today, although in most parts of Britain their significance has been co-opted by Guy Fawkes Day, which falls in the same period—an odd case of the "British" state twisting a Celtic tradition to further its own propagandistic aims! Even so, the image of the fire is still firmly associated with the season, and retains its powerful symbolic charge. During the last century the practice of lighting bonfires on Calan Gaeaf was still common in parts of Wales, though its connotations had more to do with protection than with renewal. The coincidence of the lifting of Otherworld barriers and the triumph of the Dark created a climate of unease, as entities with non-human or even anti-human associations were made capable of affecting the lives of human communities. Chief among these beings was the Hwch Ddu Gwta (the tailless black sow), of whom we shall speak again shortly. The bonfires dispelled the Darkness in which such images were most likely to be perceived.

Among the crowd of unsolicited and sometimes unwelcome Otherworld visitors to the human sphere were, as we have pointed out, the dead of the Tribe. It was the duty of the living to show their returned ancestors proper respect and hospitality. Doors and windows were left unlocked or unfastened as an invitation for such spirits to enter. It seems that the prevailing image for this visitation of the dead was that of a great *slua,* or host, of (usually) invisible people wandering through the countryside from house to house, with those belonging to each house remaining there to share the festival with their kin. Food was set aside to be consumed by this "silent company;" in Wales, this was *bwyd cennad y meirw*, the "food for the embassy of the dead;" in Brittany, it was *boued gouel an Anaon,* "the food for the feast of the dead," and it was forbidden for the living to touch any of it for the duration of the feast. Tangi Malmanche's play *Marvailh an Ene Naoniek, The Tale of the Hungry Soul*, provides a vivid illustration of the curse that, according to folk belief, would descend upon anyone impious and greedy enough to eat the food of the dead; he would be barred, after his own death, from partaking of it himself. We find here the Celtic demand for balance and symmetry, with events in the world of the living determining events in the world of the dead, and vice versa. Sometimes this symmetry would express itself in a somewhat different fashion, as in many versions of the *cennad y meirw* custom, which allowed food to be shared with the dead by sharing it with the living. The *cenhadon y meirw*, "messengers of the dead" would go from door to door and, chanting an appropriate rhyme, beg for specially prepared "soul cakes"—called *pice rhanna* in South Wales—which they, as fleshly representatives of the giver's dead relatives, would then eat. In this case the food of the dead, instead of being taboo, would become a sacrament for the one ritually intended to consume it. Often the *cenhadon* would consist of the poor and weak in the community, so that entertaining the dead would also turn into a manifestation of social solidarity, a strengthening of the Tribe. In all the sayings and songs associated with the custom in Wales the term *rhannu*, "sharing," is ubiquitous, showing the importance of that concept at the ritual's heart. Although Christian moral ideals no doubt helped to reinforce the practice, its origins almost certainly preceded Christianization.

As in the case of many other culture areas where a feast of the dead plays an important role, such as Madagascar and parts of the native Americas, hospitality for one's dead kin meant not only the presenting of food and drink but also all the emotional implications of a family reunion. There would be communion and conversation with coevals, and the satisfaction of seeing the growth and vitality of new generations. In this context the merrymaking during the Samhain parties held by extended families in farmhouses is literally intended for the amusement of the dead, as similar practices elsewhere make clear. One of the pastimes most commonly indulged in at such parties throughout most of the Celtic world—wherever older traditions have not given way to the commercial imagery of an Americanized Halloween—is bobbing for apples. Although there are fairly obvious reasons why apples should be featured prominently in the feast—they are, after all, the last fruit to be gathered before the harvest season is ritually closed—subtler symbolic correspondences linking them with the world of the dead seem to be at work here, as well. Apples exhibit the three primal colors (red skin, white flesh, black seeds) and, like all other natural phenomena with this property, are a manifestation of Otherworld power. We have seen that the dead are thought to eventually reach Eamhain Abhlach, the land of apple trees, where Manannán Mac Lir has prepared the Otherworld Feast for their eternal enjoyment, and it is possible that the Otherworld apples, eaten by the worthy dead, were considered to be the agents of that final spiritual transformation. What exactly the picking up of a floating apple without the help of one's hands was intended to represent—apart from being an occasion for uproarious fun—is no longer clear, but it does seem to be another case, like the *cennad y meirw* custom, of events in our world meant to mirror events in the other, taking advantage of the momentary removal of the barrier between the two. The apples in the bucket are, to the inner eye, the apples of Afallon. Perhaps the game was thought to help the dead arrive at the end of their Otherworld journey; perhaps it called a blessing of the dead upon the living. Some Scottish versions of the custom certainly suggest an Otherworldly ordeal by Fire and Water (the two operative elements in Celtic tradition) patterned after beliefs about the soul's journey; after bobbing for apples (the "trial by water"), a stick with an apple at one end and a lit candle at the other was suspended from a rafter, and young people had to leap and catch the apple with their teeth, without getting singed by the candle-flame!

Partying and merrymaking bring us to the third theme of the Samhain celebration, that of Dissolution. Breaking the laws of socially approved behavior and giving spontaneous vent to one's more animal feelings is, for many, what the festival is all about. In some parts of the Celtic world this means shattering the veneer of Calvinistic decorum imposed by an often rather anti-Celtic "new order." Young people can turn the tables on their elders, especially if they feel that their needs have been unjustly belittled or dismissed. Ungenerous or unkind people will, no matter how much social prestige they command during the rest of the year, have their turnip fields torn up this night. Tricks of all kinds, some malicious, some innocent, are played on neighbors, who are usually prepared for it by the spirit of the season. Exploiting the widespread fear of supernatural invasion, bands of revelers disguise themselves as the wandering dead (perhaps an echo of the *cennad y meirw* custom), or as sinister Other-world creatures. In Ireland the *buachaillí tuí*, their features obscured by masks of straw, suggest the spirits of the Land freed from their indenture to the Tribe by the end of Harvest. Sometimes the disguises are simply meant to be outrageous. The most significant and ancient in this range of customs appears to be cross-dressing—young people of opposite sexes swapping each other's clothes. In Wales such groups of young people going about on Calan Gaeaf dressed in clothes appropriate to the opposite gender were called *gwrachod*, hags or witches. While on the one hand this was surely meant to evoke the heightened activity of magical practitioners—perceived by folk tradition as a dangerous and alarming presence—on this night of Otherworld contact, there could have been a more profound significance to the imagery, related to the gender-switching theme commonly associated with world shamanism. In many Native American and Siberian traditions the shaman, by abandoning the behavioral and dress codes socially appropriate to his or her sex, transcends the existential limitations of gender and becomes capable of experiencing human nature as a balanced whole, establishing a polarity in his/her self, rather than remaining identified with only one half of a pair of opposites. The dissolution of the incomplete and spiritually unproductive social persona allows the emergence of a fresh identity more open to Otherworld gifts, and thus capable of magical influence on the environment. The *gwrachod*, by reflecting this theme, illustrate one possible application of the Dissolution that is one of the principal forces at work during the Samhain period.

Also dependent on the Dissolution is the Theme of Timelessness, underlining the fact that it becomes possible, at the year's turning point, for people to step outside their locus in the present moment and perceive the line of Time in its larger context, with both past and future visible. In practical terms this translates into an opportunity to perform divinations. Practices intended to foretell the future were one of the main pastimes indulged in at Samhain parties everywhere in the Celtic world. The vast majority of the recorded practices have to do with predicting marriages; through certain *piseoga* one is granted either a waking or a sleeping vision of one's future marriage partner, or the behavior of certain objects in a ritual setting—a pair of hazelnuts bouncing as they crack with heat on a hearth, for instance—is used to gauge the romantic prospects of a specific couple in the community. In past centuries, when arranged marriages were the norm in rural society and young people had little opportunity for independent romantic involvements, questions about one's marriage—about one's entire sexual future, by implication—were understandably a priority when divinations were performed. Today, as sexual relationships have become mostly the result of personal choice, marriage divination has lost the powerful appeal it once had. Still, the timelessness of Samhain invites us to look beyond the present, and there are plenty of causes for anxiety and factors outside our control that can motivate us to make use of divinatory methods.

(It should be mentioned here that folk tradition has associated divination with any calendar date thought to be the beginning of a new cycle. As, through the influence of non-Celtic social elites, the importance of Samhain as the New Year waned and other dates took over that role, the Samhain divination customs migrated [at least in part] to the new dates. For example, the Manx custom of the *quaalt-agh*—the first visitor to a house on the morning of a new cycle, whose appearance conveys something of the character of events in the period to come—became attached to the Gregorian New Year, though it is in spirit a Samhain custom.)

Also associated with divination but of independent ritual interest to us is the Welsh custom of making a *stwmp naw rhyw*, "mash of nine sorts," for the Calan Gaeaf household celebration. The fact that it contains *nine* specific ingredients (potatoes, carrots, turnips, peas, parsnips, leeks, pepper, salt, and milk) at once implies that it has a symbolic significance. Nine, in Celtic tradition, is a number of great power, being an extension of three, the number of dynamic efficiency and completion. Actions performed nine times, or objects occurring in groups of nine (triple triads), have the magical ability to manifest Otherworld patterns in this world. Not surprisingly, many of the divination rituals of the season refer back to this theme, deriving their efficacy from ninefold repetition. It is thus the number of its ingredients that allows the *stwmp naw rhyw*, when a wedding ring has been hidden in it, to tap into the ambient Timelessness for a marriage divination. Even apart from its divinatory function, it (or something like it) may have been a ceremonial dish since ancient times. In a related custom from Dyfed, ". . . *nine* girls used to meet to make a pancake with *nine* ingredients in it" (Owen, 1959). This, again, was used for marriage divination. The nine girls are without a doubt a reflection of the Nine Maidens who fan the Cauldron of Inspiration with their breath, and who are themselves a tripled manifestation of the Goddess-as-Triad. As a group, the girls would have become identified with the Goddess, and thus fit naturally into the Otherworld context in which true divinations are made.

Most forgotten of the Samhain themes today is the Theme of Sacrifice, except insofar as certain rural communities—especially in Ireland—still conduct their yearly slaughter of food animals during this season. Traditionally this takes place on Martinmas, November 11, close to the former date of Samhain according to the Julian Calendar. For the ancient Celts, whose wealth was in their herds and who gave a special importance to everything concerning their animals, Samhain signaled the return of the herds from highland pastures to the vicinity of human settlements, where they would be sheltered and fed on hay and grain during the cold season. All animals deemed not worth keeping through the winter were slaughtered at this time, but the nature of the event was religious as much as it was utilitarian. The life-energy in the flowing blood sank into the earth, an offering to the spirits of the Land, the Fomorian masters of fertility and blight, as payment for their cooperation during Harvest, and as propitiation to ensure the growth of crops in the coming year. Even as late as the nineteenth century the sacral nature of the bloodletting was still being expressed in tradition. As Amhlaoibh O Súilleabháin remarked in his diary in 1830, *"Is gnách fuil do dhoirteadh, oíche Fhéil Mártan."* (It is usual to shed blood on Martinmas Eve.) In Kildare—and perhaps in other parts of Ireland—a cock would be killed, brought indoors, and its blood sprinkled at the four corners of the house, as protection against malign influences related to the functions of the four quarters. Members of the household then ate the bird, as a ceremonial meal. A pig, however, seems to have been the more common sacrificial animal in this context in more ancient times. The sixteenth-century lexicographer Domhnall

O Dábhoireann, who refers to the Martinmas pig as *lupait*, is of the opinion that it was an offering "to the Lord" (*don tigerna*). In all these customs the importance of sending a blood-gift, as a guarantee of fertility, to Otherworld powers is the dominant motivation.

Of course, in an even more remote period, it was a human being whose blood would be offered to the Land and whose spirit would be sent to speak to the powers on the Tribe's behalf. Not only do both written and oral tradition maintain this, but there is archaeological evidence of widely differing sorts, as well, from the bog-drowned corpse of Lindow Man, suggesting a dignified, highly ritualized and perhaps voluntary death, to the grisly and messy pit-sacrifices of Swanwick and Holzhausen, in which people were crushed to death at the ends of stakes. Lindow Man may have been an educated, spiritually prepared sacrifice, destined to be an articulate ambassador in the Otherworld, whereas the pit victims were probably slaves, captives, or outlaws, more expendable gifts to the Fomorian lords underground. In Lindow Man's stomach were found mistletoe leaves (perhaps chewed for narcotic effect, and also perhaps used as a theological symbol) and a burned piece of bannock, which he had drawn in the lottery that designated him as the victim. Until quite recently in Scotland the custom of the bannock lottery survived as a game, in which the chooser of the burned piece would no longer be killed, but only teased and chased about the house.

The animal sacrifices of the Samhain season were again an occasion for sharing within the community; wealthier households were expected to make gifts of meat to families who had few or no herd beasts to spare.

Behind this wealth of ritual motifs, the mythology of the Goddess and her changing consorts seems very distant. Yet it is not quite obscured: Cernunnos, in the guise of Gwyn ap Nudd, leads the Wild Hunt through the skies with the darkening of the year, as he prepares to return to his home in the Otherworld. The prey he hunts is not explicitly identified, but it does not take much digging into tradition to understand that they are the year's dead, wandering as forgetful animal shapes that must be herded into their rightful Otherworld places. As Cernunnos is reunited with the Goddess, his antlers—his "cuckold horns," even though they are the fruit of a spiritual evolution—fall off. In parts of southwestern Brittany this last motif is reflected, with the coming of winter, by the ritual baking of pastries called *kornigoù*, little horns. Perhaps another echo of this theme can be found in the *bonnach Samhuinn*, the Scottish Samhain cake which is made by a circle of maidens passing dough to each other deosil, and which is solemnly named after a cuckold in the community!

As for the Maponos, he has vanished, or lies dead. There were probably, as we have seen, many variant descriptions of the manner of his passing. One of the most ancient, perhaps, is associated with the story of Diarmaid and Gráinne. While the main characters in the story are mortal humans living in a specific historical period, they are clearly acting out the parts of divine archetypes. Diarmaid—his role confirmed by his status as fosterling to Aonghus, the original Green Man himself—is the Maponos who steals away the King's daughter (i.e., sovereign-Goddess) Gráinne from her husband Fionn, who has obvious Cernunnos-like traits. At last Diarmaid is forced by his *geasa* to participate in a hunt for a boar who is destined to die at the same time as the hero himself, and who of course causes his death (after which Gráinne goes back to Fionn). Thus, the demise of the Maponos at Samhain is marked by a boar hunt, just as his triumphal return at Bealtaine, as we shall see, also entails the pursuit of a supernatural boar. The Cosmic Boar Hunt manifests itself at both hinges of the year, moving in opposite directions: at Samhain the Boar goes down into the Dark; and throughout the *giamos*-season, in our rituals, we will invoke the boar-image in the Southern Quarter.

Reunited with the Cernunnos, the Goddess's nurturing aspect becomes hidden in invisible dimensions of the Otherworld. To the external world of the senses she now presents a harsh, unmotherly appearance—expressed, for instance, by the image of the Hwch Ddu Gwta, whom we have seen lurking in the darkness at the edge of the bonfires. The Sow is a perennial Dark form of the Goddess, the unloving mother who devours her young; yet she is also a symbol of fertility, and promises us that, despite her forbidding exterior, she will become the source of returning life. We must learn patience and trust, knowing that through the cold, leafless days the process of generation goes on, unseen.

Now that we have examined the traditional meaning of Samhain through the fundamental Themes that give focus to its rituals, how are we to celebrate this feast effectively today? Thanks to the Halloween celebrations that are still so much alive in most Celtic and ex-Celtic communities, we have a ready-made context in which to place our own rituals, and we can take our initial cues from the imagery and mood we find in such local practices. Most surviving Halloween customs, however, tend to emphasize the Theme of Dissolution (and perhaps that of Timelessness) at the expense of the Themes of Renewal, Hospitality for the Dead, and Sacrifice. It is these latter themes, then, that we will have to concentrate on to ensure a proper ritual expression of the meaning of the Samhain season.

As the focusing image of Renewal, there should, in accordance with the old traditions, be a bonfire. If the circle can be held outdoors in a sufficiently large space (i.e., in an open field), this should pose no problems, and the fire can do a great deal to energize the imagination of the participants. But if the ritual has to be conducted indoors, a substitute will have to be found. The best substitute is most likely to be a large candle centrally placed, from which smaller candles will be lit to symbolize the home fires (torches will be used if one has a bonfire). Céli Dé Circle used a large red candle bearing a representation of Cernunnos with antlers on one side, and without antlers on the other.

Cernunnos should, in general, be returned to his position of pre-eminence at this turning point of the year. To further express the Theme of Renewal, the circle should have as one of its ritual props a figurine representing Cernunnos, hornless so that his transition from *samos-* to *giamos-*state and vice versa can be dramatized by affixing or removing antlers. Céli Dé Circle used a facsimile of the cross-legged Celtic statue from Oseberg in Norway, which is particularly appropriate in its design. The "antlers" can be represented in a variety of ways. Most effective, perhaps, is a pair of oak twigs still bearing dried leaves. They can be taped in place, or fitted into holes on the statue's head, if such are present.

To honor the "silent company" of the visiting dead, a banquet of "soul-cakes" or similar fare must be prepared and placed within the ritual area. One can add to this a *stwmp naw rhyw* or other ceremonial dish prepared in a corresponding manner, to be partaken of by the living members of the circle later on. This can also, if desired, be used for divination, in which case a token will have been hidden inside it.

Before the beginning of the ritual, participants may well have spent a part of the day enthusiastically expressing the Theme of Dissolution, and may be coming to the circle intoxicated by stimulants psychic or otherwise, dressed in outrageous attire, and generally divorced from mundane concerns. This is perfectly appropriate, but also makes it all the more necessary to launch the ritual with some striking, sobering element that will shift the mood dramatically and put the focus on the other themes of the feast. After invoking the Quarters (where, to signal the coming of the Dark season, the Boar will be placed in the South for the first time, and the Stag in the West), the Theme of Renewal is introduced suddenly by the recitation of a text dealing with the shift in season and the implications of the *giamos*-phase of existence. Fortunately, Celtic literature is particularly rich in vivid, powerful poems on the theme of Winter. Good choices for this ritual circumstance would be the eighth-century Irish *Scél lemm dúib*, or the Welsh sequence attributed to Llywarch Hen beginning with *Llym awel, llwm bryn*. Their diction and imagery are simple but intensely effective, hyperbolic yet completely sincere, unwaveringly tuned to the archetypal dimension they seek to express, all of which makes them excellent ritual material. The recitation may be done by the ritual leader, or by some other circle member chosen for special vocal or dramatic talent. Translation into an imperial language may be provided then, if necessary. One can, of course, use a text specially composed for the occasion, if the creative resources for this are genuinely available, but care must be taken, to ensure the effectiveness of the ritual moment, that ambition not exceed means. Modern compositions by poets of middling experience tend to sound wordy and diffuse when compared with the concentrated force found in Celtic tradition. While original material may be introduced with perfect appropriateness into other parts of the ritual, many groups may prefer to entrust the initial invocation to the tried-and-true power of a traditional text.

With this opening, the imagination of the participants should have built up an inner environment of cold, darkness, silence, and all-enshrouding snow (even if the weather outside bears no resemblance to this!). Images of light, of action, and of striving will are released into the darkness, and vanish. What is left is the essence of *giamos*-being: not-doing, attentiveness, passive learning through intuition. Indeed, in such stillness new things will be given the opportunity to grow; new life will take root and become manifest. The soul of the Tribe thus attunes itself to the processes at work in the Land; the marriage of God and Goddess is assured, as it must be at the beginning of each new cycle.

But the new cycle is to begin in earnest—and the lighting of the bonfire will be the outward sign of that event. Fire burns away the old, provides focus and energy for the new. It should be lit, if possible, by a woman, symbolically manifesting the Goddess, who is the granter of any renewal. Then the other participants should come forward to light their own fires from the sacred fire at the center. For indoor rituals, a practice originated by Céli Dé Circle (and eventually incorporated into the New Year festivities of the Celtic League American Branch) is to have white, black, and red candles available. Each participant chooses a candle according to the symbolic attributes of its color: white for those who, in the course of the coming year, will seek to emphasize conscious, rational, God- or *samos*-dominated aspects of their lives; black for those who feel closer to the unconscious, intuitive, Goddess- or *giamos*-dominated aspects; and red for those who wish to draw their energy from the tension at the interface of the two aspects. As each small candle is lit, the power generated by the God-Goddess pair is invoked to lend strength to an individual purpose.

Since, in the early celebrations of Samhain at Tara, ex-votos or other sacrificial objects are known to have been thrown into the fire, this is a good point in the ritual to introduce the Theme of Sacrifice. Of all the themes pertaining to the feast, this is perhaps the most difficult to integrate into a modern context. Blood sacrifice is, of course, both repugnant and morally impermissible for the vast majority of spiritually aware people today. Yet if one thinks on the meaning of the old sacrifices, of what they sought to accomplish, of the spiritual dynamic that was involved, it is not at all hard to come up with equivalents to which the modern consciousness can respond. To send an emissary to the Otherworld, while representing a wholehearted "giving" to hidden powers of something essential to oneself, can be done very effectively on a psychic level—and using ancient methods, at that. What will be offered, then, will be inner faculties that one wishes to have change, even as the year is changing. If the ritual is outdoors, the sacrificial object should be a small bundle of leaves and straw, previously charged by meditation on the specific qualities involved. As each person comes to light his/her torch, the bundle is dropped into the bonfire, and whatever it represents is translated to the Otherworld by the archetypal function of the flames. If the circle is indoors, and a large candle is standing in for the bonfire, the sacrificial object will be, more practically, a tiny scrap of paper on which a single word has been written. Thus, these essential qualities of one's self—talents, energies, passions—will be given back to the universe to pursue the never-ending task of its recreation, for, in the old mythologies of the Indo-European world, the universe owes its existence to a primal Sacrifice.

The main focus of the remainder of the ritual should be hospitality for the dead, which is in many ways the most personally involving aspect of the feast. The materialism that the last few centuries have encouraged in Western culture has led to a widespread inability to face the emotional consequences of death, to deal with the pain of separation other than by denial or forgetting. Samhain comes to remind us of the Celts' radically different attitude toward such things. While sorrow and pain are in no way glossed over, one's relationship with a dead kinsman or friend is not seen as ending with his physical disappearance, but is known to continue on a different plane; and when the turning of the year dissolves the boundaries that normally exist between the planes, the renewal of conscious contact with the departed is actively sought. To welcome the dead back in the Celtic spirit, therefore, we must overcome the fear that we might suffer the pain of separation anew by remembering our departed loved ones too vividly. The understanding that the apparently rigid structure of our material universe proceeds from and is contained within the in-

finite potential of the Otherworld, and that death is a transformation, not an ending, will help us combat that fear.

Before communion with the dead can occur properly, the Silent
Company must be explicitly invited into the circle to partake of the
offerings that have been prepared for them. J.A. Johnston (Kaledon
Naddair), writing in *Inner Keltia*, devised a modern ritual for this
purpose which, though it suffers from wordiness in some places and
refers to an idiosyncratic theology that some Celtic groups might not
like to embrace, still provides an excellent pattern that can be elabo-
rated on at will. We here offer Céli Dé's variation on this theme,
which again can be embellished and restructured by other circles according to their tastes and needs.

Lighting a large candle or torch from the central fire, the ritual
leader faces the southwest, the direction most propitious to Otherworld contact, and holds up the light to shine into the darkness that
hides the dead. The Silent Company is called upon, entreated to
come, and the divine powers that watch over the dead are asked to
release their hold on those that will be invited. Then the entire circle participates in the Building of the Bridge that will span the gap
between our world and that of the departed—a gap made much
smaller by the Samhain break. We circumambulate the ritual area
three times, pausing briefly at the end of each round, first to announce that work on the Bridge has begun, then to declare that the
Abyss is half spanned, and finally to celebrate the completion of the
Bridge. The circumambulations should be done without chanting;
the only focusing device should be a relatively slow, stately percus-
sive beat (best geared to the heartbeat) performed by the marchers
on drums, rattles, or any kind of resonant surface. This facilitates the
inward-turning dynamic of the ritual, the spiraling back to the center in which the stillness, dark, and repose of *giamos*-existence can be
found. As the Bridge nears completion, each of us may speak, aloud
or in silence, the names of those dead loved ones we are specifically
inviting into the circle.

Once the Bridge is complete, the psychic inward spiral on which
we have been meditating as we walked is also finished, and we are
deep within ourselves, in that state which most perfectly attunes us

to the Otherworld. So the coming of the Silent Company finds us in the condition best suited to receive them: the living are still enough, in their minds and spirits, to present no barriers to communion with the dead, and the dead are thus able to view the world of form with the eyes of the living. Each of us, fully open to those we have invited, converse with them in the Otherworld's silent language. There may be startling inner discoveries, emotional outbursts, spontaneous manifestations of long-repressed psychic realities, all of which are to be accepted as natural and proper on this occasion. Death, we must realize, is but the *giamos*-phase of our being, a necessary and benign change from the tension of material activity. It is a preparation—a gestation—for something else, something that our imaginations, fed only on earthly experience, cannot shape convincingly for us, and it is this deficiency which is at the root of our fear, sadness, and anger when we think of the dead. But the language of myths and symbols, operating beneath the surface of consciousness, conveys the truth to that part of ourselves which can receive it.

When one's direct conversation with the dead has come to a satisfactory conclusion, this can be indicated by a change in position, such as the lowering of hands that previously had been held crossed over the chest. Once all have shown a sign of their return from the presence of the Silent Company, the circle leader sprinkles water on each participant, expressing by this lustration the nurturing power of the Goddess, the life-giving moisture of her Cauldron, which gives seeds the strength to grow even as they lie dormant during the Dark season. We are reminded that *giamos* is not mere cessation of process, that growth will occur even in repose.

The feasting can then begin, living and dead partaking of the gifts side-by-side. A plate of "soul-cakes" or similar items will have been prepared especially for the dead, while the living will share a different ritual dish. If this is used for divination, as described above, it will help circle members gradually retune their minds to more mundane concerns. This then can lead naturally into any number of games and pastimes traditional to the feast, which can be indulged in (for the entertainment of the dead) both before and after the actual closing of the circle. At closing, though the powers of the Quarters will be dismissed as usual, the dead will be invited to stay and enjoy the hospitality of the living for as long as it is permissible—that is, for the three-night duration of the ritual period.

Before the end of the ritual, we must remember Cernunnos and his crucial role in the events of the feast. Two circle members will approach the Cernunnos statue, each grasp an antler, and pull them off. Cernunnos is then transformed, free to return to the Goddess and perform his creative function in the Otherworld—even as, to our eyes, the Land sleeps.

Fear of darkness and fear of death are closely related. Through the symbolic power of this ceremony we are a little better prepared to confront the season of darkness and death without fear.

Deuoriuos (attribution uncertain)

Alban Arthan—DECEMBER 21 *(Winter Solstice),* 25 *(Christmas)*

> *O kanañ Nouel e penn an ti,*
> *Un aval melen a blij din,*
> *Un aval melen pe arc'hant,*
> *Pe ar verc'h henañ mar d'eo koant!*
>   —Breton carol

(As I carol at the end of the house, I'd like a yellow apple; a yellow apple, or money—or the eldest daughter if she's pretty!)

One of the festivals identified by name in the Coligny Calendar is *Deuoriuos Riuri.* If M. Kerjean-Lemaître has been correct in translating *Riuros* as the "frost month" (by analogy with Gaelic *reo*, Welsh *rhew*, Breton *riv*) and in identifying it with, roughly, a period covering most of December, then Deuoriuos (*Deuo-ro-iuos*, great divine feast) would seem to coincide with the Winter Solstice, and to have been the Old Celtic name of that festival (although there is no consensus on this matter among Celtic scholars today).

All the solar feasts derive their ritual importance from a totally predictable, astronomically determined phenomenon: the changing ratio in length between days and nights, which we choose to cele-

brate at its extremes and midpoints. The focus is on the human response to Light and Darkness as psychic environments. As diurnal
creatures, we feel most comfortable when extended periods of daylight keep our surroundings safely visible to us and encourage us to
longer spells of activity; conversely, prolonged subjection to darkness
can bring about insecurity and depression. Even though, as we have
seen, the Celtic worldview takes light and darkness to be coequal
manifestations of the *samos-giamos* alternation and affirms their complementarity and necessity to each other, their effects on the psyche
are a part of human nature and cannot be discounted. The return of
light cannot help but be a joyous occasion; and the return of darkness, even when softened by reassuring imagery, is rarely faced without some misgivings and trepidation.

The Winter Solstice, then, is the darkest point of the year, the
complete triumph of night; yet the very moment of its triumph is
also that of its defeat, since it is the turning point that will bring the
Light back. Although the psyche knows that it still has several
months of darkness to face, it begins to orient its energies toward the
return of the Light by a spurt of *samos*-related ritual activities, reinforced by a mythological script full of bright, happy images. Thus the
deadening effect of darkness—even though one must continue to
endure it—is robbed of much of its power. One is made confident
that the seed of Light, sown in the womb of the Dark, will grow
and, in its appropriate season, bloom.

What would be a traditional Celtic response to the ritual demands of this stage in the year? On the one hand, the question is
complicated by the overwhelming influence of Christmas, both as a
religious and as a commercial phenomenon. There is not, of course,
in this day and age a Celtic community anywhere that does not associate the Winter Solstice first and foremost with Christmas and
with the imagery that the dominant culture, through institutions and
the media, has associated with that feast. Buried beneath the mass-
culture layer we can usually find some elements dating back to the
earlier history of the community, but these have at best only a tenuous life on their own, being rarely thought of as anything but local
addenda to the celebration of the international holiday.

On the other hand, however, since the observance of the Win-

ter Solstice is not based on the social heritage of any particular culture, but on a general response to external phenomena that is not
culture-specific, there is a remarkable unity to the ritual patterns of
celebration that various cultures (at least in the West) have come
up with in relation to it. Elements that dramatize the power of light
in darkness—whether Christmas-tree lights or bonfires or candles—
are found everywhere. So is the encouragement of family solidarity and the giving of gifts. Even the mythological themes that serve
to validate the celebration tend to be similar in outline: a Child of
Light—the returning Sun—is born at this darkest time in precarious
circumstances, but as we embrace him in our affection and love he is
allowed to grow and to finally reveal himself in the Light season.
Whether one thinks of the child as Jesus or Lugh or Mabon—however important such a question may seem in terms of personal religious allegiance—makes no difference at all in practice. Thus, the
successive layers of imagery that exist together in all the solstice traditions of a community tend to reinforce each other, and there is no
reason to reject any one of them as "foreign" and therefore negative.

The native versions of the myth of the Child of Light—which
we know both from medieval literature and from recent folklore—
center on the rebirth of the Maponos, the "Great Boy" or "Great
Son," the youthful Summer God who rules the realm of *samos*-expe-
rience and who has, as we have seen, died or otherwise vanished at
Samhain. In *Culhwch ac Olwen* he is still called by his ancient name,
Mabon ab Modron, "Great Son of the Great Mother," who was
stolen *yn teir nossic*, "when three nights old" (i.e., after the completion of the customary three-night ritual period) "from between his
mother and the wall," and was freed just in time to perform a necessary role in removing the Summer Maiden Olwen from the control
of her earth-giant father. In the *Pedeir Keinc* he also appears as Pryderi, stolen at birth from his mother Rhiannon by an Otherworldly
claw and rediscovered only on May Eve. And if we accept that the
High God Lugh, who fulfills a different mythological function, shares
many traits with the Maponos, we will find the same pattern in his
birth story. In Irish folk-sources we are told that he was fathered secretly by Cian (one of the Tuatha Dé Danann, the "Tribal" gods)
upon Eithne, the daughter of Balor (the champion of the Fomorians

or earth-giants) in order to fulfill a prophecy according to which Balor would be slain by his grandson. So to evade Balor's murderous fear, the child had to be spirited away at birth, and given in fosterage to Manannán Mac Lir, the host of the Otherworld Feast in the Land of Apples, and to the Leinster queen Tailtiu, until he had grown strong enough to challenge Balor and fulfill his destiny. Even in the scantier Welsh version there is an echo of this: Lleu is born as an un-formed "thing" (*pethan*) from his unsuspecting virgin-mother Arian-rhod, and is at once snatched up by his uncle Gwydion and hidden away, to be later revealed full-formed. Needless to say, the story of the Christ Child, born in obscurity, spirited away to Egypt to evade King Herod's wrath, then returning in power to redeem the world, has been a part of Celtic tradition for well over a thousand years and is so close to the native stories that, instead of competing with them, it continues to.empower them, to keep us in touch with the mythic pattern they express.

Although it is the longest-night aspect that gives the Winter Solstice its ritual importance, the actual celebration did not limit it-self to one day but extended over a more or less long period—some-times going beyond the familiar "Twelve Days of Christmas" to cover a full three weeks! In traditional rural society it was not the in-timate family holiday it has become, but involved a great many com-munal activities, often conducted outdoors. These, drawn eclectically from many cultural influences, varied from community to commu-nity, though they usually included sporting events, musical perfor-mances, processions, divination, and, of course, plenty of food and drink. The custom of burning the Yule log, though of Germanic ori-gin, became naturalized in some Celtic areas, sometimes taking on features that made it continuous with pre-existing Celtic tradition. In parts of Scotland, for instance, the log was carved in the shape of a woman, the *Cailleach Nollag*, "Christmas Hag," and her slow burn-ing over the peat fire represented the defeat of the Goddess in her sterile and forbidding aspect, the days of her reign numbered with the birth of the Child of Light.

Two customs, however, stand out among Celtic Christmas festiv-ities, and seem to stem from an indigenous heritage: the Procession of the Mari Lwyd and the Hunting of the Wren (although the latter custom may be ultimately of Scandinavian provenance). They are often quite separate in practice, yet appear to be linked in symbolic terms.

The Mari Lwyd ("Grey Mary" probably also "grey mare") is still carried house-to-house at some point in the Christmas season in various districts of southern and central Wales. She is a monstrous figure consisting of a horse's skull mounted on a pole, the carrier of which is usually hidden by a blanket to give the impression of a giant human with an animal head. The lower jaw is hinged so it can snap open and shut, and sometimes the eye sockets are fitted with glass eyes for a more striking effect. Ribbons stream from her, bells jingle around her, and in some communities the members of her escort are decked out in a variety of grotesque costumes. In the past one of the items carried in the procession was the *Aderyn Pica Llwyd* ("grey magpie") an artificial bird on a stick hung with apples and oranges. At each house the leader of the procession knocks on the door with his staff, and the group sings a stanza requesting permission to enter for themselves and the Mari. The household replies with a stanza expressing suspicion and demanding assurances that the Mari will not cause violence and disorder if she enters; this leads into a long musical dialogue which culminates in the opening of the door to admit the Mari. She, of course, forgets her promises and goes lunging about the room, snapping at the people of the house (especially the women), who pretend to be terrified. Often a little child will stand in the Mari's way and feed her a cake or candy, whereupon the monster is suddenly subdued.

Considered in the most general terms, this ritual fits into a broad continuum of "hobbyhorse" customs found all over rural Europe. Many localities, from England to Poland, have a festival (usually during the "Dark" half of the year) in which a group of mummers going from house to house includes an artificial horse (or some other type of horse disguise) that pretends to attack women, often unwed women in particular. Sometimes, as in parts of southern Germany, the role is taken up by "devils" or other fantastic maskers. The meaning of such a ritual seems to go back to a common Indo-European heritage of symbolism and belief. The Land-spirits who govern fertility—from the Centaurs of Greece to the divine Ashvins of India—were imagined with horse-like traits, and whenever their power was to be invoked equine imagery would be used. In the darkest heart of winter, when life's generative power seems to be at its lowest ebb, it would have been particularly appropriate to call up the primal guardians of fertility from the Land and associate them with the Tribe's own symbols of generation, the women. The Celts, whose mythology is replete with figures like *Eochu* and *Echbél* and *March*, certainly share in this conceptual pattern and must have taken their hobbyhorse rituals from this common store of tradition. Yet there are aspects of the Mari Lwyd ceremony that suggest a more intimate Celtic frame of reference.

For one thing, whereas in other countries the hobbyhorse is either of indeterminate gender or is explicitly male (as befits a figure who symbolically inseminates women), the Mari is in all cases specifically stated to be female. She is, then, the Great Mare, the *Epona*, the Land-goddess herself, not just one of the Land-spirits in her retinue. Both Giraldus Cambrensis's scandalous account of the investiture of an Irish king, and the majestic form of the White Horse of Uffington, carved into a chalk down in the old territory of the Dobunni, illustrate the importance of the Great Mare as an image of the Land-goddess who grants sovereignty by her union with the sacred King of the Tribe. Yet, even when she is granted a variety of animal attributes, the Land-goddess, in accounts of her interaction with the Tribe, is usually conceived anthropomorphically. What, then, conditions her appearance in animal form?

The most obvious clue comes from the First Branch of the Mabinogi: Rhiannon, "Great Queen," who first appears to her husband, the land-ruler Pwyll, riding by in typical Epona style, is herself demoted to an equine role when her newborn son, Pryderi, is stolen by Otherworldly powers, and she is accused of having murdered him. She is made to stand by the mounting-block (*yskynvaen*), and offer to carry guests on her back. In the Third Branch, when both she and Pryderi (now an adult) are prisoners in the Otherworld fortress of Llwyd fab Cil Coed, they are forced to wear horsecollars (*mynweireu*) about their necks. In both episodes, the implication is that the Goddess and her son (the newborn Pryderi is recovered by Teyrnon in the company of a magically stolen foal) are actually transformed into horses; and this is, in fact, confirmed by variants in oral folklore, especially from Brittany. The precise reason for this reversion to animal state is nowhere made clear (except insofar as, in the general structure of the narrative, it reflects Gwawl's revenge upon Rhiannon and her family, using Llwyd as his proxy); but if, as Caitlín Matthews has suggested, Rhiannon and Pryderi are meant to represent Modron and Mabon *(Matrona* and *Maponos)*, the Great Mother and the Great Son, it could be explained by its function within the larger mythological and ritual context. The birth of the Light-Child—who is to become the Maponos, the vigorous, youthful ruler of the *samos*-half of the year—takes place when the nurturing, humanly attractive aspect of the Land-goddess is dormant, replaced by the Sow, the Hag, the Goddess in her inimical aspect (perhaps represented, in the First Branch, by the serving women who engineer Rhiannon's humiliation). It is the ascendancy of the Hag which in fact forces the eclipse of the Mother, expressed by the loss of human faculties, as the character is taken over by its animal attributes (animal nature = *giamos*; human nature = *samos)*. The human, Tribe-oriented face of the Goddess will return only as the year approaches its Light half. Llwyd, the "Grey One," is the figure who holds the key to the changes.

Looking at our solstice ritual again in the light of this material, we realize that the Mari Lwyd is, in the midwinter season, a mother who has been separated from her child. This at once brings to mind many figures from other mythologies, grieving Mother-Goddesses wandering over a barren land in search of a vanished loved one (child or consort) who is linked to the power of fertility: Demeter and Persephone, Isis and Osiris, Nanna and Balder, Lemminkäinen and his mother . . . in the case of Demeter and Isis, the wandering goddesses acquire a retinue of companions who take on individual significance in the myths. Might not the tale of Rhiannon—or of the archetype she represents in Celtic lore—once have contained just such an element, surviving to the present day in the ritual that it inspired? It is her foal that the Grey Mare, or Great Mare, seeks in house after house, and the strange guizers who accompany her, ringing bells, fiddling, and waving ribbons, are the Otherworld helpers— their identities unknown to us in this specific context, but doubtless

much like the "magical companions" so common in folk tradition—
who support her in her exile. Of course, despite the possibility of
such associations, the ceremony still clearly functions as a generic
"hobbyhorse" ritual, aimed at restoring fertility or reactivating the
powers of generation. Even in exile, unable to manifest herself
openly in nature, the Land-Goddess can still transmit her "horse energy" (*eoghus*) to those who need it, and does so with typical "hobbyhorse" boisterousness.

Whether or not the Mari Lwyd ceremony and the tale of
Rhiannon and Pryderi are in fact historically linked, the mythological and poetic links are increasingly obvious, and cannot be ignored.

The other Christmas custom that has special significance in
Celtic tradition is "Hunting the Wren" (*Shelg yn Dreean*, in Manx).
This, a truly Pan-Celtic ritual, was done in essentially the same way
in Ireland, Scotland, Wales, and the Isle of Man, and there is reason to
believe that it was once known in Brittany as well. It has survived
best in southwestern Ireland, where competing *dreoilíní* ("wrens"),
i.e., ritual fraternities, sometimes make lavish expenditures on cos-
tuming and music. In its earliest attested and simplest form, the ceremony—always held on December 26, Saint Stephen's Day or "Wren
Day"—began with the pursuit of a live wren which was eventually
killed with stones. The wren's corpse was then placed in a box or
cage luxuriously decorated with evergreen branches, colored ribbons, and fruits (called a *perllan* or orchard in Welsh), which was
fixed to the end of a pole and paraded about from house to house by
a company of costumed dancers, singers, and musicians. The specific
composition of the cast varied but, at least in Ireland, it always included a transvestite *cailleach*, "hag," and a hobbyhorse called the *Láir
Bhán*, "White Mare." Wherever they were let in, the "wren boys"
would put on a performance of dance, clowning, and music new and
old (some of it referring specifically to the occasion), and then beg
for money to "bury the wren." In fact, this was more precisely money
not to bury the wren, since the wren's corpse was thought to bring
bad luck, and in some communities the mummers would, in revenge, finally dispose of the bird's body on the land of the most
miserly or discourteous householder they had encountered during
the day. In other areas the wren's burial was in itself an elaborate rit-

ual, leaving the body in a liminal place (i.e., on a shore, neither in land nor sea) where its influence was neutralized. Sometimes, in addition to the cup or purse that held the money they collected, the wren boys carried a large bowl which, more often than not, was used to beg for drinks—but, in some significant instances, was filled beforehand with a wassail-mixture that was passed around, to be sipped for a fee.

Why make a wren the focus of this merrymaking? The wren does figure prominently in folk tradition as a divinatory bird (therefore placing it in the druidic or bardic class of beings), and is the protagonist of a widespread folktale—doubtless the remnant of a very old mythology—that explains its title of "King of All Birds." In a contest of who could fly the highest, the wren stowed away on the eagle's head and, once the great bird had reached the limits of its strength, emerged from hiding and flew up higher than any other bird, thus winning supremacy over all the feathered folk, despite its tiny size. There is a striking similarity here with the symbolic attributes of another fixture of the Christmas season, the mistletoe. Although it is the smallest of "trees," the mistletoe grows in the crown of the tallest tree, the oak, and is thus the closest of all trees to the heavens. Eagle is therefore paired with wren, and oak with mistletoe, and both pairs correspond to each other, in the realms of bird- and tree-imagery respectively. The entire symbolic complex seems to be associated with the God Lugh, the most powerfully realized divine figure in Celtic tradition, and the original Child of Light. In the Fourth Branch of the Mabinogi we see Lleu as a child gain his name by his skillful casting of a stone at a wren (an obscure reference, perhaps, to "hunting the wren"); and later, betrayed by his wife Blodeuwedd to his rival Gronw, who pierces him with a spear, he turns into an eagle and flies away. Still in eagle-shape—though suffering from putrescent wounds—he perches in the top of a tall oak (in the place of the mistletoe!), where his uncle Gwydion, led by a sow (the Black Sow of the barren season), finds him and restores him to his original form. And in the iconography of the First Golden Age of the Celts, at about the time when Lugus/Lugh is becoming established as a divine figure of intertribal importance, mistletoe-leaves, birds, the horse, and the World Tree appear as a cluster of related symbols. The "little" God who eventually slays the champion of the Earth-giants and becomes ruler over all other gods is thus perceived to be, in his double guise of trickster and magical being, like both the wren and the mistletoe. Surely the druids derived a wealth of wisdom from this imagery; we can only—alas!—recapture fragments of it.

A further illustration of the wren as the representative of the Tribe-god holding the Land-spirits at bay can be found in one of the variants of the classic Scottish tale *Cath nan Eun*, "The Battle of the Birds." A wren agrees to become a farmer's servant. As he is threshing the grain, a mouse devours every wheat-kernel that drops on the ground. The mouse ignores the wren's warnings until the wren, losing patience at last, calls all the birds together and declares war on the mouse and his kind. The insatiable mice at once bring to mind the Third Branch of the Mabinogi, where they are an Other-world invasion sent by Llwyd ap Cil Coed, and are defeated by Mana-wyddan, a craftsman-figure very much on the Lugh model. They are an obvious Fomorian symbol, and the battle of the birds against the rodents can at once be seen as a transposition into animal imagery of the conflict between the Tuatha Dé Danann and the Fomhoirí, the Tribe-spirits and the Land-spirits. The hero of the story, Mac Rìgh Cathair Shìomain, arrives when the battle is all but over and the only combatants left are a raven (again, a creature historically associated with Lugh) and a snake (clearly a Land-symbol). By taking the raven's side he is led into an initiatory adventure that need not concern us here; but we have now been given ample mythological evidence of the wren as a Lugh-symbol in active conflict with Fomorian powers. Whether or not the wren dies in the battle is not stated; but clearly it was expected to do so on the Winter Solstice.

But why, if the wren represents the Child of triumphant Light, must it be killed? The mistletoe, too, is cut, and hung from the rafters as decoration, or as a fertility-talisman under which young couples kiss. Usually, in such situations, we must look to an earlier tradition of sacrifice. The recipients of blood sacrifice are, invariably, the Fomorian powers, the Land-spirits whose insatiable greed and indifference to human concerns always endanger the survival of the Tribe.

Bloodletting is associated with solar energy in many cultures. In

Middle America—to give a particularly spectacular example—the grim round of human sacrifice was expressly intended to keep the sun strong; if not well-fed on blood, it might never reemerge from the dark Underworld into which it descended at night. The brightness of blood, gold, and solar light were imaginatively linked, and could transform into each other; thus, gold condensed the healing and life-giving properties of sunlight into metallic form, while blood could fuel the warmth of the sun itself. Blood was, therefore, given to the spirits of the deep earth who held the sun in time of darkness. The Celts clearly shared in this symbolism, and we can indeed find other applications of it in their Winter Solstice ritual. Until the last century bloodletting was a component of Christmas (or Saint Stephen's) celebrations in many parts of Wales. In some communities this was confined to the bleeding of livestock, and could be explained as a kind of folk medicine; but in other places it was a ritual involving humans exclusively—sometimes one single individual designated by lot or chance (e.g., the last to wake in the morning), who was scourged with a holly branch until blood flowed, and sometimes the entire community, who struck each other with holly in mock combat. In all cases the "holming"—as the practice came to be known in English-speaking districts—was explicitly intended to draw blood.

We should, at this point, take notice of the role played by that other fixture of the Christmas season, the holly. Well known to the Celts at an early stage of their tradition (as the Old Celtic name *kolennos*, prickler, suggests), the holly tree acquired, by virtue of its characteristic traits, a religious significance. Like all evergreens, which somehow are capable of defying the influence of the *giamos*-season on the plant world, it became a symbol of divine vitality, of immortality transcending the cycles of nature. And, like all creatures that display the three sacred colors—in this case, "black" (i.e., dark green) leaves, white blossoms, and red berries—it was a special manifestation of divinity. But singling it out in either of those categories are its thorns, which are capable of drawing blood and suggest the various applications of that activity in the human realm, whether for military or ritual purposes. So the holly is the divine sacrificer among trees; and its placing at the darkest moment of the *giamos*-season, presiding over the blood-nourishment of the reborn Sun, seems eminently appropriate.

Returning to the Pryderi story in the First Branch, we see that bloodletting is also mentioned in the context of Pryderi's birth; the serving-women bathe the sleeping Rhiannon's face and hands with blood, so that others will believe that she has slain her own child. The blood in fact comes from a newborn puppy. According to some researchers, the dog is an animal associated with Lugh, and with all divine or heroic figures modeled after him. Could we, again, have here an echo of a blood-sacrifice that must occur when the Child of Light is born? Although elsewhere in the story Pryderi is equine, like his mother, Celtic divinities usually have more than one animal manifestation, and it seems very plausible that here bitch and puppy are a reflection of Great Mother and Great Son, just as, a little later, are Teyrnon's mare and her foal. Could not, then, the puppy be a creature of like-nature with Pryderi who is substituted for him, not only as the Mabinogi's plot requires, but also as a sacrifice? We cannot know for certain that the story was ever conceived in this way historically, but as we journey through the maze of mythological and ritual imagery, motifs echo each other and point to other correspondences further on, creating patterns that are compelling in their appropriateness.

It should, however, be evident to us by now that both the Mari Lwyd and Hunting the Wren rituals are linked together by common motifs and related mythological references, and that at one time they may well have been parts of a single ceremony. In the Irish wren tradition, we have seen the Mari Lwyd appear as the Láir Bhán, while in the Mari Lwyd pageant the Aderyn Pica Llwyd on its beribboned perch is very similar to the wren in its *perllan,* pear orchard. In a modern revived tradition it could be illuminating to combine the two ceremonies, underscoring the strength of their mythological imagery in the context of the season.

From this overview of Celtic Winter Solstice customs we can now extrapolate the themes that must be expressed in a Celtic celebration of "Deuoriuos." The following appear to be of paramount importance:

1. The Theme of the Child of Light. The spark of light and life born at the moment of Night's triumph must be made to survive and grow, in spite of the inimical forces arrayed against it.
2. The Theme of the Exiled Mother. The power of generation and growth is unable to manifest itself outwardly, but it is still active on a hidden, not easily recognized level.
3. The Theme of the Sun-Sacrifice. The newborn light must be given energy from a source similar to itself.

As with Samhain, the continued importance of this festival in our communities provides us with a ready-made framework for celebrating it. Virtually all Christmas customs (except, of course, for the purely commercial uses of the holiday, which fortunately are still no more than a media veneer over deep-rooted traditions) contribute something appropriate to the spirit of "Deuoriuos." In the measure that circle members experience them as embodiments of that spirit, all such local customs can and should be used. Both the Christian and the non-Christian motifs contained in the traditions will be of value to all since, as we pointed out earlier, they have a common source, a common goal, and reinforce each other. The "Christmas spirit" is older than Christianity, although it obviously loses none of its force in a Christian context.

But, again, we will want to develop, as a supplement to the community or family traditions we have inherited, ritual statements that will express the uniquely Celtic understanding of this season's sacred meaning. The following suggestions, taken for the most part from Céli Dé Circle's experience, may serve as inspiration.

Since this is the moment of Night's triumph, let us begin our ritual in absolute darkness. As we did at Samhain, let us impress upon our inner eye the purest representations of *giamos*-reality: night, cold, silence, motionlessness, all the outward signs of death. The circle leader may help us by verbally evoking these things, or we can, after some practice, build up the images by ourselves. An unbroken pall of snow lies over the entire Land; the kindly Lady, whose gifts we could rely on during the bright season, is hidden, and only the Hag or Sow shows us her face. At this still point, where any hope of motion or growth seems to be denied, what can we do but yield to the hypnotic spell of the Winter power?

But out of the Otherworld comes the counterpower, the spark of *samos*-energy that will impel events in the direction of light and life again. From among the oranges which, studded with cloves, will go into the wassail bowl, we have chosen one and stuck a candle into its top. The candle is lit; where, a moment before, total night reigned, a small pool of wavering light has appeared. We pass the orange—the little Sun—from hand to hand around the circle, slowly and reverently at first, then faster and faster, perhaps with chanting and exhortations as our passion in celebrating the light grows and gathers energy. When the energy has reached its peak and the whirling of the light around the circle can get no faster, the orange is taken to the center of the ritual space and used to light a large candle there. Now we have our new focus of *samos*-reality, a light to guide our waking consciousness, keeping the darkness at bay.

Now the story of the Child of Light is told. We have many versions to choose from in Celtic tradition; indeed the term *mabinogi*, in Welsh, seems originally to have designated such a story. We can tell the story of Mabon and Modron, or the more fleshed-out version in which they are called Pryderi and Rhiannon. We can tell the folk-version of the birth of Lugh, in which his father Cian steals through the Fomorian darkness to make secret love to Eithne daughter of Balor, and winds up fathering not only the Child of Light but also the race of seals (from the habit of telling this story Céli Dé Circle came to associate seals with "Deuoriuos," and used them as a solstice decoration motif!). Or, we can use the Welsh counterpart of the story (if we leave out the element of Arianrhod's unwillingness, which belongs in a different ritual setting), where the water-child Dylan is Lleu's seal-brother. Even the birth of Fionn Mac Cumhail is appropriate here; and there are a number of miraculous births recounted in local folktales that clearly fit the theme of the Child of Light, and can be adapted to our ritual.

But almost as soon as he is born, the Child disappears. Pryderi is stolen by the monstrous Otherworld claw, while Rhiannon sleeps, drenched in puppy-blood. When three nights old, Mabon vanishes, no one knows where. Lugh is taken to the paradise of Manannán to

protect him from the wrath of his Fomorian grandfather. Lleu, un-
formed at birth, is hidden by his uncle Gwydion in an incubator-
like chest. Fionn, after magically escaping the king's attempt to drown
him, is concealed by his Amazon foster-mother in a forest tree; and
so forth. The telling of the story should end climactically with this
eclipsing of the desired Child (paralleled, perhaps, by a partial obscuring of the candlelight), creating an atmosphere of mild anxiety
and anticipation.

Now strange figures appear in the half-darkness beyond the circle: a giant shape with a head like a grinning horse's skull, surrounded by smaller companions in outlandish clothes. They stop at
the circle's edge, unable to proceed farther without permission. A
spokesman for the mummers' group then asks that the Great Mare
and her retinue be given leave to enter the circle (one can use the
traditional verses from the Welsh ceremony, or improvise something
new, with more allusions to the mythological sources). Those in the
circle at first feign fright and disgust, but eventually relent and let the
Mare in, only to have her rush about threateningly, lunging and
snapping at the company. At last a woman stops her, speaks to her
soothingly, tells her that her Child is not lost but will grow and reveal himself when the year reaches its bright half. The Mare is
calmed (although she may be allowed to behave in tricksterish fashion at later points in the ceremony), and the mummers who accompany her can now sing and play instruments as they parade around
the circle to display their "wren" in its *perllan*. One of the mummers,
disguised as a hag (or perhaps a sow), periodically attempts to attack
either the Mare or the wren, but is fended off by the others.

The wassail bowl, filled with mulled cider and brandy—gener-
ously spiced—and an assortment of fruits (there are many recipes for
this; the most characteristic ones come from Scotland), is held out to
each circle member, who sips it as he or she comes to greet the
wren. Thus the drink of the Sun—the energy of growth, the *samos*-
power—passes into us. Céli Dé Circle used mistletoe to symbolize
the Divine Child, and placed it on a bed of branches representing
the three primordial colors: silver fir (white), yew (black), and holly
(red). This could, in variant forms of the ritual, be substituted for the
wren, or be shown to the Great Mare to quiet her frenzy.

Gifts, twinkling lights, seasonal songs—all the things that appeal to the childlike, impressionable part of ourselves—should be allowed to work their full effect upon us, ensuring that the seed of Light is firmly planted and that the Darkness will have no power to prevent its growth. And for those who wish to include the specifically Christian aspect of the feast in their celebration, that is, again, perfectly appropriate.

Imbolc (Oímealg)

Lá Fhéile Bríde, Laa'l Breeshey, Gwyl Mair Dechrau'r Gwanwyn, Goel Kantolyon, Gouel Varia ar Goulou.—FEBRUARY 1–2

Gach 're lá go maith
óm lá-sa amach
agus leath mo lae féinig.
            —Brigit's Promise on Her Day

(Every second day will be fine from my day onwards, as well as half of my own day.)

The feast known in Middle Irish as *Imbolc* is the second of the four great Quarterly Feasts of the Celtic calendar, and marks the midpoint of the *giamos*-half of the sacred Year. A widespread folk etymology in modern Irish explains the name of the feast as *i mbolg* "in the belly"—a very apt expression of the symbolic meaning of the holiday, of Winter pregnant with Summer—but in fact it seems to be derived from the root *m(b)lig*, "milk," and means something like "lactation." An alternate form of the name was *Oímelc* (modern form *Oímealg*), which reflects Old Celtic *Oui-melko-*, "ewes' milk." Traditionally the feast was supposed to coincide with the first flowing of milk in the udders of ewes, a month or so before the lambing season. This fairly inconspicuous sign of returning fertility was the first in a series of events that heralded the awakening of life in the Land and urged the Tribe to engage in a new cycle of activities.

Imbolc, then, is the first day of spring, as the second quarter of the Celtic Year (*earrach, gwanwyn* or *nevez-amzer*) is conventionally referred to in English. To those of us conditioned to think of spring as specifically the time of new leaves and flowers, the choice of cold and snowy February as the date of its beginning might seem a little odd. But, by now, we should be used to the Celtic concept of things beginning in darkness, in the Goddess's hidden womb. The Fire of Spring is lit in secret, while Winter still rules in the world above. The signs of Winter's demise are small and obscure—the ewes' lactation, for instance—but for those who can read them they are a sure guarantee that the cold and snow will not last. In the Coligny Calendar the month in which Imbolc would fall is called *Ogronios*, which (by analogy with *Samonios,* "end of summer") seems to mean "end of the cold." It is quite possible that the druids of southern Gaul called their equivalent of Imbolc *Ogronia*.

In some communities it was even considered lucky for snow to fall on Imbolc, as though all the strength of Winter would spend itself in this fashion and leave the way clear for fair weather. From the Isle of Man we have the following seasonal verse:

> *Laa'l Breeshey bane:*
> *Dy chooilley yeeig lane*
> *Dy ghoo ny dy vane.*

(White Bridget's day: every ditch filled with black or with white.) On this day of transition the snow transfigures the land and reveals it to be made up of the primal duality of *giamos* and *samos*.

The mention of Brigit leads us to discuss the figure who has come to dominate all ritual aspects of the feast, so that in most modern communities, the original name of the holiday has been forgotten and replaced with her own name. *Oímealg* is a relatively unfamiliar term to most modern Irish-speakers: everyone spontaneously refers to the feast as *Lá Fhéile Bríde*, "Bridget's Feast Day." By a wonderful accident of history, pagan and Christian traditions have completely fused in this instance, transforming a goddess into a saint of the Christian calendar without denying or obscuring any of her pre-Christian traits, so that the essence of her role in the ancient religion has not survived merely as a half-hidden substratum, muddled by later accretions, but remains focal to the celebration of the feast. Very little is known about the actual life of the fifth-century woman who founded a religious community in Kildare (*Cill Dara*, "Chapel of the Oak-Grove," suggesting a pre-Christian importance to the site), and who became the object of such intense veneration that, over the centuries, almost came to usurp the role of the Virgin Mary herself, receiving the title of "Midwife of Christ" and, by extension, "Second Mother of the Lord." One can speculate that this woman already was, before becoming a Christian and leading a Christian community, a religious figure of some kind, perhaps revered as a human manifestation of the goddess whose name she bore. In any case, the people who loved her and perpetuated her memory with such devotion seem to have thought of her entirely in terms of her identity with the goddess. And it is as the goddess—despite the Church's attempts to ground her in "historical" reality—that she survives in Celtic consciousness.

So the figure, whether goddess or saint, whom modern Gaelic-speakers call *Bríd* goes back to the *Brigantia* (or *Brigantî*) commemorated in insular Celtic inscriptions from the period of the Roman occupation, and even more directly to the *Brigindu* invoked in a famous text from eastern Gaul. Brigantia was above all the Land-goddess of the Brigantes, the confederation of tribes whose territory covered most of what is now northern England; but there is evidence that she had a wider renown, and certainly the goddess type she represents—the "Minerva" of the *interpretatio Romana*—was expressed throughout the Celtic world. Her name comes from a stem *brig-* meaning "height," often appearing in the place-name element *brigâ*, applied to hills and mountains. The derived form *Brigantiâ* would mean something like, "She who raises herself on high, who is exalted." From the evidence of the modern Celtic languages, however, it appears that the term *brigâ* originally had a much more complex meaning than just "height." Scots Gaelic *brigh*, Irish *brí*, and Manx *bree* all have the range of meanings "force, power, meaning, invigorating essence," as well as "hill"; and in the Brythonic languages, while *bre* means "hill," *bri* has the meaning "fame, respect, value." Thus, *brigâ* is both something that is "raised up," and something that imparts strength and a sense of meaning by doing so: an upwelling of force.

The *Brigantia/Brigindu* of epigraphy develops linguistically into the *Brigit* of the medieval Irish mythological texts, who in turn gives her name to the saint. The mythological Brigit is the daughter of the Dagda, a champion of the Tuatha Dé Danann (the gods of the Tribe) who was probably the main link between the Danann and Fomorian identities before the development of the Lugh mythos. As such, she is (despite her Goddess-nature which automatically links her with the Land) identified with the welfare of the human Tribe, a role confirmed by her frequent representation in triple form, mirroring the trifunctional concerns of the Celtic community: as *banfhile,* "female poet," she inspires the bards, opening communications between this world and the Otherworld, as befits specialists of the first function; as patroness of the forge and consort of smiths, she presides over the making of the weapons that warriors bear; and as healer, herbalist, and purifier of the home, she deals with the physical, health-related realm of the third function. In all of these roles fire is one of her main attributes—whether it be fire of sunlight, fire of the forge, or fire of the hearth. Even in her Christian guise at Kildare she has a perpetual fire burning in her honor, watched over by twenty women who are obviously the inheritors of a pre-Christian religious function. This fire is perhaps to be equated with the *brigâ* in her name, the energy that wells up and imparts strength and meaning. It is, in all cases, a life-giving and inspiring fire. It manifests first in the Land, awakening sleeping forces in the hidden depths, setting in motion processes that will become apparent only later in the season, and by the same token making the weather milder and more suited to human work. In this last respect Brigit makes herself known as the aspect of the Land-goddess who is most favorable to the Tribe; but her fire works directly within the Tribe itself as well, fueling all the creative endeavors—whether purely intellectual or material—that human culture can give rise to. As such, she is the universal Muse, maybe even the same as the *awen* invoked in Welsh bardic tradition.

Like all Celtic divinities, Brigit—both goddess and saint—has a number of plant and animal attributes. She is accompanied by a white cow, which symbolizes her protection of cattle—always the most prized possessions of a Celtic community—and is a manifestation of her mother *Bó-fhionn*, the White Cow who is the goddess of the sacred river Boyne. Her flower is usually said to be the dandelion (*caisearbhán* in Irish, *beartan-Brìde* in Scots Gaelic), a bloom of "solar" appearance with many medicinal properties, and which contains a milky juice, linking it symbolically to cattle; though at one time it may have been the coltsfoot (*adhann*), a somewhat similar-looking plant, also of great medicinal importance, but which flowers much earlier, often quite near the date of Imbolc. Her messenger bird is the oystercatcher—called *brìdean* (generally explained as *Brìd-eun*, "Bríd-bird") in Scotland, and *giolla Bríde* ("Bríd's servant") in parts of western Ireland—which shares its sacred status with all other beings that are naturally black, white, and red. And the snake—especially, it seems, the adder—is her divinatory animal, also linking her (by its Fomorian associations) to the mythology of the Land-powers.

In the Christian calendar Imbolc immediately precedes Candlemas, i.e., the Feast of the Purification of the Virgin. Since the traditions of Brigit have not survived to a great extent in the Brythonic-speaking countries (except in parts of Wales, where she is known as *Ffraed*), her role there has tended to be taken over by the Virgin Mary. In Wales the feast was known as *Gwyl Mair Dechrau'r Gwanwyn*, "The Feast of Mary of the Beginning of Spring." The Breton name is *Gouel Varia ar Gouloù*, "Feast of Mary of the Light," a reference to the use of candles in celebrating it (especially in its Christian form). One of the Manx names of the feast, *Laa'l Moirrey ny Goinnley*, "Day of Mary of the Candles," reflects the same custom.

The celebration of Imbolc expressed two themes: the reawakening of fertility in the Land, and the inception of a new cycle of agricultural activity in the life of the Tribe, with the figure of Brigantia—the creative force in both Tribe and Land—uniting the two as one. The goddess was invited to bless the process, granting protection from harm, as well as energy to grow. She could be portrayed ceremonially as a doll or statue, or represented by a woman who took on her role. Purification with water, the display of fire, and the making of talismans were among the main ritual gestures used to manifest her power.

Purification by lustration was one of the most basic items in the ritual vocabulary of the ancient Celts. In the case of Imbolc, hands, feet, and head were washed to consecrate them for the new cycle of work. Indeed, one of the alternative etymologies for the name of the feast is, in a medieval Irish source, *imb-fholc*, "washing oneself" (compare Welsh *ymolchi*).

The fire of Brigantia was both the fire of fertility within the earth and the fire of the sun, which gradually gained in strength as the days lengthened. The lighting of bonfires or candles was an expression of magical encouragement to the sun, as well as a sign of rejoicing at the more abundant light. Traditionally, Imbolc marked the point after which it would no longer be necessary to carry a candle when going out to do early morning work. In parts of Wales a candle would be ceremonially returned by the servants to the head of the household on this day, implying that it would no longer be needed. In keeping with the "Candlemas" imagery, candles would be lit in all the windows of the house; and candles would be carried in procession after the Christian celebration of the feast.

The talisman that granted Brigit's protection was, throughout Ireland, the *cros-Bríde* (Bridget's cross), sometimes referred to as *bogha Bríde* (Bridget's bow) or *crosóg* (little cross). This could be made from a variety of materials—usually plaited rushes, but also straw, cord, sedge, or vine bound around a wooden framework—and could take on a variety of shapes. The most familiar model is no doubt the four-armed "swastika" made of rushes, which was used particularly in Ulster, though it was known elsewhere as well. It was a symbol of the perpetual cycle of the seasons, of the certainty that light and summer would always return, and its four arms reflected the four-sided structure of the Celtic Year—though it also had a three-armed counterpart, which placed the symbolic stress on Brigit's triple influence on the activities of the Tribe. The *cros Bríde* could also look like a true Celtic cross, or be a much more complex figure made up of several crosses.

Another important talisman consecrated at this time was the *brat Bríde*, or "Bridget's mantle." This was a length of cloth or ribbon left exposed at the window during the night of the feast to absorb the power of the goddess/saint as she became manifest during the ritual.

It would then be worn for protection, or used in healing rituals, and its potency could be renewed year after year at this time, with some sources stating that it took seven years for a *brat Bríde* to attain the full extent of its curative properties.

The ceremonies for welcoming Brigit into the house and obtaining her blessing varied a great deal from community to community, but they all had some elements in common, and they were all founded on the image of a wandering Brigit in need of hospitality. We have already met the wandering Land-goddess at Deuoriuos: there she was pitiful indeed, demoted to animal form, her power and identity cloaked; but at Imbolc she is stronger, certain of her victory over the darkness, and can show the Tribe her human face, conferring true blessings which are, in a sense, a repayment of our kindness to her at the solstice. Some traditions from Gaelic Scotland specify that Brigit has been shut up inside Ben Nevis by the Cailleach (Hag) until Imbolc, when her brother Aonghus (the Maponos, manifesting at an unusually early date) comes riding a White Horse out of the Otherworld to free her. In other variants it is the Cailleach herself who is transformed into Brigit by drinking from a holy spring before dawn on Imbolc.

One variant of the ceremony had a human being impersonate the goddess/saint. Usually this was the eldest daughter of the house, though other women—and even men—could play the part. She would go outdoors and gather a bunch of rushes, then return and call out on the threshold: *Téigí ar bhur nglúine, agus osclaigí bhur súile, agus ligigí Bríd bheannaithe isteach!* (Be on your knees, and open your eyes, and let blessed Bríd in!). The other members of the household would welcome her: '*Sé do bheatha, 'sé do bheatha, 'sé do bheatha, a bhean uasail!* (Thrice welcome, noble lady!) or *O, tar isteach, tá céad fáilte romhat!* (O come in, you are a hundred times welcome!). She would then enter, put the rushes under a centrally placed table, and proceed to bless the house and all that was in it, especially the food and drink, and the hearth-fire. After this the entire household would use the rushes to make *crosóga*, which were later blessed by the priest and hung up over the doors for protection against want. A significant detail of the ceremony involved contact between the *crosóga* and foodstuffs: in Derry, for instance, a large loaf of oatbread shaped like a *cros*

Bríde was placed upon the pile of rushes that would be used to make the *crosóga*; the bread was eaten by the household in a ritual atmosphere, and when it was finished the *crosóga* were made. Elsewhere the *crosóga* were placed over or under pieces of bread during dinner, or they were sprinkled with crumbs of bread—all of this pointing to the "third function" nature of the magic involved. In another variant of the same ceremony the family made the *crosóga* before calling in the person playing Brigit, who then entered the darkened room with a candle to bless the *crosóga*, the fire, the house, and the food. In some local traditions different members of the household would make *crosóga* of different sizes and shapes, with different functions.

More widespread was the representation of Brigit by an effigy called a *brídeóg*, typically a straw doll wearing a child's clothes. It would be carried from house to house by a procession of young men and women who were often themselves referred to as *brídeóga*. At each house they would beg hospitality for the *brídeóg*, sing songs, recite blessings and prayers, distribute *crosóga*, and receive some money or food for their performance. The woman who actually held the *brídeóg* was expected to possess outstanding moral qualities, and indeed to be herself something of a mirror for Brigit. One senses here the remnant of an ancient sacerdotal function; in fact, some communities dispensed with the doll altogether, and called the leader of the procession *An Bhrídeóg*, having her bear a crown of rushes, a shield, and a *crosóg* (all applicable to the pre-Christian goddess), as well as a veil. (The veil was probably an attribute specific to the Christian saint: in the *Félire Oengusso* Brigit is called *cenn cáid caillech n-Eirenn,* "the revered head of the veiled women of Ireland"; for the term *cailleach*—which has come to mean "hag"—originally meant "nun," being derived from the Latin *pallium* "veil," with the customary Irish substitution of *c* for *p.*) In much of Munster and Connacht the members of the *brídeóg* procession were, on the contrary, all men, dressed in white, wearing skirts, and pointed straw headdresses with mask-like visors, of the kind we have seen worn by the *buachaillí tuí* on Samhain and other ritual occasions. Again, they are Land-spirits, now made beneficent by their presence in Brigit's retinue, and are bringing their gift of fertility to the awakening countryside.

Each family could also make its own *brídeóg*, bring it into the house with ceremony, and leave it overnight in a specially prepared bed to bless all those present. In parts of Scotland the *brídeóg* was put to bed with a wooden wand at her side. During the night Brigit was thought to rise and strike the hearth-fire with her wand; and if the mark of the stroke could be seen in the ashes the following morning, it was an omen of good fortune. In other Scottish communities no actual doll was used, but a bed was made and Brigit was invoked three times at the door of the house: *A Bhrighd, a Bhrighd, thig a steach: tha do leabaidh air a chàradh!* ("Brighd, Brighd, come in: your bed is ready!") Candles were lit at the window and around the bed, and left to burn all night. On the Isle of Man the head of the household would stand on the threshold with a bunch of rushes in his hand and invoke Brigit by singing:

> *Brede, Brede, tar gys my hie,*
> *Tar gys my hie ayns noght;*
> *Foshiljee yn dorrys da Vrede*
> *As lhig da Vrede çheet stiagh!*

(Brede, Brede, come to my house, come to my house tonight; open the door for Brede and let Brede come in!).

The rushes were then strewn on the floor to make a passage for Brigit, and later gathered together to make a bed for her.

Besides the effigy of the goddess, the *brídeóg* party originally also carried a ritual implement called the *crios Bríde,* (Bridget's belt). This was a large hoop of braided straw decorated with four woven crosses marking the quarters of its circumference. According to the form in which the custom survived in Connemara and the Aran Islands, the women in the procession would carry the *brídeóg* while the men would hold the *crios.* At each house they visited, the inhabitants would be invited to pass through the *crios* in order to obtain supernatural blessings, especially blessings of physical health. The bearers of the *crios* would introduce the ritual by reciting a verse like the following:

> *Crios Bríde mo chrios,*
> *Crios na gceithre gcros.*

Eirigh suas, a bhean an tighe
Agus gaibh trí h-uaire amach.
An té 'rachas tré mo chrios,
Go mba seacht bhfearr a bheidh sé bliain ó inniu.

(My girdle is Bríd's girdle, the girdle with the four crosses. Rise up, woman of the house, and go out three times. May whoever goes through my girdle be seven times better a year from today.)

Men would pass through the *crios* sideways, beginning with the right foot, while women would bring it down over their heads, and then step out of it. For maximum effect the ritual had to be repeated three times. Clearly the hoop is a representation of the birth canal—more specifically, the birth canal of the Land-goddess who is the archetype of fertility and the source of all physical benefits—and the ceremony is meant to be a rejuvenation, a rebirth from the goddess's womb. At one time it may have been the central element in the Imbolc celebration, but its very pagan flavor probably made Church authorities uncomfortable during the standardizing period of the Counter Reformation, and where it survived it did so only on the condition that the ritual appeals to the Goddess be tempered by Church-approved prayers to the saint.

To complete our inventory of the ritual objects associated with Imbolc, we must mention an odd artifact recorded only from Leitrim, but which may represent an ancient and formerly widespread tradition. Strips of peeled rush-stems, taken from among those used to make *crosóga*, were pasted with sticky starch onto a board, in the shapes of a disk, a half-disk, four seven-rayed stars, and a ladder with three rungs. The entire figure was called "the sun, the moon, and the stars," and it was displayed together with the *crosóga*. It seems likely that we have here the remains of a ritual to a divinity (or divinities) once invoked together with Brigit, but whose memory faded and survived only in a few communities—where it was sheltered, as it were, under the saint's mantle.

As with all of the Quarterly Feasts, which weaken our conventional time-space continuum by beginning a new cycle or sub-cycle, some divination was done on Imbolc, though not as assiduously as

on Samhain. In Wales, for instance, two candles would be lit and
placed on either side of a chair. Each member of the household
would sit in the chair, take a drink from a horn goblet, and throw the
goblet over his or her shoulder. If the goblet landed upright, it was a
good omen; if its opening was to the floor, it was a sign of early
death. The two candles, in this case, define a liminal state in which
the consultant is neither in this world or the Otherworld, and the
throwing of the goblet past this threshold places it under Otherworld conditions where it can react to future events.

But the most famous and mythologically charged instance of
divination on this day involved Brigit's oracular serpent. In Scottish
tradition the serpent was believed to emerge, by the influence of its
divine mistress, from the hill in which it was hibernating. If weather
conditions were favorable, it would become active and presage an
early thaw; if it returned to its hole, winter would keep its grip on
the land for another month. The *Carmina Gadelica* have preserved an
invocation to the serpent on this ritual occasion:

Moch maduinn Bhride
Thig an nimhir as an toll.
Cha bhean mise ris an nimhir,
Cha bhean an nimhir rium.

(On Bride's morn the serpent will come out of the hole. I will
not harm the serpent, nor will the serpent harm me. [In some other
versions the serpent is addressed as *rioghan,* "queen."])

It may well be that in pre-Christian times some communities
possessed an actual snake, looked after by religious functionaries, to
be consulted as an oracle on this holiday. In Ireland, famous for its
lack of snakes, it was a hedgehog (*gráinneog*)—also a chthonic animal—
whose behavior provided folk with a weather forecast on Imbolc. A
number of animal species—varying according to the composition of
local fauna—may have served this purpose in different Celtic communities since ancient times. And, of course, the tradition has migrated to America, in the form of Groundhog Day.

Feasting was also an integral part of the celebration. Brigit's visit and the blessing of the *crosóga* were usually followed by a solemn, candlelit family dinner. *Bairín breac*, a cake-like bread containing candied fruits, was a staple for the holiday in Ireland. In Brittany, it was more customary to make crêpes (*krampouezh*), which, because their shape suggests the solar disk, have been a ritual spring dish in many parts of the Western world. Other communities made pancakes on Shrove Tuesday, closer to the period of the Spring Equinox.

Somewhat obscured by the agricultural imagery the feast has come to emphasize, yet central to its full meaning, is Brigit's blessing of the forge fire. Since the very origins of metalworking the function of the smith has, in most traditional cultures, acquired an aura of Otherworldly power. Because the smith transforms an apparently useless natural feature (metallic ore) into an immensely powerful and useful substance (metal) not found in nature, his work becomes a symbol of the culture itself, of the Tribe's ability to take material from the Land and transmute it into something new, uniquely of the Tribe's realm. So the Land-goddess's blessing of the smith's fire and of his tools becomes a blessing on the Tribe as a whole, a renewed validation of the marriage between Tribe and Land, implying that the Tribe has permission to transform certain aspects of the Land— provided, of course, that the Land's structural balance is not upset by such activity. Brigit's association with smithery is, as we have seen, an ancient one, and has extended to her Christian legend, for the saint's principal collaborator in her community at Cill Dara was Saint Connlaed (Conleth), a smith.

Through Brigit's approval of the smith's "making," then, the Tribe is given leave to work its own transformation upon the Land. The main elements of this transformation will have to do with crops and food production, so agricultural tools (also products of the smith) will be blessed at this time. As the sun grows warmer, the frozen soil thaws out, ploughing and sowing can begin, inaugurating the cycle of nurture and growth that will bear fruit on Lúghnasadh, the polar opposite of Imbolc in the Celtic Year.

If, then, we look back on the ritual elements we have enumerated, we can see them all reflecting one basic concept, that of *increase*, particularly in the material realm. The unending sunwise rotation of the *cros Bríde* imparts life-giving energy—the *brigâ/brí* that gives the goddess her name—to everything that comes into contact with it. Other talismans may, as representations of her or of her attributes, acquire the same power to bless and heal, but it is all a manifestation of this one energy, traceable to one divine source. The *brigâ* empowers both Tribe (by giving inspiration to human endeavors) and Land (by creating circumstances conducive to growth), and in so doing makes a Bridge between them. We are, on the one hand, revealed to be composed of the same material substance as the Land we live on, physically at one with it, growing and developing by the same processes that promote growth in all living organisms; and, on the other hand, that mental activity, that expression of self-identity, which seems to characterize the Tribe exclusively, is shown to be energized in precisely the same way, and by the same power. This realization, through ritual, of the fundamental unity of existence—in spite of the duality we experience in everyday consciousness—is a joyous, deeply affecting event. We must remember, in our modern celebrations of Imbolc, to express this unifying function of the *brigâ*, the Goddess-energy.

The Imbolc rituals that have survived until recent times in Celtic communities are, as we have tried to show, so rich in content and so clear in structure that we really have no need to reconstruct or reinvent any material for the feast. It is a question of choosing which local tradition, or which combination of traditions, we wish to follow. If a circle is lucky enough to be established in a community where ancient Imbolc traditions are still alive, those are definitely the ones that should be adopted. We may find it useful at this point, however, to review the ritual elements that express or magically encourage the central theme of increase on this day:

1. Ablution, to wash away elements (linked to the *giamos*-state) that impede increase.
2. The *cros Bríde* (*crosóg*), as the primal symbol of the source of increase; or, alternately, the *brídeóg*, representing the Goddess herself.
3. The *crios Bríde*, as the magical agent for bringing increase into the lives of the participants, by means of a ritual passage through the source of *brigâ* (the Goddess's womb).

4. An object to be charged by the energy of the ritual in order to conserve that energy for future use. This can be specifically the *brat Bríde*, or simply *crosóga*.

We will now outline an Imbolc ritual based on practices that developed within Céli Dé Circle, and which can be used as inspiration for future rituals, though like all other material in this book it is not meant to exclude different approaches that are consistent with Celtic tradition. More versions of the Imbolc ritual exist in various communities than could possibly be used on a single ceremonial occasion.

The ritual is set to begin after dark. A supply of *crosóga* will have been prepared by circle members: as many small ones as there will be participants in the ceremony, one large one that will be carried by the *brídeóg* party or the individual impersonating Brigit, and (if desired) four more of intermediate size for the four Quarters. An abundance of candles also should be made available, preferably in solar colors, from bright red through orange and yellow to white. One much larger than the others will be brought in by the Brigit-figure, and will be placed in the center, as a focus for the ritual; the others—to be lit from this central candle—will be held by the participants, but also should be placed wherever possible around the ritual space, to provide, at the appropriate moment, an intense and joyous illumination. Food and drink for the feasting are laid out on a brightly-colored cloth in the middle of the ritual area. Somewhere near them there also should be prepared a *crios Bríde*—a hoop large enough for a person to step through—with a framework of rope, wicker, or wire, decorated with a variety of ribbons, scarves, or similar items; each participant should contribute such a decoration to the *crios*. Participants are clad, insofar as possible, in light, *samos*-oriented colors.

After establishing sacred space in the usual manner, the ritual leader walks out to the southern edge of the circle and, holding either a bunch of rushes or a finished *crosóg* in his hand, sings an invitation to Brigit to enter into the assembly (he may use the Manx invocation, or one like it). The circle member impersonating Brigit appears from the outer darkness carrying the large candle and the large *crosóg*. Stopping at the edge of the circle, she calls on all present to be prepared to receive her, and is formally welcomed by all. A variant of this, stressing the trifunctional specialization of Brigit, would have three people, each representing a different aspect of the Goddess, appear and be welcomed in turn. In this case each might be carrying a *crosóg* of the three-armed variety, drawing attention to their relationship with the three functions of the Tribe. As the large candle is brought in and put down in the center of the ritual area, all participants should open themselves imaginatively to the power of the light, using it to dispel the passivity of the *giamos*-state in themselves even as it dispels the darkness with its coming.

The Brigit (or the three Brigits) then bless the Quarters with the *crosóg*, focusing each blessing on the Tribal function associated with that quarter. Beginning in the West, she, as *banfhile*, grants an increase of inspiration to the intellectual, poetical, and teaching activities of the first function. In the North, as patroness of the forge and consort of smiths, she guarantees the protection of weapons—actual and spiritual—to those who defend the Tribe and deal with conflicts. As healer and expert in the knowledge of herbs, she extends, in the East, her life-giving power to those who work at healing and nurturing the physical body. And finally, turning back to her entry-point in the South, she conjures increase into the Land itself. (If Brigit is represented as a triad, all three Brigits should come from their respective quarters to the South and speak the blessing together; and they should, in place of the three-armed *crosóga* they held previously, perform the blessing with a four-armed *crosóg*, symbolically associated with the Land.)

If desired, a "guardian" may be appointed to each Tribe-related quarter, representing the actual agent of its specific function (in symbolic terms, its "Danann-god"). The three of them light their candles from the fire the goddess has brought, and then pass the fire on to other circle members in their vicinity, who pass it on in turn until all the candles prepared around the ritual area are blazing brightly.

Now it is time for each circle member to receive individually the goddess's gift of increase. But before this can be done one must cleanse away the static *giamos* elements that control the present situation and provide no energy for growth. Taking up a basin of water, the ritual leader presents it to the person on his right as *tobar Bríde* ("the well of Bríd"), the source of the primal purifying water. That person washes his hands and face (and, if possible, his feet!), enhancing the act for himself as much as possible through imagination, then presents the basin to his right-hand neighbor in the circle, who after washing passes it on, until all present have performed the rite.

The ritual leader and an assistant then hold up the *crios Bríde*, and all pass through it in the prescribed manner (right side first for men, women feet-first). The procession to the *crios* should have the character of a slow, meditative line dance; it is best accompanied by a steady drumbeat, and perhaps a chant of the Hebridean type. All pass through the *crios* three times, concentrating each time on the renewing energy granted by the goddess through this ritual gesture; and upon his/her third emergence from the goddess's womb each participant receives a small *crosóg*, which must be meditated on briefly, visualizing it as a turning wheel that generates bright solar light by the very force of its turning. A shaft of warm sunlight should be seen flashing out from the center of the *crosóg*, to be absorbed by the energy-hungry elements of one's body. When all have completed their third passage, two other circle members take up the *crios* so that the ritual leader and his/her assistant can go through themselves.

The main portion of the ritual is now finished, and the circle members can give themselves over to quiet feasting, before the ceremony is officially closed. Each decorative item on the *crios* will be returned to its owner to be used as a *brat Bríde* throughout the year, for healing of aches and pains. The same items should be placed on the *crios* year after year, to increase their potency in this regard.

Although we are, on this day, only halfway through the Dark Half of the Celtic Year, all ritual endeavors will, from now to Bealtaine, focus on the strengthening of the Light, and on the encouragement of growth and activity. The Land-goddess's fire has been kindled, the blaze is spreading, before long the thawed earth will part to reveal the first green shoots.

Midspring

Alban Eilir—MARCH 21

Howl sowth, tor leun, pareusi an gwenton.
                                    —Cornish Saying

(A southerly sun, a full belly, prepare the Spring.)

There is no clear evidence that the Celts gave any special ritual significance to the actual date of the Spring Equinox. No name for such a feast can be found in any branch of Celtic tradition, and no Celtic community makes a specific commemoration of it. Most customs associated with the concept of Spring seem to have gravitated either toward Imbolc (the date of its inception) or toward Bealtaine (its culmination, and passage into Summer). It is possible to suppose, from the lack of evidence, that there was in fact no date of ritual importance between those two feasts.

Yet, there are a few factors that could lead us to reconsider such a position. First, although the Four Quarterly Feasts of the Earth cycle were clearly the preeminent ritual occasions of the Celtic Year, we know that the solar feasts had, at an early stage, acquired some significance in Celtic tradition, and that, although the two solstices are the only dates that continue to be commemorated almost everywhere, a variety of sources show that the Autumn Equinox was once, in some communities, celebrated quite lavishly. For the sake of symmetry, then, it would seem likely that some attention would have been paid to the date of the Spring Equinox, as well. Second, March 25 is Lady Day, and we are used to major Marial holidays indicating the former presence of a goddess-centered feast on the same date. And finally, no less than three major Celtic saint's days that have become national holidays—Saint David's Day, Saint Piran's Day, and Saint Patrick's Day—occur in March, and may have attracted to themselves some of the ritual material that would once have been used to celebrate the middle of the spring season. An Irish rhyme from Connacht points to a traditional solar quartering of the Year (*ráithí cama,* "crooked quarters") that coexisted with the *ráithí fírinneacha* or "true quarters" based on the Earth Feasts:

Ráithe ón Nollaig go Féile Phádraig,
Ráithe ó Fhéile Phádraig go Féile Seáin,
Ráithe ó Fhéile Seáin go Féile Mhichil,
'S ráithe ó Fhéile Mhichil go Nollaig.

(A quarter from Christmas to Saint Patrick's Day, a quarter from Saint Patrick's to Saint John's, a quarter from Saint John's to Michaelmas, and a quarter from Michaelmas to Christmas.)

One must also point out that, for the past thousand years at least, the celebration of Easter has come to dominate spring ritual activity in the Western world. Placed originally in this season for historical reasons (although it was linked with the Jewish lunar festival of Passover, itself determined in relation to the Spring Equinox), the Christian feast's theme of renewal and triumph over death was certainly in tune with its position in the yearly cycle, and could be easily wedded to local pagan customs. As in the case of Christmas, however, the very importance of the festival of Easter and its linking to international rather than community religious observance have encouraged the migration of Easter customs—even those with pre-Christian origins—and made it harder to trace their individual provenance. The "Easter bunny" that has become the main focus of the Anglo-American commercial packaging of the feast goes back to a Germanic mythology of Spring: he is the *Österhase* or "Easter hare," the fertility animal who accompanies the Goddess of Spring and Dawn—and the Old English name of that goddess (Eostre) has remained as the name of the feast even in its purely Christian form. Although this imagery is by now familiar throughout the English-speaking world, including the English-dominated Celtic lands, it cannot be assumed to represent a Celtic view of Spring ritual.

Easter eggs, however, even though they belong to that same commercial "mythology," seem to have been so widespread in early European village traditions that they very well may have been a part of the Celtic heritage before Christianity. The egg, after all, is a very basic symbol of life returning from a period of concealment in darkness—a little external womb, as it were. We have already mentioned the strong appeal all such womb imagery had for the Celts. Tantalizing hints in the works of classical writers and in early Celtic iconography suggest that the druids may have had a tradition of the Cosmic Egg out of which the world as we know it hatched, much as in a number of other religions that may have been in contact with them, such as Orphism. In any case, the display of brightly painted eggs does not seem out of place in a Celtic celebration of Spring. From a comparison of many Easter egg customs throughout Europe, it would appear that red—the color of life at its most intense and creative—was originally the universal color for eggs used in this ritual context.

From the carnival customs of Shrove Tuesday through the rigors of Lent (with, in some communities, a "Mid-Lent" break on Laetare Sunday that can almost become a second carnival) to the floral processions of Palm Sunday and the final rejoicing of the Resurrection, the rituals of the Easter season are spread out over a period of some six weeks, which makes it difficult to relate any of their elements, varied as they are, specifically to the Spring Equinox. Some of the Shrovetide rituals (which usually fall in February) may well, as we suggested in the preceding section, represent Imbolc material that has migrated to the later date—as in the case of the "solar" pancakes (Shrovetide fare in Wales and Ireland, among other places). Ceremonies involving the display of flowers or other plants, usually nearer the end of the season, may be Bealtaine customs celebrated earlier than the traditional date.

Yet there is one south Welsh custom associated with Shrovetide that does seem to have a direct application to the Spring Equinox. Two teams, assembling in the village square, engage in a football match that extends across the entire territory of the community, and may last all day. The object is to kick the ball—an inflated bull's bladder covered with leather—past one or the other end of the town. All the young men, divided into two teams, participate in the game, and are fed throughout the day on the ubiquitous vernal pancakes. The solar symbolism of ball games is well attested from many traditions around the world—we need mention only the famous Meso-american examples—and in the Welsh case the solar references are clear enough that we can identify it as a Celtic manifestation of the same concept. The ball is the Sun, and its passage across a goal line represents the Sun's passage across a decisive boundary between light and dark. Such a ritual is, of course, particularly suited to the time of the equinox—with the Tribe as usual, ceremonially echoing a process in the Land, and gaining a sense, through the ceremony, of magically participating in the process. The fact that football games are, in a number of Celtic communities, specifically associated with one or several of the solar feasts further encourages us to relate this particular custom to the Equinox.

Also perhaps a vestige of Midspring is the Welsh Good Friday custom of distributing cross-buns after the church service—not to be eaten, but to be preserved as healing talismans. The association of the cross on the buns with Good Friday is obvious, yet noted Celtic scholar Trefor M. Owen, following Laurence Whistler, has suggested that "wheaten cakes marked with a cross may have been eaten at the Spring Festival in pre-Christian times before the Gospel suggested another meaning"(Owen 1959). The original meaning of the cross here may have been the year—in this case, the solar year—divided into its quarters. The *crois Phádraig* that used to be made on Saint Patrick's Day—an equal-armed cross, often with a circular framing device, in "Celtic cross" fashion—may have been a related motif. The Sun's passage across the most important points in its yearly jour-ney was perhaps visualized as a ninety-degree turn of the cross on its axis.

Another ritual of spring renewal which became aligned with the date of Easter was the Breton custom of breaking old pots on Quasi-modo Sunday (the Sunday after Easter) to shouts of *Kazimodo, torr ar podoù!* (Quasimodo, break the pots!). The pots (in most cases already well-worn and broken) were suspended from strings, and young men, blindfolded, attempted to hit them with sticks.

This is, all in all, meager material to build a ritual with, but we can supplement it with our understanding of the mythology of the season. On Midspring we cross the final hurdle separating us from the Light half of the year. From this day on, victory for the Light is

assured, and we have only a triumphal march left to the final en-
thronement of Summer on Bealtaine, and the banishing of the last
vestiges of *giamos*-consciousness. Every week will bring new signs of
triumph, as spring flowers push up out of the ground and the buds
open on the trees. The Summer-Lord, the Maponos, the Sun-Child
who was born in the depths of winter and then hidden away, has
come of age and awakened to his true nature. It is our participation
in his awakening and the beginning of his triumphal progress that
should be the focus of our ritual observance of this feast.

The image of the Sleeping Lord is a powerful element in the heritage of all Celtic communities: whether he is King Arthur or Fionn
or a nameless chieftain from the forgotten tribal past, Pan-Celtic folklore speaks of discovering him in a cave, hidden from the world of
exoteric manifestation, sometimes surrounded with sleeping companions or with treasures of a bygone Golden Age. To wake him is a
revolutionary act, a literal turning of the world on its hinges. On a
cosmic scale, it can be seen as a return of Celtic self-awareness and
self-empowerment, but even in the seasonal context the return of
samos-consciousness must be interpreted as a call to action, to apply
to the world what has been learned in the meditative state of the *giamos*-phase. The return of Light is the return of hope at all levels of
being.

Thus, we have the following three elements as a framework for
our ritual:

1. The Waking of the Sleeping Lord.
2. The Game of the Boundary Between Dark and Light.
3. Symbols of Fertility to Come (eggs, flowering bulbs, etc.).

The ritual area should be decorated with light, solar-oriented
colors. Yellow daffodils are especially suitable. A basket of red painted
eggs (covered with a cloth until the appropriate ritual moment) is
placed in the middle of the space, together with a plate of thin pancakes.

After the usual opening procedure, the ritual leader leads the
other participants in a meditation on the Sleeping Lord. All see
themselves, with their inner eye, going down a narrow passage deep

into the ground, into damp darkness lit only by fox fire. As the passage levels out we find ourselves entering a tall vaulted chamber extending out indefinitely before us, and lit very dimly from an unseen source. The world of everyday consciousness is high above us, and we are cut off from it by a great weight of earth; in this deep place only eternal archetypes are found, capable of bringing about fundamental change.

Then we discern, resting on a great stone slab in the chamber before us, a giant human figure. As we come closer, we see it is a rather young man lying with his arms folded across his chest like a figure placed over a tomb, yet we can sense that he is not dead but in a deep sleep. The man is clad in rich robes and decked with ornaments that suggest a ritual role in some very ancient context; we realize he must have been a sacred king when he was in the world. All around the great body lie weapons—a sword, a spear, a dagger, a bow—which themselves possess an aura of magic that makes them seem more than mere instruments of battle.

Looking into the giant king's face, we are moved not only by his Otherworldly beauty, but also by traces of mysterious, ancient suffering. His banishment from the world of surface consciousness was effected by some violent means, which has left memories of hurt. If he were to wake, would remembering that hurt bring back the pain? And if he were in pain, what path of action would he take on returning to the world of form? Would the weapons that are a part of his inheritance—tools of magical power, with creative potential—be turned to destructive ends?

We ponder these questions even as we come to grips with our own feelings for the sleeping giant, our desire to see him restored to health and strength so that the entire world of nature—including ourselves—could, by coming under his leadership, regain the energy it needs for growth. We are greatly attracted to the intense vitality we can sense pulsing through his huge form, dammed only by the barriers of sleep, and we long to break those barriers so that the vitality might be bestowed freely upon us. We realize, then, that we ourselves are to be the primary interpreters of that vitality to the world around us, and that the way in which the energy will be used—whether creatively or destructively—depends on our own fundamental moral decision. If we have learned to deal positively with the sense of hurt and deprivation the ego often feels when our being enters the *giamos*-state, we need not carry any of that hurt over to the time when it is appropriate for us to return to the *samos*-state. By accepting as a necessity the periodic alternation of the two states, we accept all the feelings that are associated with each of them in its due season.

Our hesitations gone, we wake the Sleeping Lord of Summer. His eyes open to meet our gaze with love and gratitude, acknowledging us as kin. We watch him rise and fill the chamber with light as the solar vitality in him fills his body and shines forth. Soon the light has become so bright that it appears to dissolve the stony ceiling of the cave, allowing the Lord's giant form to pass upward to the world of blue sky. In this exhilarating mood of triumph we follow him and find spring flowers and new green leaves breaking through everywhere in the conquering sunlight.

At this point the meditation can turn effortlessly into a processional, accompanied by a simple chant.

The Game of the Boundary can, if the ritual is done outdoors, be expressed as an actual ball game, though if space is more limited it can be turned into a tug-of-war, with Summer and Winter teams trying to drag each other across a line in the center of the ritual area. This contest may be used as a form of divination, with the outcome prefiguring either the actual weather of the month to come (i.e., whether the spring will fully establish itself early or late), or the extent to which *giamos*-energies will give way to *samos*-energies in the life of the circle or the community.

Before the end of the circle, all participants receive one of the red painted eggs from the basket.

Bealtaine/Calan Mai

Bealltainn, Boaldyn, Calan Me, Kala-Mae—MAY 1

Harddwas teg a'm anrhegai,
Hylaw wr mawr hael yw'r Mai.

Anfones ym iawn fwnai,
Glas defyll glân mwyngyll Mai.
> —Dafydd ap Gwilym

(It is a fair, handsome youth who gave me gifts, a handy, generous great man is May. He has sent me proper currency, pure green leaves of May's gentle hazels.)

Introducing the second half of the Celtic Year—the Light season of *samos*—the feast of Bealtaine almost equals Samhain in importance. Since their function in the calendar is similar (creating a passage between *samos* and *giamos*, in one direction or the other), the ceremonies associated with Samhain and Bealtaine often parallel each other. Both feasts involve bonfires, contacts with the Otherworld, the Cosmic Boar Hunt, and an interaction between the Cernunnos and Maponos god-forms. Although, unlike Samhain, Bealtaine is not specifically mentioned in the Coligny Calendar, it is clearly a very ancient observance, fundamental to the Celtic ritual cycle. The modern name of the feast in the Goidelic languages appears to be derived from an Old Celtic *Belo-teniâ*, "(bon)fire of Belos (i.e., the Bright)," the latter name being evidently (despite some arguments to the contrary) a variant form of *Belenos*, a god of solar healing associated with cattle, whom we will discuss more fully below. In medieval Irish sources the holiday is often referred to as *Cétshamain*, from Old Celtic *Kentu-saminos*, "first of Summer"—although Cormac's Glossary, the ninth-century classic work, interprets it (through folk etymology) as *cét-sam-sín* 'first of summer weather.' This name survives today as *Céitein*, the Scots Gaelic name for the month of May. All the Brythonic languages, more influenced by Roman concepts, call it "first day of May," using the Latin name for the month. In the Coligny Calendar, the month which is the polar opposite of *Samonios* (end of Summer) is *Giamonios* (end of Winter), suggesting a name *Giamonia* for the feast among the druids of southern Gaul.

With Bealtaine the *samos*-mode of being at last fully establishes its dominance; actions that have been in gestation, contemplated in imagination only, can now be expressed in the world of form. We have entered the season of action and energy. Yet even as the *giamos*-

season, beginning with the triumph of Darkness, progressed to an ever-greater outward-moving affirmation of Light, so the *samos*-season, after an initial reveling in the triumph of Light on Bealtaine, gradually comes to turn more and more inward, letting in aspects of Darkness even while the *samos*-mode of willed action remains dominant.

The traditions of Celtic and formerly Celtic communities have provided us with a rich substructure of mythology to explicate the ritual celebration of the feast. In Ireland, whereas Samhain was associated with the sites of Tara and Tlachtga, the main rituals of Bealtaine were focused on Uisnech. Not far from Tara on the plain of Meath, Uisnech was considered to be, in ritual matters, its polar opposite and complement. Tara was the place of the High King and the warrior-aristocracy, but Uisnech was the stronghold of the druids. They coexisted in friendly and necessary rivalry, neither having pre-eminence over the other, "like two kidneys in one beast," to use the terminology in *Suidigud Tellaig Temra*. On Samhain Tara was the true center, and remained so through the Dark season; but on Bealtaine the function of the center passed to Uisnech, and with that change some of the symbolic language in ritual would shift as well. Whereas Tara was four-sided, indicating the willed stability of the social order, the Stone of Boundaries, which was the ritual center of Uisnech, had five sides reflecting a different, more dynamic concept of sacred geometry. At Tara the influences governing the functions of the Tribe came together, whereas Uisnech was the meeting-point of forces at work in the Land. One could say that Tara and its ritual associations belonged to the God, while Uisnech was the province of the Goddess, but to press the point too far would be to oversimplify the structures of Celtic religion, where everything interpenetrates everything else, and nothing is only itself.

According to the Irish lore of place-names, the first Bealtaine fire was lit at Uisnech in the time of the Nemedian invasion, by the druid Mide, whose name (center; although in the story it is also punningly interpreted as *mí-dé*, ungodly, evil) is then given to the ritually preeminent central province of Ireland. Mide's gigantic bon-fire blazed for seven years, was seen in all the provinces of Ireland, and became (as in the case of the Samhain fire) the source of all the

hearth-fires in the land. Because other druids who had been at Uisnech before him protested his usurpation of their privileges, he cut
out their tongues, which he then buried beneath his seat at Uisnech.
We may have in this myth an explanation of the druids' control over
all sacred matters in society, as well as, perhaps, the memory of the
consecration of a religious site by human sacrifice. But above all it
makes clear that Bealtaine, like Samhain, is a "hinge" date of renewal,
in which a major change occurs in the cycle of the year, dramatized
by the consuming and purifying fire.

The actual nature of the change, however, the passing of *giamos*
into *samos,* is portrayed mythologically as the Sacred Marriage, the
coming of age of the Maponos and his wedding to the Flower Maiden,
the youthfully desirable aspect of the Land-goddess. This latter figure
was of primal importance in Bealtaine tradition, and manifests in
various forms in different parts of the Celtic world. In the Fourth
Branch of the Mabinogi, she appears as Blodeuwedd ("flower-face"),
created magically by Gwydion and Mâth out of three kinds of flowers (or nine, if we follow the *Câd Goddeu*) to be the bride of Lleu
(who is here made to stand for the Maponos), because he had been
cursed by his virgin-mother Arianrhod to never have a wife from a
race that now inhabits the world. By breaking the power of the
infertile *giamos*-energies that had, throughout the Dark season, controlled the manifestations of the Goddess, the Maponos triumph-
antly asserts his ability to fulfill the Third Function in the social
realm (i.e., by marrying, becoming a reproducer), and by following
his archetype all of nature finds itself in the fertile mode. Of course,
this state of things is temporary, Darkness will return, and the tale of
Lleu stresses Blodeuwedd's eventual betrayal of her husband, and her
transformation into an owl. But on Bealtaine those events are still in
the future, and we can dwell joyfully on the Young Lord's winning of
his flower-bride.

In Lleu's story the difficulties in obtaining the Flower Maiden are
not (apart from the original obstacle set by Arianrhod) significantly
developed, although other versions of the myth make it clear that
the "testing" of the bridegroom-to-be was an important part of the
way it was originally conceived. This is best illustrated by the tale of
Culhwch ac Olwen. Although we are given no specific account of her

creation out of flowers, Olwen ("white track") is as much the Flower
Maiden as Blodeuwedd, as evidenced by the four white clovers that
spring up wherever she walks, giving her her name. She is prevented
from wedding by her retentive, "Fomorian" Land-spirit father, the
Hawthorn Giant, who, although he has a floral name himself, represents the Land in its niggardly, anti-human aspect. The hawthorn,
which guards its beautiful flowers and nourishing berries with
wickedly long and sharp thorns, is an excellent symbol of the Fomorian nature, of the Land's bounty given grudgingly. It represents
the powers of the Land untamed by the Tribe, which may explain
why it was considered unlucky—especially in Ireland—to bring
hawthorn blossoms into houses. To release the Flower Maiden from
her infertility, then, it is necessary to break the Hawthorn Giant's
power, and it is the young hero Culhwch—a manifestation of the
Maponos, and Olwen's husband-to-be—who accomplishes this.
Interestingly, the Maponos is identified by name (as Mabon) in the
story, but appears as another character, whom Culhwch must free
from a mysterious prison (he has vanished, as we have seen at
Deuoriuos, since he was only "three nights old"), so that he can participate in the fulfilling of the difficult tasks set by the Hawthorn
Giant as a precondition for his daughter's wedding. It may be that
Culhwch and Mabon were originally one character, but more likely
that Culhwch represents a specific, localized narrative instance of the
Maponos archetype, and that he assimilates the full power of that archetype when he liberates Mabon from the *giamos*-state—just as, in
Tóraíocht Diarmada agus Gráinne, the hero Diarmaid is portrayed as
the "foster-son" of Aonghus an Mac Og (the Irish Maponos), and
takes on the full qualities of the Maponos archetype only after Aonghus has intervened in the story.

The main event that is required for the release of the Hawthorn
Giant's daughter is, in fact, the Cosmic Boar Hunt, that great movement—in which all the powers of Tribe and Land participate—that
catapults the world order across the line that separates *samos* from *giamos.* We have seen how, at Samhain, the Maponos is slain by the
Boar in his southward, *giamos*-directed trajectory (as in the tale of
Diarmaid destroyed by his foster-brother, the boar of Beann Gul-
bain). On Bealtaine, the Boar Hunt is, on the contrary, the Young

God's triumph, and leads up into the sunlit world of *samos*, so that the Boar's symbolic attributes shift from Underworld darkness to solar enlightenment. Culhwch's name itself means "slender pig," or, to use the storyteller's own etymology, "pig-run," and by the unusual circumstances of his birth he is made the alter ego, not only of the Maponos, but of the Boar Trwyth whom he hunts, and whom he can compel to give up the magical implements (in this case, the razor and scissors in his bristles, which will be used to "shave"—i.e., de-capitate—the Hawthorn Giant) necessary for breaking the hold of the *giamos*-power over the Flower Maiden. In our practice we will, when invoking the Quarters of sacred space, begin placing the Boar in the West on Bealtaine and keep him there throughout the Light half of the year, turning him into a symbol of enlightenment, wis-dom, and inspiration. The Stag, meanwhile, we will place in the South, the place of the Underworld and hidden things—precisely when the Cernunnos, abandoned by the Goddess in her Flower Maiden form, enters his own *giamos*-phase and begins taking on stag-like characteristics.

There are other stories that confirm these patterns in Celtic tra-dition. In Irish mythology the Flower Maiden is called *Bláthnat* (lit-tle flower), a name obviously related to *Blodeuwedd*. She is an object of contention between the great hero Cúchulainn and the mysteri-ous Underworld figure Cú Roí Mac Dáire. In some versions she clearly appears to be the wife of Cú Roí, the keeper of his Other-world castle where terrifying apparitions test the courage of heroes; in others she is said to belong by right to Cúchulainn, but is stolen by Cú Roí, and then conspires with Cúchulainn to bring about Cú Roí's death. We have here the same ambiguity that appears in the Pwyll/Gwawl/Rhiannon relationship in the First Branch of the Mabinogi, the Lleu/Gronw/Blodeuwedd relationship in the Fourth Branch, and the Gwyn/Gwythyr/Creiddylad relationship in *Cul-hwch ac Olwen*—to name only three obvious examples among many similar "triangles." The shifting allegiance of the Goddess is, as we have explained, cyclic: as Queen of the Underworld, she chooses the Cernunnos-figure at Samhain; but as Flower Maiden she prefers the Maponos-figure on Bealtaine. Cúchulainn, being the son of Lugh (and evidently representing Lugh in this context), is clearly the

Maponos here. Cú Roí, in his giant, uncouth *bachlach* form, suggests the Hawthorn Giant as well as Cernunnos (whom he resembles as master of an Otherworld stronghold), but in his possession of a weapon that can deal both death and life he seems to belong to the *Sucellos* ("good striker") god-type, which is exemplified elsewhere in Irish tradition by the giant figure of the Dagda (good god) with his club. Indeed, the Dagda and his son Aonghus are opposed in a Cernunnos/Maponos relationship; and it well may be that the Sucellos was—at least in some parts of the Celtic world—a manifestation of the "unhorned" Cernunnos.

(It should be pointed out that the tale of Cúchulainn's testing by Cú Roí, as told in *Fled Bricrend*, became the basis of the well-known Middle English story "Sir Gawain and the Green Knight." Since the name Gawain belongs to Arthurian (Brythonic) tradition, it seems likely that the story was not borrowed directly from the Irish, but from a British Celtic source. Gawain may have been a standard Brythonic equivalent of Cúchulainn; and in that case Gawain's name in Welsh tradition, *Gwalchmai* (hawk of May), very explicitly associates the figure with Bealtaine. Gwalchmai is, in fact, one of Culhwch's companions, helping him accomplish the tasks set by the Hawthorn Giant.)

Yet another significant detail may link Bláthnat with Blodeuwedd; both may have, upon relinquishing their Flower Maiden status at the end of the *samos* season, taken on animal forms. We know that Blodeuwedd turned into an owl, the creature with the prophetic voice from the Otherworld, standing on the threshold between life and death, usually (in folklore) announcing death. We have no story specifically recounting Bláthnat's transformation, but in modern Irish *bláthnaid* is one of the words for "weasel." The weasel, in Celtic tradition, has many of the same fearsome associations with the Otherworld that the owl has. It has power over life and death (as illustrated in Marie de France's tale *Eliduc*), and there are stories from oral tradition (like the one Douglas Hyde retold in *Cois na Teineadh*) about women with magical powers turned into weasels. Thus, it seems very likely that Bláthnat's story may, in versions now lost to us, once have ended much like Blodeuwedd's.

Finally, we must not forget that, besides the freeing of Mabon and the enacting of the Cosmic Boar Hunt, Culhwch must, in order to win Olwen, slay the Hag, "the Pure-Black Witch, daughter of the Pure-White Witch, from the Head of the Ravine of Worry, on the borders of Hell" (*y Widon Ordu merch y Widon Orwen o Penn Nant Gouut yn gwrthtir Uffern*) to obtain her blood. This Hag, like the Black Sow, is the sterile manifestation of the Goddess, inimical to life and growth, and she must be ritually slain before the Goddess can appear as the beneficent Flower Maiden.

The ritual celebration of Bealtaine remains an important event in the calendar of many Celtic and ex-Celtic communities. The lighting of bonfires on this day is no longer as common as it once was, for the "summer fire" has come to be more and more exclusively associated with midsummer. In the days when the economy of Celtic villages centered primarily on the raising of cattle, however, the Bealtaine fires were used to purify the herds as they were about to be driven to the upland pastures where they would spend the *samos*-season. In both Wales and Scotland the bonfire was to be built by nine men, using nine different kinds of wood—we have here, again, the significance of the number nine, which we have discussed in relation to Samhain. The fires—lit at dawn, unlike the Samhain fires, which were lit at dusk—may have been placed under the patronage of Belenos (the bright one), who appears to have been yet another manifestation of the radiant Summer Lord, in this case specifically associated with the healing powers of the sun, especially when applied to cattle. Not much in the way of mythology directly relating to Belenos has survived in later Celtic tradition (unless he is in fact the *Beli Mawr* who is the consort of Dôn, which is doubtful), but he was evidently a Pan-Celtic figure in pre-Christian times, and must have, like all Celtic god-forms, undergone cycles of death and rebirth, as evidenced by the place called the Tombelaine (allegedly *tombe-Belen,* 'tomb of Belenos') near the Mont-Saint-Michel in Brittany. In order to receive his protection cattle were driven between two bonfires, close enough to the flame to be almost singed by it. The custom gave rise to the Irish expression *idir dhá tine Bealtaine,* "between two Bealtaine fires" (i.e., between a rock and a hard place). So important was this ritual in the eyes of Celtic communities that, throughout the Gaelic-speaking world, it gave its name to the entire festival.

Humans had other ways of partaking of the healing energy of the Sun as it rose on the first day of Summer. In most places it was customary to be up before the Sun (in some cases after an all-night vigil in the woods, where young people would take part in sexual revelry), and to go to some ritually significant hilltop in the area and watch the Sun rise, bathing in its rays. The bathing also could be more literal. In the symbolic imagery of Celtic religion, the healing property of sunlight was most effective if it was trapped in water—water and fire conjoined. (The same idea is expressed in the figure of *Sulis*, the Goddess of the Medicinal Springs in Bath: a healing water divinity with a solar name.) Many people gathered the dew that had reflected the Sun's fire on Bealtaine morning, and kept it in a bottle to use for healing during the rest of the year. Others journeyed to holy wells and drank the water or poured it over themselves as the sunlight struck it. The "sun in water" was the gentle, life-strengthening Sun, not the scorching, fiery Sun of the hot days closer to Harvest, that had an entirely different ritual significance, as we shall see.

Though the cattle were dramatically purified by fire on this day, they also could be subjected to the gentler magic of the "sun in water." In parts of Scotland cow-hairs were knotted together with red string into a rope (with as many knots as there were cows in the herd), and the resulting talisman would be dragged in the May dew while chanting: *Bainne an té seo shios, bainne an té seo shuas, 'nam ghogan mhòr fhein* (The milk of the one below, the milk of the one above, into my own big pail). This would magically align the earthly cows with the divine cows who represented the fertility of the Land, and would make them give milk more abundantly.

The custom most people think of in relation to May Day is, of course, the maypole. The tall poles set up in village greens, bedecked with many colored ribbons that are elaborately woven together by young people in a dance are, however, an English custom, and are not characteristic of Celtic tradition. Equivalents to it—probably borrowings, reinterpreted in the light of Celtic concepts—are found in some Celtic communities, where the maypole is then usually a tree, either living or freshly cut. In Wales this tree is a birch, the *Bedwen Haf* ("summer birch"), although in Glamorgan the custom of dancing around the birch eventually gravitated to midsummer. In parts of Brittany the tree was (as mythologically appropriate for the day) a hawthorn, cut down for the May Day revels even as the Hawthorn Giant was cut down for his daughter's wedding. The often observed phallic attributes of the maypole can be easily linked to the Hawthorn Giant's role as phallic fertilizer of Fomorian nature. By the ritual "decapitation" of the Giant—actually a castration, though without loss of potency!—the organ of fertility is brought into the control of the Tribe, and its magic is passed on to those who dance around it. In parts of Cornwall different communities tried to steal each other's maypoles to enhance the fertility of their own fields and stock, sometimes leading to serious conflicts.

More often it is only branches of hawthorn that are ritually cut during the night before Bealtaine. Even so, their phallic symbolism remains the same. In many Celtic and ex-Celtic communities on the Continent young men gather the branches and introduce them secretly, under cover of darkness, into the rooms of young unmarried women whom they fancy. This is referred to as "planting the May," and the young woman thus honored is expected to keep the young man company during the holiday (there is the implication that, in a more innocent time, sexual favors were exchanged as well!). In Ireland the maypole was replaced by a "May bush," either a construction of hawthorn branches, or a holly bush decorated with blooming hawthorn twigs. This was further decorated with brightly colored ribbons and eggshells (an obvious fertility symbol; the shells were saved from eggs eaten on Easter), and used as the focus of the ritual dancing and revelry. Marsh-marigolds (*lus buí Bealtaine*) were also gathered at this time, and strewn across the floors of houses for luck and prosperity. But the plant whose protective influence was most consistently invoked at this time was the rowan, which had the power to dispel unfriendly Otherworld influences. Rowan branches were placed at doors and windows, singly or tied together with red strings as talismans of various shapes: on the Isle of Man, this took the shape of a cross, the *crosh-cuirn*.

In most Celtic communities some type of pageantry would be

enacted to bring to mind the mythological context of the feast. The
Flower Maiden would appear, in Ireland, as *bábóg na Bealtaine*, a doll
adorned with flowers that was carried in procession by a group of
girls (as described in the well-known Bealtaine song *Thugamar féin
an Samhradh linn*), or sometimes by a larger company featuring costumed mummers. Again, as at Samhain and Imbolc, we meet the
buachaillí tuí, the straw-masked representatives of the Land who accompany the Goddess in all her transformations. The most elaborate
of these Bealtaine pageants still surviving today is no doubt the one
that takes place in Padstow in Cornwall, with its fantastic hobbyhorse (a widespread fertility symbol linked to the Land, as we have
seen)—who, Centaur-like, pounces on unmarried women—, its
mummer figures, its unique dances and songs (featuring a maypole
and hawthorn branches), and community participation. The hobbyhorse is found associated with Bealtaine in other parts of the Celtic
world, notably in Brittany. Many of the pageant roles also remain
constant from area to area: for instance, the King and Queen of May,
chosen to represent the Maponos and the Flower Maiden on the day
of their wedding; and the Fool, who in many cases leads the procession. In Celtic tradition the Fool—as exemplified by the Arthurian
Peredur/Percival and the Gaelic *Amadán Mór*—often appears as the
agent of transformation, helping the world to break out of a pattern
because, from the start, he has never conformed to the pattern. From
the narrative of *Culhwch ac Olwen* one gets the sense that Culhwch,
almost as brash and tactless as Peredur upon his entry into Arthur's
court, was himself originally conceived as something of a Fool-
figure. In Wales the Fool (or, sometimes, this was a figure distinct
from the Fool) appeared as the *Cadi Haf*, a man partially dressed in
women's clothes to produce an androgynous effect. It seems that the
"Teaser" who leads the Cornish May processions was also, originally,
a "man-woman" of this type (he was traditionally chosen for his
burly physique and thick moustache, which would contrast with his
effeminate attire). We have already remarked, in our discussion of
Samhain, on the role of cross-dressing in ritual and its correspondences in shamanic lore. By breaking with patterns of expected
behaviour, the cross-dresser, like the Fool, makes a larger change
possible.

Also present in many Bealtaine pageants was the Hag, the inimical, infertile aspect of the Goddess, whose rule was about to end. Often the ritual depicted her destruction in some form. In Scotland the *Cailleach* (usually played by a man) was chosen by lot (using a bannock, as described in our section on Samhain) and was "killed" by being briefly cast on the bonfire. It is likely that this was once a genuine human sacrifice. On the Isle of Man the Hag appeared as the Queen of Winter, who with an army of followers did battle with the Queen of Summer (the Flower Maiden). In Brycheiniog (southeast Wales) it was the triangle composed of the Goddess and her two consorts that was dramatized: two boys were chosen to represent the Winter King and the Summer King (like Gwyn and Gwythyr), and were paraded about covered with birch branches and wearing distinctive headdresses (a crown of bright ribbons for the Summer King, a wreath of holly for the Winter King).

As at Samhain, the major turn in the cycle—the passage from *giamos* into *samos*, in this case—caused a break in the fabric of time and blurred the normal distinctions between this world and the Otherworld. Hostile witchcraft would be particularly effective during this period. Otherworld beings would be present in all their power, and magical precautions had to be taken to prevent both humans and domestic animals from falling under their spell. The erotic, fertility-oriented nature of the feast made it particularly susceptible to the birth of fairy changelings. Conversely, the close proximity of the Otherworld forces made it easier to propitiate them. In the Highlands of Scotland, where the pre-Christian consciousness survived longer than in other parts of the Celtic world, the eighteenth-century traveler Thomas Pennant observed a ceremonial offering to the divinities of the Land on Bealtaine: nine men (as opposed to the nine women we saw in some Samhain rituals) make a mixture of eggs, barley, water, and milk, some of which is poured into a trough in the ground; then cakes of oatmeal bearing nine bumps (representing nine divinities) are given, piece by piece, first to the protective powers of the Land, and then to the destructive powers (e.g., the spirits of animals that prey on sheep). Thus, both the positive and negative aspects of the Fomorian realm are dealt with.

This wealth of Bealtaine customs presents us with a wide variety of explicit suggestions on how to celebrate the feast, among which we can discern some prominent themes:

1. The Theme of the Flower Maiden.
2. The Theme of the Transforming and Purifying Fire.
3. The Theme of the Breaking of the Hawthorn Giant's Power.
4. The Theme of the Restoration and Wedding of the Maponos.
5. The Theme of the Banishing of the Cernunnos (which we will discuss more fully below).
6. The Theme of Fire-in-Water as a Healing Power.

How one expresses these themes will depend very much on one's taste and affinity, since there are so many traditional models one can follow. Again, if any Bealtaine traditions have survived in your community, they should certainly be made a part of your observances. The suggestions we give below, drawn from the author's experience with Céli Dé and other groups, are purposely loose and sketchy in order to leave individual circles with plenty of leeway to give form to their own intuitions, interests, and (perhaps) inherited material.

First, our initial establishment of sacred space and calling of the Quarters will, in a dramatic shift reflecting the change at the midpoint of the Celtic Year, place the Boar in the West and the Stag in the South. The Cosmic Boar Hunt brings the Boar—with the Maponos following—into the region of Light (represented by all three "northern" Quarters), and puts him in the fiery West, home of the wise and enlightened, of all learning and intellectual skills, and turns him, perhaps, into one of the bardic *perchyll* (piglets) whom Myrddin instructs in prophecy under the apple tree. Meanwhile the Stag descends into the Dark South, where the mysteries of the Land are kept, even as Cernunnos, unseated from his position as kingly consort of the Goddess, takes on his stag-like characteristics and becomes one with the forces of the natural world.

The main Otherworldly event that is ritually commemorated on Bealtaine is the Wedding of the Maponos and the Flower Maiden. But the Flower Maiden first must be given a shape to manifest in our world, even as Mâth and Gwydion created Blodeuwedd out of flowers (the power of growth in the living Land). Following their example, we will use flowers to invoke the presence of the Flower Maiden into our midst. The account in the Fourth Branch of the Mabinogi tells us that the divine wizards used three kinds of flowers: oak (*deri*), broom (*banadyl*), and meadowsweet (*erwein*). Whenever we see three things listed in Celtic lore, we know we are being presented with a triadic statement, linked in some way with the triplicities that, according to Celtic thought, are at work in the structure of the world. In this case, the threefold nature of the Goddess as Flower Maiden reflects the way in which she (like Brigit) interacts with the three functions of the Tribe. We are thus justified in applying a trifunctional symbolism to the three kinds of flowers. Although tradition is not definite in this regard, we can, without too much of a strain on the imagination, see the oak, with its hardwood used to make spears, as symbolic of the Second Function; the broom, with its fiery, solar associations, as expressing the First Function; and the meadowsweet, pleasantly aromatic and used in medicine, as representing the Third Function of physical healing and well-being (and by its other Welsh name, *blodau'r Frenhines* queen's flowers—(the meadowsweet can be further linked with the Goddess of the Land herself). Of course, other alignments are possible, but this is a set of attributions that squares well with traditional imagery.

Water that has been gathered in a large vessel at dawn on Bealtaine—from a holy well, or some ritually significant body of water, or mixed with morning dew—is brought into the circle from the South. In the center three trays filled with dried flowers have been disposed: broom in the West, oak in the North, and meadowsweet in the East. The vessel of water is placed between them. The passage in the Fourth Branch relating to the creation of Blodeuwedd may be read, and the ritual leader speaks of the Flower Maiden, instilling in all participants the strong desire to call that aspect of the Land-goddess into their lives and into the world around them. Then each circle member in turn comes to the center, takes a pinch of dried flowers from each of the trays and sprinkles them into the water, uttering an appropriate invocation each time. When all have done so, the Flower Maiden is declared to be present.

Then the *bábóg*, a doll decked with flowers of the season, especially white clover, is brought forward. Some of the enchanted water is sprinkled over it, enlivening it with the spirit of the Flower Maiden and, in effect, placing the identity of the Flower Maiden upon it. The *bábóg* is then carried away in procession by all the circle members singing songs associated with the feast—*Thugamar féin an Samhradh linn* is, of course, appropriate, as are any of the *carolau Haf* from Welsh tradition. At the head of the procession the *cangen Haf* ("summer branch"—a hawthorn branch ritually cut to represent the felling of the Hawthorn Giant's power) should be carried by a special officer, perhaps an androgynous "Opener of the Ways" like the *Cadi Haf*. Other mummer figures from various Bealtaine traditions can be incorporated into the procession, especially the erotic hobbyhorse with his gift of fertility.

The procession is heading for the spot where the maypole has been erected (or where the birch tree that will serve as a maypole is already growing), but suddenly a fearsome figure stands in the way. This is the *Cailleach*, the *Gwiddon Orddu*, the infertile aspect of the Goddess who rules Winter, who is hostile to the Flower Maiden's manifestation in the world and must be vanquished before Summer's influence can truly be felt in the Land. The Hag should be a cloth doll filled with grain, flowers, and all kinds of delicious foodstuffs. The manner of her defeat can be as dramatic as one wishes, or as resources allow: it can be reduced to a duel between the Hag and the *Cadi Haf*, or it can involve a confrontation between "armies" on either side. In the end the Hag is torn open, and all the symbols of fertility she had kept hidden in her belly are spilled onto the ground, to be picked up by members of the procession.

When the procession at last reaches its destination, the *cangen Haf* is affixed to the maypole, identifying it with the Hawthorn Giant's now harnessed power. The *bábóg* is enthroned by the maypole (or, if practical, at its top). A King and Queen of May—representing the Maponos and the Flower Maiden as they join in marriage—are chosen by lot, and they proceed to lead the revelry around the maypole (the weaving of the ribbons both containing and channeling the Hawthorn Giant's procreative energy) and the subsequent feasting and entertainment. May wine (flavored with woodruff, another herb associated with the holiday) is an appropriate seasonal libation. At this point, too, the multitude of Land-spirits may be propitiated by an offering in the Scottish manner, as described above.

We must not forget that, even as we celebrate the choosing of the Maponos by the Land-goddess, the Cernunnos is driven out to become an actual part of the world of plants and animals, in our very midst. We bring forward the Cernunnos statue that we used at Samhain, and the antlers that were removed from it then are now ceremonially affixed to it again. They are, on the one hand, "cuckold's horns," but also symbols of enlightenment, which can be gained in no other way but through individual experience in the world of form. As he resumes his stag nature and becomes the spirit of all wild things, Cernunnos can speak to us in an intimate fashion, out of the depths of the forest, where animals still live unmolested by man, and where paths to the Otherworld remain.

Finally, before participants leave the ritual area they must be cleansed by the Bealtaine fire. Two bonfires are lit close enough to each other that an individual passing between them will experience extreme heat. As each circle member makes his/her exit, he/she moves quickly between the fires, thinking of the last shreds of *giamos*-oriented inertia being burned away as *samos* comes to reign supreme. If bonfires are impractical, two torches, or even two candles, may be put to use with good effect.

The celebration of the Divine Wedding should be an uplifting, joyous, extroverted occasion. *Samos*-energy is active rather than reflective, oriented to kinetic rather than to verbal expression, more concerned with spreading-out than with gathering-in. It is this energy that will be furiously at work, in the Land and in ourselves, as the year moves quickly toward its climax.

Mediosaminos

Lá Fhéile Eoin, An Fhéill-Eoin, Gwyl Ifan, Golowan, Gouel Sant-Yann, Laa l'Ean.—JUNE 21 (24)

> *Fàilte ort fhéin, a ghrian nan tràth*
> *ag siubhal ard nan speur;*

'S do cheumaibh treun air sgéith nan ard,
'S tu mathair àigh nan reul.

'S tu 'laigheadh sios an cuan na dith
gun dìobhail is gun sgath,
'S tu 'g éirigh suas air stuagh na sìth
mar rìoghain òg fo bhlàth.
                                        —Carmina Gadelica

(Greetings, Sun of the seasons, as you walk in the high heavens; with your strong steps upon the high void you are the joyous mother of the stars. You lie down in the abyss of destruction without suffering harm or scathe, you rise up on the peaceful wave like a young queen in flower.)

Although we have no evidence from pre-Christian sources of a specific Celtic observance at the Summer Solstice, we can deduce its Old Celtic name—*Medio-saminos* "(of) midsummer"—from its descendants in many modern Celtic names for the month of June: Irish *Meitheamh*, Welsh *Mehefin*, Cornish *Metheven*, and Breton *Mezheven*.

As with the other astronomically derived dates in the Celtic calendar, the celebration of the Summer Solstice originally would have been very much overshadowed (if not completely eclipsed) by the Earth Feast preceding it; and indeed, many of the rituals associated with midsummer in Celtic communities today are clearly Bealtaine rituals "moved forward." However, perhaps from Roman and Germanic influence the date is now well-entrenched as an important occasion in the ritual year throughout the Celtic world, and despite much foreign admixture and confusion with Bealtaine it does retain a great deal that is significant in a Celtic context, as we shall see. One should note that, although some modern groups (especially Neo-Pagans) insist on celebrating the solstice on its astronomically correct date, folk custom has universally identified it with the feast of Saint John the Baptist on June 24, and all traditional midsummer observances thus take place on the night of June 23.

As in the case of the Winter Solstice, the importance of midsummer does not derive from any specific cultural tradition, but from an objective occurrence in the environment—the shift in the ratio of light to darkness within twenty-four-hour periods—and its universal effects on human psychology. Whereas on midwinter we saw the reign of Darkness reaching its peak and at the same time inaugurating the period of increasing Light, on midsummer the triumph of Light—and the energy it brings—is at its climax, yet contains within it the seeds of returning Darkness. The human response to this is, however, quite different from the wholehearted embrace of the change that characterizes Winter Solstice rituals, since we naturally associate Light with life and growth (and welcome it), and Darkness with death (and fear it at worst, regard it with stoicism at best). Thus our focus, as we observe midsummer, will not be on celebrating and encouraging the growing Darkness (although we should, of course, view the return of the *giamos*-energies as a natural and necessary process), but on preserving and storing as much of the nourishing Light as we can. The expansive power of *samos* begins to yield to the inward-turning influence of *giamos*, but the inward motion will, at this stage, have to do with the gathering and holding of what is valuable in the Summer season, especially the energy of sunlight itself.

This is, of course, a preparation for the Harvest. We should remember that, in Celtic tradition, although the whole period from Bealtaine to Samhain can be thought of as *samos,* each of the Year's halves are further subdivided into quarters, and the Summer season proper—the period of triumphant and unimpeded growth—lasts only until Lúghnasadh. After that comes the Harvest season (*methâ*), in which the reversal of energies is fully established, growth is checked, and the fruits of growth are gathered in, for the use of the Tribe. Thus on midsummer, although the reproductive energies of the Land are still furiously at work all around us, there is an early warning that the season for concentrating and gathering resources is close at hand.

One characteristic of the midsummer observance in the Celtic world which places it firmly within the conceptual framework of the Celtic Year—fulfilling aspects of Bealtaine, as well as looking forward to the Harvest—is the importance it gives to the gathering of medicinal herbs at this date. Belenos, the god of solar healing who is

exalted on Bealtaine, is the patron of all plants with curative properties, which begin their main period of growth with the onset of
Summer, and are considered to be ripe for the picking on the solstice. All these plants have a sacred association with the God, and are
indeed thought to be born of his flesh—being, for the most part,
yellow-hued and "solar" in appearance, as is he. The gathering of
these herbs constitutes a miniature "harvest," one conducted by specialists in a very limited context that is somehow "reserved" by its
closeness to the gods and to Otherworld power, yet does serve to
prepare the way (by ritually setting a precedent) for the larger Harvest that will feed the Tribe.

The herbalists who were qualified to identify and collect the
medicinal plants on this date originally would have belonged to the
priestly caste of the druids, and their action would—like all religious
acts—be seen to reflect a mythological model, a prototype established in the Otherworld. Indeed, in Irish tradition (albeit in a fairly
late source), we find the relevant myth. Dian Cécht, the physician of
the Tuatha Dé Danann, had a son Miach and a daughter Airmid (or
Airmeith), both of whom shared their father's healing abilities.
During the conflict between the Tuatha Dé Danann and the Fomorians Miach and Airmid went to offer their services to Nuadu, the
king of the Danann-folk who had lost his arm in an earlier battle
and had had it replaced by a wonderful silver arm that Goibniu, the
smith-god, had fashioned. Since no sacred king could rule if he was
less than perfect in body, it was not clear whether the silver arm had
in fact made Nuadu whole again for ritual purposes; and the Tuatha
Dé Danann had, in the meantime, accepted the rule of the Fomorian Bress mac Elathan, who (true to his Fomorian nature) had
proved to be unbearably niggardly, holding back the fertility of the
Land, and eventually spurring the Danann-folk (representatives of
the Tribe) to revolt. The children of Dian Cécht offered to restore
Nuadu's arm to its original state, thus making him beyond a doubt
eligible for the sacred kingship again. By way of demonstration they
"cured" Nuadu's one-eyed porter by replacing his missing eye with
a cat's eye. Then Miach recovered Nuadu's hand from where it had
been buried, placed it on the stump of Nuadu's arm, and, with the
help of incantations, made the limb whole in the space of three days.

Dian Cécht, however, was made insanely jealous of his son's talent (the relationship between them here is very similar to that between the Greek Asklepios and his father Apollo). He sent for Miach and struck him three progressively deeper blows on the head with a sword, each of which Miach was easily able to heal, until a fourth blow destroyed his brain, and with it his life. Dian Cécht then buried his son, and from Miach's grave (there are parallels to this episode in the mythologies of many cultures) grew 365 herbs, one to cure the ailments of each of the 365 "nerves" (i.e., organs) of the human body. Airmid picked them and systematically arranged them on her mantle according to their properties, but her father, unwilling to recognize his son's healing powers even in that form, overturned the mantle and confused the positions of the herbs. Thus many of the properties of herbs are no longer known (if they were, no disease would be incurable), and herbalists have had to labor through a long process of trial and error to reconstruct at least a part of the pattern Airmid discovered.

So we have Miach and Airmid as tutelary deities of herbalists, and the Airmid's mantle (*brat Airmeithe*) as a potent symbol of the herbalist's lore. Both Miach and Dian Cécht seem related to the Belenos archetype (they may have originally been cyclic alternants, like so many Celtic divinities), and the sacrifice of Miach would then correspond to the seasonal sacrifice of Belenos, whose funeral-pyre the midsummer bonfire is often thought to be. Breton herbalists (*louza-ouerien*) who have preserved something of their esoteric tradition do indeed see herbs as corresponding to the organs of a slain divinity. The sacred herbs are twenty-six in number (rather than 365!): vervain is at the head, Saint Johnswort is the blood, mugwort is at the waist, and so on. This confirms that the positioning of the herbs on the *brat Airmeithe* originally was meant to correspond to the configuration of Miach's anatomy.

A full discussion of Celtic herbalism is beyond the scope of this book. We will limit ourselves to mentioning some of the more important herbs and outlining the system of their classification. Herbs with "first-function" applications—either psychotropic herbs like henbane (called *belenountion,* "Belenos-herb," in Gallo-Roman sources) and other nightshades, or herbs with "spiritual" effects like vervain (much cherished by the druids), which produces general good feeling and protects from harmful Otherworld entitities, are usually at the head of Belenos. Herbs with coagulant and vulnerary properties are particularly useful for warriors and constitute a "second-function" class, of which Saint Johnswort and yarrow are the chiefs (though yarrow is also used for divinations and love-charms, as evidenced by the famous "yarrow spell" in the *Carmina Gadelica*). Finally, the bulk of herbs that heal diseases of the organs—especially of digestion and reproduction—are conceived as "third-function" and placed along the lower body and limbs of the figure. Among other herbs that figure prominently in Celtic lore we should mention male fern and mugwort, both highly effective against parasites; monkshood, once used to poison arrows; stonecrop or houseleek, which protected houses from thunder and also cured eye-diseases, and in parts of Brittany was so important on this herb-gathering day that it wound up being called *louzaouenn sant-Yann* (Saint John's herb); and cinquefoil, a tonic as well as a symbolically important plant because of its fivefold structure.

Even in very recent midsummer traditions the herbs of this "court of Belenos" were remembered, usually with the main focus on one or two of them. The principal among them was, almost always—as its common name indeed reminds us—Saint Johnswort. In Irish it is called *beathnua* (life-renewer), as well as *luibh Eoin Baiste* (John the Baptist's herb) and *allas Muire* (the Virgin Mary's sweat). In Welsh it is *dail y fendigaid* (the blessed one's leaf) as well as *llys Ieuan* (John's herb). While in Breton it is well-known as *kant-toull* ("hundred-holes," from the tiny perforations on its leaves, likened to wounds and interpreted by medieval herbalists as a "signature" of its vulnerary properties), its place in midsummer folklore is usually taken by a wholly fantastic plant: the *aour-yeotenn* or "golden herb," which shines like a little sun in the darkness on Saint John's Eve (and at no other time), and cannot be found without special visionary skill. It may be that the *aour-yeotenn* is itself a representation of Saint Johnswort (as well as other "Belenos" herbs), seen from an esoteric, magical viewpoint. All the herbalist traditions associated with midsummer stress the importance of following proper procedures in harvesting the plants, treating the operation as a magical ritual: usually (not always) it is to be done with the left hand only, while wearing special loose-fitting garments, not touching the plant with metal, and not leaving any part of the plant broken in the ground, etc. A chant would sometimes accompany the rite, such as the Scottish one recorded in the *Carmina Gadelica*:

> *Eala-bhi, eala-bhi*
> *Mo niarach neach aig am bi*
> *Buaineam thu le mo làmh dheas*
> *Tasgam thu le mo làmh chlì*
> *Ga ba cò a gheabh thu'n crò an àil*
> *Cha bhi e gu brath gun ni.*

(Saint Johnswort, Saint Johnswort, I deem lucky the one who will have you; I harvest you with my right hand, I store you away with my left hand; whoever finds you in the fold of the young animals will never want for anything.)

While this esoteric prefiguration of the harvest was being enacted by religious specialists, a more exoteric approach to the spiritual realities of the season would be taken by the bulk of the Tribe, focusing on the building of bonfires. This remains an important facet of midsummer in many Celtic communities to this day. Customs relating to bonfires are remarkably uniform throughout the Celtic world. The bonfire was circular in shape, was built on a ritually significant spot (e.g., near a holy well, at a crossroads, on the border between people's homes—the Tribe—and cultivated fields—the Land—etc.), was lit precisely at sunset, and was blessed to consecrate its powers to the protection of the growing crops. In some places a particular individual (*giolla an teine,* in Gaelic) was appointed to oversee the building of the bonfire, and to watch over it once it was lit. That this was probably the survival of an old religious function is reinforced by the Breton custom of the *Tad-You*, a person who not only oversaw the operations but also recited prayers over the flames, in particular blessing the sprig of furze (a solar plant) that was used to light the entire bonfire. The fire, of course, was—beyond the mythological explanation of an ancient personage's funeral pyre—

an evocation of the Sun's energy, necessary for the growth of the crops but soon to lose its own impetus. In order to amplify the effects of this energy and ensure its survival through the period of increasing darkness, the young people of the community would play boisterous and reckless games with the fire far into the night. Brands were taken from the bonfire and thrown high up into the air. In some ex-Celtic areas of the Continent wheels—commonplace solar images—were set on fire and rolled down hills. More recently the technology of fireworks has been put to use to further enhance the expansive atmosphere. Throughout the Western world this particular ritual mood has come to attach itself to secular Summer holidays, like Bastille Day or the Fourth of July.

Since the proper growth of the crops was, at this season, the community's greatest concern, much effort was made to extend the magical influence of the bonfire into the surrounding fields. Embers from the fire were (despite the risk!) thrown into the corn; or, for safety's sake, it was only the ashes that were scattered over the crops on the following day. Most often the fire would be taken through the fields symbolically, in the form of a winding procession carrying torches (*soip Sheáin*) which, after the completion of the ritual, would be attached to fences and walls and left to burn all night. Thus, the Sun's fertilizing power, imagined as the element of Fire, was, at its highest point within the year, brought into union with the energy-hungry matter that served as the Tribe's earthly nourishment.

As the night wore on and the flames of the bonfire got lower, individuals would seek the midsummer blessing for themselves by leaping over the fire. People about to experience a major change in their lives—whether marriage, or a far journey, or new work—were especially encouraged to perform this ritual. Just as the Sun, on the point of entering its waning period, magically stored the *samos*-energy that would ensure its survival and return, so did those who leaped over the fire take that energy into themselves to store as a protection for when they would be faced with the darkness of uncertainty. To be blackened by the fire was an omen of good luck.

Of all the solar feasts in the Celtic calendar, the Summer Solstice was the one most charged with Otherworldly influence. Welsh tradition counted it as one of the three spirit-nights (*tair ysbrydnos*) of the year—the other two being, of course, Calan Gaeaf and Calan Mai. The thinning of the boundary between our world and the Otherworld again made circumstances appropriate for divination, and beings foreign to our reality could manifest in our space and time. Since not all such visitors were friendly to humans, some measures had to be taken to protect against them, as on the other "spirit-nights." In parts of Munster the mallow (*hocas fiáin*) was singled out as a source of magical protection on midsummer: groups of young people went out to the marshes to pick mallow leaves on the eve of the feast, and later touched their friends and relatives with them, thus passing on the protective essence. Eventually the leaves were thrown onto the bonfire, adding to its potency.

Some of the Otherworld visitors, however, were desired presences on this night, and some effort was made to attract them. In parts of Brittany the curious custom of sounding the basins (*seniñ ar c'hirinoù*) aimed at bringing together beneficial spirits, especially ancestral spirits. Large copper basins containing coins or pebbles were filled with water, and groups of reed-stems were placed horizontally across their openings. While one person kept one end of the reed-stems flat against the edge of the basin, another would, with wet fingers, push the stems rapidly back and forth. After a while, in expert hands, the stems would begin to produce a deep, far-carrying buzzing noise, not unlike a bull-roarer. When the spirits were felt to have arrived, the *Tad-You* led the assembly in a procession three times around the fire, after which the "fire verses" (the *gwerzioù an Tan*) were solemnly recited.

From the account we have just given we can see that the feast is characterized by the following themes:

1. The Theme of the Affirmation of the Sun's Energy.
2. The Theme of the Esoteric Harvest: the Herbs.
3. The Theme of the Protective Fire.

To celebrate midsummer today as a Celtic circle, many of us have, again, community traditions to build on. Lighting bonfires on Saint John's Eve is still a widespread custom throughout the Celtic world, so that our own bonfire can be made to fit comfortably into that pattern; and a bonfire should indeed, if at all possible, be the focus of our ritual on this night of all nights. But what if—a possibility we touched on earlier—our circle meets in a place where lighting a bonfire would be impractical or dangerous? If so, the fire should be presented in a more manageable form, but the basic structure of the ritual we are about to discuss can remain for the most part unchanged—whether it is done outdoors or in, with a bonfire, or with candles.

After defining the ritual space in the usual manner, the leader (or cantor) will turn to the East and sing an invocation to the Sun, turning the imagination of all participants to the beautiful, nurturing, loved aspects of solar energy. Probably the best text for this occasion is the invocation *Fàilte ort fhéin, a ghrian nan tràth* from the *Carmina Gadelica*. The circle will then meditate on the significance of this moment in the year: the apex of the Sun's power, radiating its growth-inducing energy at all living things, about to turn into its decline, gradually yielding to the inward-facing immobility of Darkness. Yet Light and Darkness are not mutually exclusive, for each will always contain the seed of the other, and each provides the qualities necessary for nurturing the other. Thus, we know that the growing Darkness will not extinguish the Light but turn it inwards, where it will fertilize the *giamos*-womb of the Land and lead to the birth of new life.

But because we acknowledge that Light is the stuff of life—even though it needs Darkness to grow in—and that our consciousness cannot exist except in Light, we now reinforce the reserves of Light within ourselves. The central bonfire is now lit—either a true bonfire in the traditional style, if the ritual is outdoors, or else eight large candles in a circle. Each participant then brings forward his own individual source of illumination—a torch, a candle or, better yet, a sparkler or some similarly theatrical device—and lights it either from a torch that has been kindled from the bonfire, or from the candles that substitute for the bonfire. This lighting should be accompanied by expressions of joy and excitement, and lead to a dance in which the fires are woven in and out with near-reckless exhilaration. At this point of the ritual, the participants become Fire, their

of beginnings and sustained growth. As the dance winds to a close,
each participant concentrates on the flame he/she is carrying, drawing all the power of this miniature Sun into the depths of the psyche,
where it will shine in spite of the surrounding Darkness. Once we
have a secure grasp on this image, each one of us can, when it feels
appropriate, extinguish the outward manifestation of our individual
flame.

The *brat Airmeithe* is then laid out just to the south of the central
fire. The mythological prototype of the ceremony is explained, and
herbs that have been ritually gathered are disposed upon the *brat* according to their functions, preferably by circle members who have a
special interest in herbalism or natural history. Before each herb is
put in its proper place it should be raised up for the entire circle to
see, as a short piece of alliterative poetry in a Celtic language (with
translation in an imperial language if necessary) is recited, describing
that herb's mythological/ritual associations and its medical properties. When this has been done for all the herbs, there may be a short
closing invocation of the Belenos-power, the healing Sun.

Then the rest of the circle can be devoted to feasting and merrymaking; but before the formal closing of the ceremony there must
be a blessing of the Tribe by fire. Once the flames of the bonfire have
died down sufficiently, everyone must jump over them, drawing in
the essence of the Sun from the singeing heat. At the moment of
leaping one should visualize a new beginning, with the power of fire
making it real. Couples who feel their destinies bound to each other
can make the leap together. After closing, the fire can, if local circumstances permit, be taken through the fields in the ancient way.

The intensity of the fire's heat reminds us that the Sun, after this
date, will gradually lose its nurturing aspect. Although the earth will
be green and growing for several months yet, the Sun's increasingly
scorching rays may threaten to overheat it, and endanger the survival
of the crops as harvest nears. It is with the Sun's Dark aspect and its
conflict with the Tribe's needs that the next Earth feast largely concerns itself.

Lúghnasadh (Lúnasa)

Lúnasdal, Laa Luanys, Calan Awst, Gouel an Eost—AUGUST 1

Léighidh mi mo chorran sios,
'S an dias biadhchar fo mo ghlac,
Togam suas mo shuil an aird,
Tionndam air mo shail gu grad,

Deiseil mar thriallas a' ghrian
Bho 'n airde 'n ear gu ruig an iar,
Bho 'n airde tuath le gluasadh reidh,
Gu fior chré na h-airde deas.

            —Carmina Gadelica

(I will let my sickle down as the nourishing ear is in my hand, I will raise my eye to the heights, I will turn quickly on my heel to the right—as the Sun travels from the eastern quarter to the west—from the northern quarter, with a smooth motion, to the true center of the southern quarter.)

Although it has not left quite the same mark on the traditions of modern Celtic communities as the three other Quarterly Feasts, the feast of Lúghnasadh is nevertheless the culmination of all of them, the final fruit of the process that has been developing throughout the year. The Harvest—the season inaugurated by Lúghnasadh, for summer proper lasts only through July—has been anticipated by all the rituals performed on the previous feasts: it represents the successful outcome of the year-long relationship between Tribe and Land. Although the name of the season that begins in August really means "autumn"—Gaelic *foghmhar* is from an earlier *fo-gemur* (under/at the edge of winter), and Welsh *cynhaeaf* is originally *cyn-gaeaf* (before winter)—in the modern languages these terms have come to denote the actual activity of the harvest, for nothing else was of comparable importance during this period. Even the Breton term *an eost* was originally derived from *Augustus* "August," yet now means "the harvest."

Although we have no mention of the feast in truly ancient sources, the form of its name seems archaic. It clearly refers to the god Lugh, and Cormac's Glossary interprets the second element in the name as *násad*, glossed *cluiche nó aonach* (game or assembly). It would thus reflect the funeral games Lugh is said to have instituted in memory of his foster-mother Tailtiu, perpetuated by the sporting events and assemblies that have continued to characterize Lúghnasadh festivities in historical times. An earlier name for the feast in poetic contexts is *brón Trógain,* "the sorrow of Trógán," with the second element suggesting Old Celtic *trougâ*, itself meaning "sorrow," although it is also explained by an early Irish *troghan* meaning "earth." One thus cannot escape the suggestion that the feast had strong funerary associations, even though the mood of its actual celebration has always been, as we shall see, one of exuberance and joy.

According to some current interpretations, Lúghnasadh would fall in the month *Edrinios* of the Coligny Calendar. This is reinforced by the Cornish name of the month of July, *Gortheren*, which seems to have originally meant "against/before *Edrinios*." If *Edrinios* was, in an earlier form, *Ædrinios* (as it is indeed spelled in some sections of the Coligny Calendar), it would be derived from the stem *aid-* "fire, intense heat" and would mean "the end of the heat," a direct counterpart to *Ogronios,* "the end of the cold." Since the end of the summer heat does play an important role in the symbolism of Lúghnasadh in all its ritual manifestations, it is quite possible that the druids of southern Gaul once called the feast *Ædrinia*.

For our extensive knowledge of the ritual and mythology of Lúghnasadh today we have to thank Máire Mac Néill's wonderful study, *The Festival of Lughnasa* (1962), which must be consulted by anyone seeking factual information on this aspect of Celtic tradition. We will here follow the broad outline of the pattern she has revealed, while extending many of the mythological implications and exploring applications of the ritual to present-day needs.

As we have seen, the Samhain-Bealtaine axis in the wheel of the year represents a cycle of events occurring within the Land, and not in itself dependent on any activity of the Tribe. Imbolc and Lúgh-nasadh, on the other hand, are linked as the initiation and the out-come of the Tribe's "dialogue" with the Land, expressed in the form of the agricultural cycle. The figure presiding over the inception of the cycle at Imbolc was Brigit, the aspect of the Land-goddess most auspicious to the Tribe's concerns. Now, as the cycle reaches its final phase, the presiding deity becomes Lugh, the God of the Tribe who is uniquely gifted to have power over the Land.

Lugh's rise to prominence as a theological concept and the spread of his cult throughout the Celtic world can be charted from about the middle of the Iron Age to the fall of the last Free Celts. Much of the ideals of Celtic civilization, of what was most elevated and forward-looking in the Celts' view of themselves, came to be bound up with his image. Numerous place-names throughout central and western Europe (especially places called *Lugudunon,* the fort of Lugus [Lugh]) testify to his importance in the consciousness of Celtic communities—the foremost of them being of course the city of Lyons, the Gallo-Roman *Lugdunum,* which was once the capital of Gaul, and is still, to some extent, the magical heartland of that region. His Old Celtic name *Lugus* appears to mean "lightning, illumination"—and while there is, as we shall see, a purely meteorological application of the name that is relevant to the celebration of the Harvest, it is evident that it had a far broader range of more abstract associations linking it to all the capabilities of the human mind. Lugh displayed the epitome of intelligence, illustrating the primacy of mind over matter, of brains over brawn—a trait which, for all his awe-inspiring transcendence, gave him some of the endearing qual-ities of a folk trickster. Where Brigit, the Muse, provides the sheer energy needed for creative endeavor, Lugh, the perfect craftsman, knows how to shape that energy flawlessly. The *interpretatio Romana,* drawing on the versatile and tricky side of his character, turned him into Mercury, thus giving that god-name an unprecedented impor-tance in those parts of the Empire that had a Celtic population. The affection in which he was held is still evident in the images and tra-ditions that have survived. However, to understand his particular role in the rituals of Lúghnasadh, one must delve deeper into his mythol-ogy.

The relatively large amount of material about Lugh in Irish literature and folklore (completed by what we have about his Welsh counterpart Lleu in the Fourth Branch of the Mabinogi) is proof in itself of his preeminent position in Celtic tradition. Countless local variations of his story must have existed and are now forgotten—though here and there fragments may survive reassigned to some other character, as in the case of the Cornish "Jack the Tinkard" story associated with the Lúghnasadh festivities at Morvah Fair. In a late Iron Age context it appears that, like the Germanic Odin, Lugh had prophetic ravens as one of his main attributes, although that aspect of the tradition is no longer found in the medieval literary sources. While the remaining variants do not always agree with each other in matters of plot and detail, the overall patterns they present give us a consistent picture of the mythological themes involved.

We have already seen that Lugh's birth comes at a time of tension and danger. Since the invincible Fomorian champion Balor, whose eye burns to cinders anything he looks upon, can be slain only by his own grandson, the Tuatha Dé Danann undertake to make his daughter pregnant as a way of engineering his defeat. Thus Cian son of Dian Cécht enters into a secret liaison with Eithne, daughter of Balor, and Lugh is conceived. But it is the name *Eithne* ("Kernel") that reveals the full significance of the episode, for it denotes precisely that part of Fomorian nature that the human Tribe absolutely must control: the crops. Eithne therefore represents the realm in which Tribe and Land necessarily meet, and where the conflict between them, though inevitable, must be resolved. By partaking of both a Danann (Tribe-oriented) and a Fomorian (Land-oriented) heritage, Lugh becomes the figure best equipped to resolve that conflict. He also emerges as the positive counterpart of Bress mac Elathan, the Fomorian High King of Ireland who, like Lugh, is part-Danann, part-Fomorian (but with a Fomorian *father*, placing his allegiance on the other side), and whose rule, characterized by blight and famine, the Tuatha Dé Danann are trying to end—unsuccessfully, because of Balor's invincibility. Since his existence is a threat to the status quo, the infant Lugh is at once in danger of his life—like every saviour-hero, every Child of Light, as we saw at Deuoriuos. He must be hidden, and like the infant Maponos, vanishes from the world—a fact which, aided by Lugh's solar ("*samos*-like") attributes, makes it easy, as we have noted, to identify him with the Maponos figure in general. It does seem that, in some later literary traditions (as in what we can gather from the fragmentary Welsh material), the distinction between Lugh and the Maponos may have become blurred. Given the fluid and non-categorical bias of Celtic religious thinking, this is not entirely inappropriate; yet if one considers his specific role in the ritual Year, it is clear that Lugh transcends the *samos/giamos* alternation of the divinities associated with Samhain and Bealtaine, and that his main function is to be the eternal champion of the Tribe.

Lugh is first fostered to Manannán Mac Lir, the host of the Otherworld Feast enjoyed by the blessed dead in Eamhain Abhlach, the Land of Apples. Manannán (who is also the local patron deity of the Isle of Man, as well as of the Isle of Arran in Scotland) appears in Irish tradition as an Otherworld ruler with links to the Tuatha Dé Danann yet not embroiled in their conflicts, though some sources suggest that he was once a figure of the same general type as Lugh, skilled in crafts and the powers of the mind (this is especially evident in his Welsh counterpart, Manawyddan ap Llyr). From him the child Lugh will learn the skills that will earn him the title of *ildánach,* "many-gifted." In the Irish stories it is only the first-function talent of poetry that he is specifically said to acquire in Manannán's realm (Eamhain Abhlach is the source of all bardic inspiration, the storehouse of the unconscious), allowing him to announce on his coming to Tara: *File meise a hEamhain Abhlaigh ealaigh iobhraigh,* "I am a poet from the Land of Apples, rich in swans and yew trees." In the Welsh version of the tale, Lleu is taken in charge by his uncle Gwydion (who, again, appears to be a version of the same god-type, an older counterpart of the hero) and initiated into all three Tribal functions, originally made inaccessible to him by the curse of his virgin-mother Arianrhod (an ambiguous curse, for it in effect "consecrates" Lleu to the Land-goddess, ensuring that he will not enter the world of the Tribe save through her). Through Gwydion's clever trickery, Arianrhod is compelled to give her child a name (first function) and weapons (second function). He gains a wife (third function) only when the Goddess ceases to appear in the story as Arianrhod, and (through the magic of Gwydion and his uncle Mâth) takes on the

more appropriate form of the Flower Maiden—i.e., the Divine
Bride. The Irish Lugh also gains a consort, Nás (as the Gaulish Lugus
has Rosmerta).

After his apprenticeship in the Otherworld, Lugh is fostered a
second time, to the Fir Bolg Queen Tailtiu, who dies as a result of
the effort she expends clearing the central plain of Ireland for cultivation. The place of her death becomes the site of the *Oenach
Tailtenn*, the great assembly (said to have been instituted by Lugh in
her memory) held by Irish High Kings on Lúghnasadh. This tradition clearly relates Lugh's story to the realm of the Tribe/Land interface, the saga of the crops, and also conforms to a pattern found
throughout the Celtic world: the spot where a legendary female figure dies a violent death becomes the ritual center of a community.
In Tailtiu's case the reason for her death is not altogether clear within
the logical structure of the myth, but the parallel origin-myth of
Oenach Carmain (the Lúghnasadh assembly of Leinster) is more
transparent: Carman invades Ireland with her three sons Dian (Fierce),
Dubh (Black), and Dochar (Harm) to destroy the crops, and is beaten
back by the Tuatha Dé Danann, with Lugh among their leaders. She
is kept as a hostage (i.e., bowing to the authority of the gods of the
Tribe), and eventually dies in the oak grove that will become the site
of the assembly. She is thus explicitly the anti-human, "Fomorian"
aspect of the Land-goddess, which must be neutralized before the
side of her that is favorable to the Harvest (the "Eithne" aspect) can
manifest. Lugh plays a major role here, and there are other local variants of the myth, as we shall see.

At last Lugh comes to claim his place among the Tuatha Dé
Danann in Tara. None may enter Tara unless he has a craft, but since
Lugh is now past master at all the activities of all three functions (as
is no one else among the Tuatha Dé Danann), he is hailed as the
Samildánach (totally gifted), and in effect supersedes all the other
Tribal gods. He is now the all-purpose God of the Tribe, ready to
champion the Tribe's cause. In the ensuing battle of Maigh Tuireadh,
the final apocalyptic confrontation between the divinities of the
Tribe and those of the Land, he faces his grandfather Balor and destroys the baneful Eye with a slingstone. The Fomorians are thus no
longer invincible, the blight-causing power of Bress Mac Elathan is

broken, and the fruits of the Land again flow freely: the Harvest is secure.

Yet there is another twist to the story. Lugh, like all Celtic gods, has a cyclic existence. From the Metrical Dinnshenchas we know that his consort Nás was unfaithful to him with Cearmaid Milbhéal (honey-mouth), a son of the Dagda (and therefore, one assumes, a form of the Maponos, like Aonghus). Lugh spears Cearmhaid, who is eventually nursed back to life by his father's magic; but Cearmaid's own sons, the Three Gods of Danu, decide to seek revenge, and one of them, Mac Cuill, kills Lugh. In the more fleshed-out Welsh version, Blodeuwedd (the Flower Maiden) has an adulterous liaison with the beautiful huntsman Gronw Pebr, and for love of him discovers how her husband Lleu may be killed. Having manufactured an enchanted spear and gotten Lleu in the complicated and unlikely situation that makes him vulnerable to weapons, Gronw strikes his rival, but Lleu turns into an eagle and flies away (birds being a common symbol for souls in the Otherworld state). His uncle Gwydion searches for him and, led by a Sow (the Goddess in her Dark, devouring aspect), finds him perched in a great oak tree (the World Tree, spanning many worlds with its height), shedding his rotting flesh for the Sow to eat (freeing his spirit for rebirth). Gwydion restores Lleu to human shape and nurses him back to health so that, a year later, he can confront Gronw and kill him with a spear.

What we have here, clearly, is the basic myth behind the Lúghnasadh ritual: the God of the Tribe and the God who, in alternating forms, is the consort of the Goddess within the Land, are (despite or because of their obvious similarities; they can be said to be mirror-images of each other) rivals for the Goddess's favor. To ensure a successful Harvest, the Land-goddess must temporarily give her allegiance to the God of the Tribe rather than to the Maponos who is normally her consort at this time. The Maponos will, of course, steal her back; many sites of Lúghnasadh celebrations are associated with stories of a woman snatched into the depths of the earth by an Otherworld suitor. In the beautiful story *Tochmarc Étaíne*, the Goddess Étaín, once loved by the God Mider in the fairy fort of Brí Léith, becomes incarnate as a mortal woman and marries the King Eochaid Airem (stallion-like ploughman). Mider eventually finds her and, despite Eochaidh's opposition, manages to restore her memory and entice her back to his Otherworld realm. Eochaidh makes war upon the *síd* to regain his wife, is foiled once by being given Étaín's look-alike daughter, but finally gains the upper hand and obliges Mider to undertake certain tasks favorable to agriculture. In a very similar Welsh story known to us from fragments, Arthur's Queen Gwenhwyfar is seduced by the Otherworld chieftain Melwas (usually interpreted as a Cornish form of *Maelwas* "lordly lad"—although if it means "honey-lad" it would be an interesting link to Cearmaid *Milbhéal*) and carried away by him. It is not entirely certain how Arthur gets her back, but it is probably the adventure alluded to in the mysterious poem *Preiddeu Annwn*, "The Spoils of the Otherworld." Both Eochaid and Arthur, as High Kings, embody the God of the Tribe; and Eochaid's title *Airem* (ploughman) is even echoed by the pun that links Arthur's name with the word *arator*. Like Lugh, they rescue the fertile aspect of the Land-goddess from the control of purely Land-based (Fomorian) divinities, and make the Harvest possible for the Tribe. An echo of the same theme is certainly present in the Third Branch of the Mabinogi: the Otherworld ruler Llwyd ap Cil Coed steals away Rhiannon (the Land-goddess) and her son Pryderi into his magic fortress, and they are delivered only when the craftsman-god Manawyddan (i.e., Manannán) has defeated an army of mice (Land-spirits in animal form) sent to destroy his crops.

Whatever name may have been applied to the God of the Tribe in various local traditions, Lugh is the archetype behind them all. He is the saviour-hero, the bringer of happy endings, the embodiment of a new synthesis that transcends earlier problems. Very likely the elaboration and dissemination of his cult by the druids was associated with a wealth of theological speculation. In his daring "leaps"— an element stressed in several traditions about him—he even reminds one of the Vedic Vishnu, whose "steps" create space where there was none, permitting the defeat of the cosmic destroyer Vṛtra. It is quite possible that druidic thinking about Lugh was developing along similar lines, and that, if the religion of the Free Celts had been left to evolve on its own, Lugh would have come to play a role as universal and pervasive as Vishnu does in modern Hinduism.

Lugh's adversary, the ruler of the Land, is given many different names and forms in more recent Lúghnasadh customs. Over much of Ireland he was thought of as Crom Dubh (the black bent one), and the last Sunday in July was referred to as *Domhnach Chroim Dhuibh*. He often had a destructive bull who had to be stopped by the Harvest champion, and it is possible that a bullfight or bull-sacrifice at this date was intended to be a reenactment of this myth. Frequently the negative aspects of the Land-goddess were also portrayed as active opponents of the hero: we have already mentioned the myth of Carman in Leinster; in the area of Cruach Phádraig in Mayo we are told of the "devil's mother," the dragon-like *Caorthannach*, who had to be imprisoned beneath the waters of a pool (the natural habitat of Fomorian beings); and the *Cailleach*, the sterile Hag, appears again, here and there, as a force to be neutralized before the Harvest can be safe. The defeat of the power of blight in the shape of a dragon is significant, for it links up all the legends of heroes and saints (all ultimately avatars of Lugh) who fight with dragons or other serpentine beings.

The most famous of Lugh's opponents in literature, Balor of the Evil Eye, is perhaps the easiest one to relate to the specific ritual circumstances of the festival. The heat of the Sun, once welcome when it served to drive away the deadly cold of winter, comes to acquire, as the summer wears on, an intensity that is itself excessive and life-denying. There is now a surfeit of *samos*-energy, which is more likely to scorch the crops than to help them grow; and nothing is more desirable at this time than a dose of cooling *giamos*-energy, in the shape of the August thunderstorms that clear the air and put an end to the sultry "dog days." Thus does Lugh ("lightning" is one meaning of his name) quench the fire in the eye of his grandfather Balor (the "dog day" period was, in Scotland, referred to as *an t-Iuchar*, now the modern Scots Gaelic name of the month of July; and it is curious to note that Iuchar is one of the three sons of Tuireann who are Lugh's enemies in *Oidheadh Chloinne Tuireann*). Thunderstorms and heavy rain were considered to be very auspicious at the time of the festival, and presaged a good harvest. There is generally a ritual preoccupation with water on Lúghnasadh, contrasting with the emphasis on fire on Imbolc and Bealtaine—fire and water being, as we have seen, mated opposites in Celtic thought. Just as, on Bealtaine, cattle were driven

close to the flame of the bonfires to receive protection from supernatural harm, so on Lúghnasadh the horses of the community were
purified by being driven through water; in a highly ritualized "race,"
men rode naked across a lake or river, making sure the horses were
largely submerged and made to swim. Since cattle were usually symbolic of the powers of the Land (with bulls exemplifying the destructive aspects, cows the nurturing aspects), and horses represented
the Tribe and its sovereignty, there seems to be a reunion of opposites achieved here on a number of levels: the normally "water-
identified" cattle (river-goddesses could be portrayed as cows; and
there are many tales of "magic" cattle emerging from pools and lakes)
are healed by exposure to fire, while the "solar" horses need to be
brought into contact with water. This ritual theme could, in a sense,
be related to Lugh himself, with his dual Danann/Fomorian nature.

On the opening day of the festival, communities would assemble
on a high place—i.e., a meeting-ground of the earth and sky, the
proper locus for a manifestation of Lugh. Particularly appropriate
were hills or mountains that had a well (a Goddess/Fomorian motif)
near their summit. There essentially three types of rituals would be
performed: dramatic enactment of mythological material associated
with the season; inauguration of the Harvest through enjoyment of
first fruits (both wild and cultivated); and activities symbolic of continued fertility in the Land.

Pageants depicting local versions of the Lugh story were evidently once an important part of the season's ceremonial ritual, with
mummers representing all kinds of monsters, and perhaps an actual
bull used in a combination of bullfight and animal sacrifice; but over
the centuries the more blatantly non-Christian material was phased
out, doubtless through the Church's influence. The aforementioned
"Jack the Tinkard" plays performed at Morvah Fair in Cornwall
constitute an exceptional survival. Various local traditions suggest
that the God of the Land was often represented as a sculptured stone
head on the summit of the hill, probably in many cases a two-sided
"Janus head" (like the famous one from Roquepertuse) reflecting
the god's dual aspect, looking simultaneously towards the *samos* and
giamos poles of the yearly cycle; and the individual playing the part
of Lugh in the pageant would somehow interact with this sculpture,

demonstrating (by leaping over it, for instance) his victory over what it symbolized (on the other hand, the double figure could also represent Lugh's own ability to cross boundaries and exist in two realms at once). The spectacular *Men an Toll* (perforated stone) at Morvah, believed to have curative properties and set between two other standing stones, is almost certainly a reminder of one of the final episodes in the Fourth Branch of the Mabinogi, in which Lleu's rival Gronw Pebr, about to suffer Lleu's revenge, asks to have a stone placed between him and the avenging spear, only to have the spear pierce the stone and kill him anyway. Outside Cornwall, the only sort of mythologically-inspired pageantry to survive into recent times was the ritualized faction-fighting that would take place in many parts of Ireland on this day. Pitting against each other (usually with staves) the young men of two communities (or two territorial subsets of a community), with the victorious group claiming better luck with the harvest in the coming year, this ritual was obviously an enactment of the conflict between the two groups of gods, as in the battle of Maigh Tuireadh.

Since the main theme of the feast was the successful reaping of benefits from the Land by the Tribe, the communal enjoyment of first fruits was the high point of the day's ritual. This would include both cultivated crops and wild-growing edible fruits, which also were made accessible for the Tribe's use by Lugh's intercession (at Samhain, as we have seen, they would revert to the control of the Land-spirits). Even if, because of weather conditions or other circumstantial factors, the full harvest would not begin until later, it was absolutely necessary to gather and ceremonially consume a small portion of the crops on Lúghnasadh. In Ireland over the last two hundred years the main crop has, of course, been potatoes, but in earlier times and in other regions the focus was on the grain crops. In some traditions, Otherworld beings—like the Manx *fennodyree*, a brownie-like "wild man"—were thought to begin the Harvest on a subtler plane, "preparing" it before the human Tribe took over in the physical realm. The actual cutting of the first sheaf was, needless to say, a highly ritualized gesture: in Scotland the head of the kin-group would, facing the Sun as it rose, cut the sheaf with a sickle and then hold it up to the sky, turning three times sunwise on his heels while chanting the *iolach buana* ("reaping paean"). This first harvest then would be quickly made into cakes which would be brought up to the ritual site on the hilltop or mountaintop and consumed by the entire community. It was a particularly joyous occasion since, in many rural areas until recently, food reserves from the previous harvest would be running out by the end of the summer, and people would be hungry (the Irish expressions *Iúil an Ghorta* —"July of the Famine"—and *Iúil an Chabáiste*—"July of the Cabbage," the only food still available—reflect this). The wild foods traditionally gathered and eaten on this day were blueberries (or other berries of the genus *Vaccinium*); so closely associated, throughout the Celtic world, was this activity with the feast that in some places it gave it its common name (in parts of Ireland the day was called *Domhnach na bhFraochóga,* Blueberry Sunday).

The third element in the day's ritual concerned some form of fertility magic performed by the young people of the community. The scandalized comments of some Victorian observers suggest that sexually explicit activities went on, but most likely it was no more than erotic banter accompanying symbolic gestures. Making flower garlands was a part of it; in one version of the ritual, the boys made chains of flowers or blueberries with ragwort-stems and offered them to the girls. In other versions, one girl in particular was enthroned on a stone seat (often a feature of Lúghnasadh ceremonial sites) and offered flowers as though she were a goddess—and indeed she *was* a representation of the fairy-queen Aine (whose name is perhaps related to Eithne's), the Land-goddess in her positive aspect. A different kind of fertility ritual associated with the feast was the Welsh game *rhibo,* in which a boy and a girl were tossed on the linked arms of six other young people. In all cases there was a general atmosphere of happy dissolution, with much dancing and singing.

Another ritual use was made of flowers on this day; flowers that had been worn on the way up to the ceremonial site were solemnly buried, as a sign that summer was over. The act of burying the flowers was a way of damping the *samos*-energy in the environment, while ensuring that it returned to the Land to promote fertility later on.

Finally, an important aspect of Lúghnasadh, as the day of the

Tribe's victory, was the consolidation of the inner structure of the Tribe, the reaffirmation of solidarity between the Tribe's members, achieved through the *aonach* or "assembly." Because of the opportunity such assemblies offer for commercial transactions, the word *aonach* has come to mean "fair" in the market sense, but originally it meant something more like "reunion," derived as it is from *aon,* "one." It drew together the inhabitants of scattered, isolated farmhouses and gave them the sense of belonging to a larger unit, descended from a common ancestor, with a common set of traditions. Tribal chieftains and provincial kings all sponsored *aontaí* on various scales. They were, in many ways, showcases for the creative element in the Tribe's culture: poets presented their latest compositions, musicians entertained, craftsmen showed off their handiwork. It was, on a different level, another harvest of fruits whose generation was prepared at Imbolc—for Brigit, as we have seen, is the originator/Muse of cultural creativity, as well as the energizer of growth in the Land. After the conquest of the Celtic lands and the disappearance of their native rulers, the *aontaí* were left without sponsors and were reduced to informal singing and dancing at Lúghnasadh sites.

We now can recapitulate the rather well-defined themes of the Lúghnasadh ritual:

1. The Assembly on a Height.
2. The Pageant of the Triumph of Lugh.
3. The Solemn Reaping and Enjoyment of First Fruits, Cultivated and Wild.
4. The Racing of Horses (Tribe-symbolic) in Water (Land-symbolic).
5. Men and Women Paired in Fertility Magic.
6. The Burial of Flowers: End of Summer.
7. The Reaffirmation of the Tribe's Order.

The themes and the manner of their ritual expression are so constant throughout Celtic tradition that it would seem wise to follow them as closely as possible in our circle's modern practice. If there is a high place in your area that is known to have been used for such rituals by past generations, that is, of course, where the assembly should be. Or there may be a high place that has no extant tradition attached to it but that "feels" right, fulfilling all the requirements of a Lúghnasadh ritual site. Of all the Year's ceremonies, this is the one that gains most by being held outdoors, and every effort must be made to arrange for this, even by an urban circle.

Prior to assembling in the ritual area, a sampling of the Land's "first fruits" must be gathered: a fruit or other food plant that grows wild in the area, and whatever crop plant is getting ripe at the time of the festival. If the circle is based in a farming community, this poses no problems. If not, appropriate items should be obtained from a farmers' market that sells local produce. The food, of course, should be prepared and in edible form before the ritual.

A cauldron filled with water should be on the site. Also at hand should be the flower-filled water that was used to create the Flower Maiden on Bealtaine. The circle's four "Treasures"—sword, cauldron, stone, and spear—should be present, since they will figure in the ritual.

After establishing sacred space, the circle leader proclaims the opening of the Harvest, invoking the power of Lugh to claim the fruits of the Land for the Tribe, and perhaps reciting some relevant portion of a Lugh legend. If the circle's resources are limited, the mythological recitation may suffice, but in most cases some type of pageant or dramatic presentation will be given to make the triumph of Lugh more vividly real to all. A mummer playing the part of Lugh confronts the varied array of Fomorian powers, masked as dragons, bulls, or other shapes known from folk sources. The God of the Tribe dispatches all of them with a mixture of force and trickery. The last episode features Balor of the Evil Eye: Lugh eventually vanquishes him as well, but the other circle members join in, uniting as the Tribe against this great enemy of theirs. As Balor falls the fountains of the sky are loosed, and as a sign of this the water from the cauldron is splashed haphazardly over the circle members, adding to the riotous atmosphere and momentarily joining the energies of Tribe and Land.

A shallow hole is then dug, and the flower-water saved from Bealtaine is poured into it, and covered over. All present call out their farewells to summer, for the cooling water of *giamos* has been invoked and will exercise ever more influence as the days grow shorter. By the burial of the flowers the Flower Maiden has been dismissed: the Goddess now rules as Queen of the Harvest, enticed into serving the Tribe by Lugh's charisma. An effigy of the Goddess in her new guise can be set up and decorated, or a woman can play her part, led to her appointed place in the circle by the mummer who played Lûgh; the vessels containing the first fruits are then placed at her feet. A game of *rhibo*—a couple bounced on the arms of three other couples—or some other ritual associated with fertility is enacted before her.

The ritual leader picks up each of the vessels in turn, holding them up to the Sun and turning deosil three times, while chanting an appropriate invocation—perhaps a variant of one of the Harvest invocations in the *Carmina Gadelica*. Then each vessel is given to whoever is standing in the eastern quarter, who eats some of the food and passes it on sunwise until it has gone around the whole circle (the vessels may be passed around the circle three times, if there is enough food). Thus, the Harvest is inaugurated as the Tribe lays claim to the year's first fruits.

The structure of the Tribe—the conceptual world it inhabits—now must ritually be strengthened, to protect those aspects of it that allow it to coexist successfully with the Land. Under the guidance of the circle leader, all participants meditate on the sacred space they are in. At the four quarters the Forts of the Treasures are imagined in vivid reality, each of them a portal for a specific Otherworld influence on the Tribe: courage and endurance from the North, fertility and material comfort from the East, inspiration from the South, intellectual acumen from the West. The divine powers that play a part in the ritual life of the Year are visualized as present in this framework; to deepen their trance state, circle members can softly vibrate the names they use for these various figures.

Now that the circle has reaffirmed the mythic structure in which it operates, the Treasures that symbolize the authority to act in all the Tribal functions are reconsecrated by being presented to the mythological guardians of those functions. A circle member in the North takes up the sword and offers it to the Lord of Battles, reciting an invocation of second-function virtues. As all focus on the scene with their inner eye, the Lord of Battles is seen to take hold of the sword, bless it, and give it back for the circle's use. In similar fashion the cauldron is offered to the Lord of Riches, the stone to the Great Mother, and the spear to the Many-Gifted Lord. At the conclusion of the rite, all four Treasures are placed reverently around the central axis of the ceremonial area.

Once the most basic principles of the Tribe's existence have been made secure again, members of the Tribe can come together to share their diverse gifts in a spirit of unity. The rest of the day can be spent in enjoyment of poetry, music, or any other area of art in which some circle members display creative talent.

The Harvest is a period of bounty, a long-awaited satisfaction of hunger and want. It is a time of hard work, but work done in joy, for the worst threats the malignant powers in the Land can deploy against the Tribe are now left behind.

Mid-Harvest

Alban Elfed, Lá Fhéile Michil, Gwyl Fihangel, Gouel Sant-Mikael, Goel Myghal, Goeldheys—SEPTEMBER 21 (29)

> *V'eh sheeyney magh er lare yn lheeannee*
> *As ceau yn faiyr er y çheu chiare;*
> *O hug eh yindys orrin nurree*
> *As t'eh mleeaney foddey share.*
>
> —Manx Song About the Fennodyree

(He was stretching [his arm] out in the middle of the meadow, and casting the grass to the left side; he was wonderful to us last year, and this year he is far better yet!)

Although the specific date of the Autumn Equinox was not marked by any ritual in Celtic tradition, there is evidence that, at some point roughly halfway between Lúghnasadh and Samhain, communities would involve themselves with a ceremony that reflected the processes then at work in the year. This was usually a conclusion to ritual themes invoked at Lúghnasadh, and focused on the end of the main harvest activities (i.e., the grain harvest), although it did not imply the end of the entire Harvest season, which continued until Samhain. In the Coligny Calendar the date of *xv Cantli* is glossed as *tiocobrextion*. If some current interpretations of the calendar's dating system are correct, this would usually fall on or about September 29; and if the name of the ritual is a dialectal development from *teg(es)okomrextion* "setting the house in order," it would be an apt description of the spirit of a "harvest home" celebration, wrapping up agricultural activities for the year.

September 29 has, today, become the Feast of Saint Michael in the Christian calendar. There are strong pre-Christian associations with this motif. The image of the archangel Michael fighting the Satanic dragon was easily assimilated, in Celtic minds, to the image of Lugh who himself struggled with dragon-like Fomorian powers. Saint Michael thus became an acceptable Christianization of Lugh, and assumed most of Lugh's characteristics and ritual functions. The high places associated with Lúghnasadh celebrations came to be known as "Saint Michael's Mounts," and there are many of them throughout Celtic and ex-Celtic lands (though in Ireland, where traditions about Saint Michael did not penetrate until fairly late in the Middle Ages, Lugh survived in folk consciousness under his original name). Michaelmas, then, by putting the ritual focus on a figure widely assumed to be the same as the one presiding over Lúghnasadh, was interpreted as a part of the same Harvest-identified ceremonial cycle, and indeed as the closure of the processes set in motion on Lúghnasadh.

In northern Scotland, where climate made it impossible to begin the harvest as early as August, Michaelmas actually took the place of Lúghnasadh as the solemn beginning of Harvest activities, incorporating most of the ritual elements discussed in the preceding section, such as the festive assemblies on heights, the ritual gathering of first fruits, and the "watering" of horses. The archangel Michael was invoked in terms that clearly revealed him to be the heir of Lugh.

In most of the Celtic world, however, the grain harvest would be over by the end of September, and Michaelmas would be an appropriate date to celebrate the successful conclusion of the Tribe's dealings with the Land. But the very act of ending the harvest was in itself an event fraught with metaphysical dangers and linked to Otherworld influences. Reaping the fruits of the soil was, however one went about it, an act of violence against the Land-deities, even if Lugh's victory allowed one to escape, for a time, the consequences of such violence. The gathering of the very last fruits threatened to tax the Fomorian reserves of fertility, and lead to future blight. Also, the last sheaf of the harvest was felt to concentrate in itself all of the properties—fertility and blight combined—of the Fomorian realm, and its proper disposal was of paramount importance to ensure continuing good relations with the Land. The potency of the last sheaf passed magically into the reaper who cut it, so that he became a figure of ritual significance for the rest of the season.

The ceremonies attending the cutting of the last sheaf were remarkably uniform throughout the Celtic and ex-Celtic lands. It was important that the identity of the one who cut it be determined by chance. In some areas this was achieved by having all the reapers turn their backs to the last standing patch of grain and throw their reaping-hooks blindly behind them, until one of them at last cut the sheaf. In other places the reapers were blindfolded. With the cutting, the Land-spirit who had been providing the corn with the energy to grow found itself separated from the continuum of the Goddess's realm, so that special pains had to be taken to ensure, by ritual means, that it did not simply dissipate in isolation and thus squander the Land's fertility. An appropriate vehicle had to be devised for it, a symbolic form that would express its identity and maintain its living presence within the community. So the last sheaf was plaited into a figure, a "corn dolly," representing the spirit it was intended to house. This was often an animal, usually an animal strongly associated with the Land-goddess—the hare, because it would actually hide among the grain, was an obvious favorite. In western Cornwall the last sheaf or "neck" was called the *penn-yar* (the hen's head). But in Wales the Goddess's transformation into a mare was such an important and well-known motif that the figure made out of the last sheaf was called the *caseg fedi* (harvest mare). When the "dolly" was a human figure, she was always a representation of the Land-goddess, whether as an agent of fertility or of blight. In parts of Scotland the two aspects were very clearly differentiated: if the harvest was judged to have been a good one, the figure was said to be that of a young woman (the Harvest Queen, the Goddess as a fertile and friendly being), but if the harvest had been bad, the "dolly" was called the *cailleach* (the sterile Hag, inimical to human needs). Most communities kept the figure for a full year, burning it ritually at the conclusion of the following harvest, as soon as a new "dolly" had been made. In the meantime, it would be stored in a space significantly related to the third function: in a tree (returning it, partially, to the Land), in a kitchen, in the church (where the harvest implements were blessed), or among the stock seed kept to be sown the following spring, where it would be expected to "teach" the young grain the power of growth, passing on some of its essence. The *cailleach*, not being associated with fertility, was often disposed of differently, usually by burial—and since the spot where she was buried would, of course, take on her sterile characteristics, unpopular or niggardly landowners could suffer by having the *cailleach* secretly buried on their property. There are also indications that the *cailleach* could be used in more sinister forms of black magic.

The reaper who had cut the last sheaf was, as we have noted, at once invested with a special role. He became the guardian of the *babban* or *cailleach* or *caseg fedi,* and, as such, received particular favors from the Otherworld (he could, for instance, expect a wish made at that moment to come true); but he also was made into something of a figure of fun, and a game would ensue in which he tried to bring the "dolly" into the village secretly, avoiding those who were lying in wait to pour water on him and his charge. In some communities water was poured on the "dolly" systematically, outside the context of any game, suggesting that the custom began as a necessary fertility ritual, and only later acquired the character of a contest.

The conclusion of the grain harvest was celebrated with a community feast, the ancestor of the "harvest home" feasts that still subsist in rural areas, usually as acts of thanksgiving under the auspices of the parish church. In Cornwall this was called the *Goeldheys* or "feast of ricks." The "corn dolly" originally presided over this feast as its guest of honor. In many communities carrots—because they were being gathered at this time—featured prominently as a ritual food; and in Scotland their phallic appearance was invoked in fertility magic, as women dug them up with spades (associated with vaginal symbolism) while chanting:

> Torcan torrach, torcan torrach
> Sonas curran corr orm!
> Micheal mil a bhi dha'm chonuil
> Bride gheal dha'm chòmhnadh.
> Piseach linn gach piseach,
> Piseach dha mo bhroinn;
> Piseach linn gach piseach,
> Piseach dha mo chloinn!

(Fruitful cleft, fruitful cleft, the good fortune of pointed carrots be upon me! Brave Michael [i.e., Lugh] will endow me, bright Brigit will aid me. Increase of a generation be every increase, increase to my womb; increase of a generation be every increase, increase to my children!) The *struan Mhichil*, a cake made for the occasion, was triangular and intended to suggest a vagina.

In West Munster the feast was described as the *clabhsúr* (closure). The men of the community, who had just completed the work of the harvest, made a show of threatening to destroy all their agricultural tools if the women did not prepare a feast for them. After much ritualized banter, in which the tools were tentatively thrown on the fire but were rescued at once by the women, concrete plans were made for the feast. This is a fascinating instance of a Celtic mythological pattern expressed as ritual: within the context of the classic Tribe/Land dichotomy the men (the "God" aspect), representing the activities specific to the Tribe (the tools), demand from the women (the "Goddess" aspect) that which can be given only by the Land (food).

After the gathering-in of the crops the year can be said to come to its own *clabhsúr*, both in terms of the Tribe/Land relation in the agricultural cycle and in terms of the *samos/giamos* cycle within the Land. With the equinox the "Dark" again gains the upper hand, *giamos*-energy becomes ever more prominent in the daily rhythms of the natural world, and the energies of the human Tribe must strive to realign themselves with the changing order of things. The very act of gathering in, of turning inwards, is the main characteristic of *gi-amos* (as opposed to the expansive, outward-turning quality of *samos*), and once the collecting and storing activities of the harvest have been completed, the "Dark" season can fully establish itself, gifting the world with a necessary period of inaction, contemplation, and rest. In mythological terms, this means that the Maponos, the Summer Lord of growth-energy in whom all the qualities of *samos* are manifested, must be made to yield his position as consort of the Land to his dethroned rival. We already have seen some of the ways in which this theme could be expressed in Celtic tradition. Perhaps the most elegant is the one that uses the motif of the Cosmic Boar Hunt, which brings in the summer season on Bealtaine, but gives it the opposite result, slaying the Maponos. The best-known version of this story—which we have already mentioned—is the death of Diarmaid (foster-son of Aonghus and thus himself a version of the Maponos), who had eloped with Gráinne (as Land-goddess) after she had married Fionn (the Cernunnos). Seeking revenge on Diarmaid but unable to kill him himself, Fionn manipulates the younger man's *geasa* (taboos that govern his behavior in relation to the Otherworld influences in his life—i.e., innate talents or sacred vocational commitments) to make him participate in a hunt for a magical boar with venomous bristles. As a hunter-warrior within the Fenian system, Diarmaid cannot refuse to join in a hunt. Like the summer-hero Culhwch (whose birth and name made him a "pig"), Diarmaid is intimately related to the Boar: they are foster-brothers, and destined to die on the same instant. This destiny, of course, comes to pass, and Gráinne, after mourning Diarmaid, returns to Fionn (the Winter consort). Thus the Boar Hunt is enacted again, but leads in the opposite direction, into the *giamos*-realm of death and repose; and when we reopen the ritual Year on Samhain, we will again begin to invoke the Boar in the South, the *giamos*-direction.

The principal themes expressed in this ritual period, then, are the following:

1. The Preservation of the Land's Fertility in the form of the Last Sheaf.
2. The Closure of the Year with a Communal Feast.
3. Setting the conditions for the coming Triumph of Darkness.

If we live in an agricultural community, our celebration of the *clabhsúr* can very literally follow the pattern described above, and incorporate any other elements that may have survived in local tradition. If our circle meets in an urban setting, or if none of its members are in any way involved in food-producing work, the concept of the Harvest and the Tribe's interaction with the Land will have to be represented in a new way. We can, as was suggested for Lúghnasadh, go to the nearest center of agricultural production and obtain the makings of a corn dolly and a feast; but, whereas the "first fruits" specifications of the Lúghnasadh ritual could be interpreted broadly to mean any crops harvested within the first few days of the season by any farmers in a given area, such an interpretation applied to the harvest's end would dilute the very specific sacrificial meaning of the Last Sheaf. To recapture that meaning in ritual, we will have to explore the nature of the circle's interaction with the Land, in what precise way the circle is benefiting from a Harvest of its own. We can remind ourselves of the fact that everything we create, even if it is with our minds (simply because they are inseparable from our bodies), depends on sustenance from the Land, and that the fruits of all our occupations are, in that sense, a Harvest. They have been made possible by the nurturing energy of Brigantia, the figure we honored at Imbolc, the beginning of the Tribe/Land cycle. Thus, anything that represents the fruit of our labors—that is, the truly satisfying result of work one freely identifies with—can be brought to be shared and blessed at the Michaelmas feast. And anything that manifests the Land's presence as the backdrop to our activities—any "found objects" that are not man-made—can be used to make a vehicle for the Land-goddess's power, to be present at that feast.

During a specified period just before the actual celebration of the holiday, we should go about gathering the materials for such a vehicle—our equivalent of a "dolly." The choice of specific objects will, of course, be purely intuitive: a twig with berries, fallen leaves, feathers, strips of bark, and the like. Once they have been gathered, chance should again determine who the final "reaper" will be. One may decide that it is the last person to have found an object within the prescribed period; or we can use one of the traditional methods described above, with the combination of the found materials standing for the "last sheaf." The designated *gille na caillí* makes a "dolly" out of them and carries it to the spot where the feast is to be held, dodging other circle members who make a game of spraying water over him and his charge.

The *babban* is ceremonially enthroned at the head of the feasting table, which has already been decked with seasonally appropriate foods. Before partaking of the offerings, however, we must acknowledge the tools without which they could not have been obtained. Circle members now bring to the table an object that each thinks of as a tool of their trade. The ritual leader blesses the tools by sprinkling them with water from the lustration bowl. This can be done in silence, or a brief blessing can be spoken.

All now take their places at the feast, but since the gathering-in of the harvest is an event that signals the return of *giamos* to dominance within the energies of the year, and indicates that the face the Land presents to the Tribe is about to change fundamentally, we should meditate on the mythological subtext of these things, so that we partake of the feast in a proper frame of mind. Just as we woke the sleeping lord in midspring to affirm the triumph of *samos*, so on Mid-Harvest we bid farewell to the Maponos, whose rule must be cut short to allow the full establishment of *giamos*.

We see ourselves, in our mind's eye, traveling through a great forest. It has been a prosperous summer, the signs of successful growth are everywhere: a dense leafy canopy, fruits hanging from many branches, ubiquitous bird song, frequent indications of animal presences. The sun shines brightly, the air is pleasantly warm, though no longer hot. This, we feel, is supreme well-being: the sense of having reached fulfilment, of having accomplished all that one had set out to do.

But we soon notice that not all is well in the forest. A break appears in the trees; a great swathe has been cut by some inexorably violent passage. Trunks have been knocked down and trampled underfoot to make an ugly, inchoate mess where nothing can grow. An aura of fear hangs over the scene. The disturbance stretches like a great highway, with no beginning and no end that we can see. It strikes us as a massive denial of the growth and well-being we had seen around us before.

Looking ahead along the path of the destruction, we spy some movement and color. Coming closer, we identify an armed company on foot, appareled in a way suggesting one of the Golden Ages of the Celtic past. The obvious leader of the company—who turns to greet us—is tall beyond mortal height, and has the radiant vitality of a god. His summery aura at once warms our hearts, and we feel drawn to him; it is obvious that he, like the hero Diarmaid, has a *ball seirce* (love spot) that can compel the affection of those who look upon him. We feel sure that he, of all beings, can restore order to the unpleasant chaos we have discovered.

Yet the longer we gaze at him, the more certainly we realize that his radiance is not at its full strength, that a weariness and sadness are beginning to lie heavily upon his features. And we learn from him what has come to pass: a great Boar, an archetype of destruction from the Otherworld, has become manifest in the Land, and it lies on the Lord and his company to confront the monster, for there is a deep bond between the nature of the Lord and the nature of the Boar. That bond is not such, however, as to ensure the Lord's control over the Boar. A chill passes over us as, looking into the Lord's eyes, we understand that, although the Hunt must be enacted and all must do their best, the outcome is already known: he will die.

We rebel at the thought of losing this being who seems so much to be the embodiment of all our hopes. Yet the look in his eyes has a finality with which we cannot argue. With immense regret, we are forced to tear our hopes away from him, to convince ourselves that we can no longer follow him to victory.

Yet we cannot deny our love for him. We wish to express this love by giving him a parting gift, and we discover that we are indeed carrying such a gift; the Land-goddess, his consort, entrusted us with a green flowing mantle, an image of the power of Summer, for him to wear on this last Hunt. He takes the gift from us happily, with a look that acknowledges the kinship between us. Then he and his company continue on their way, and we are left alone.

The sky turns dark and stormy. A cold wind begins to blow. The western horizon has taken on the color of blood, and from that quarter we see approaching, borne on the fierce wind, a great billowing shape which we know to be the Lord's mantle—yet as it comes nearer, it dissolves into a multitude of brightly-colored dead leaves, which whirl about and eclipse the gloomy landscape behind a riot of joy-inspiring beauty. We gaze in wonder at how the moment of death, which we usually think of with sadness, could give rise to a vision of such invigorating delight, manifest only at this time.

The meditation ended, the ritual leader pronounces a blessing on all present and their households, perhaps using one of the Michaelmas blessings in the *Carmina Gadelica*. And the actual feasting will conclude the ritual.

So the year returns to Darkness, where it had its origins. But in that Darkness, as we now know, are the seeds of new life, and a Light waiting to be reborn.

We have here, then, a compendium of traditions concerning the great turning points in the year, preserved for us by Celtic-speaking communities. The individual traditions have entered the continuum of Celtic culture at various times and from various sources, but they have fit themselves into the context of the great, comprehensive mythical schemes of thought that underlie the Celtic way of looking at things, and have both enriched and reaffirmed that central identity. They have given rise to a pattern of ritual observance that has, in one form or another, been a part of Celtic life for many centuries. Where this pattern has survived, Celtic culture, as a rule, remains strong; conversely, where it has been eroded by pressures from outside, the sense of Celtic identity is fading, and all aspects of its cultural heritage are in disarray. It follows that a conscious, intelligent reaffirmation of the pattern will do much to restore a sense of confidence to Celtic consciousness.

As we have stated repeatedly, nothing that has been presented here is meant to be taken in a dogmatic, prescriptive way. The suggested rituals are no more than that: suggestions on how to flesh out a traditional pattern in new contexts. Others may come up with better ways of expressing that pattern. Individual circles will undoubtedly either "paganize" or "Christianize" the rituals, depending on their members' orientation. And elements suggested by the Land itself—local events in nature, synchronous with the festivals—can be worked into the rituals: the first blooming of a particular species of flower, for instance, or the first appearance of a certain migratory bird.

It is this attention to the Land that is the most important byproduct of observing the ritual cycle of Earth and Sun. As the exigencies of the rituals force us to be aware of the seasonal changes in the Land in an intimate way, we may be better defended when the purely Tribal preoccupations that now dominate our lives—the state that defines our civil rights, the corporations and bureaucracies that employ us, the landlords to whom we turn for shelter, the markets that determine our wealth—tempt us to forget her.

CHAPTER FOUR

The Cycle of the Moon

Ll existence is propelled by cyclic rhythms, ranging from the unimaginably vast to the unimaginably tiny, from the explosion and implosion of universes to the nanoseconds-long birth and decay of certain subatomic particles. In between are those rhythms that human beings can readily perceive, and which serve to pattern their lives. The solar year, containing within its limits a full cycle of reproductive activity in nature, is perhaps, as we have seen in the preceding chapter, the most basic and influential cosmic cycle in human experience, since it is the measure of the agricultural process, which is necessary to the Tribe's survival. We have discussed the *samos-giamos* alternation within that cycle—a period of growth and expansion followed by a period of stasis and recollection—and noted the importance of that concept in the Celtic consciousness, which sees in it the most fundamental organizing principle in the universe.

Every cycle in our environment follows this structure; indeed, the human psyche needs to experience this kind of rhythm for its well-being. And other cycles besides the solar year play a significant role in ordering our existence—most notably, the waxing and waning of the Moon. Each lunation imitates, in miniature, the pattern of the year, with its waxing *samos*-period, its moment of glorious fullness, then its waning into *giamos*, ending in a complete disappearance into darkness from which the cycle begins anew. Countless folk customs in many cultures testify to the powerful effect these phenomena have on human life, as the phases of the Moon are used to determine the appropriateness of a wide variety of activities, with the waxing moon promoting growth and the beginning of new projects, while the waning moon favors endings and the banishing of unwanted influences. Between twelve and thirteen complete lunations occur within the period of the solar year; although each one of them follows precisely the same pattern, the very different situation each presides over in its relation to the much slower rhythm of the Sun's journey lends it an individual character, so that various cultural traditions have ascribed separate names, qualities, and influences to all twelve or thirteen of them, and have often devised specific rituals for each one.

The Celts, of course, shared in this wealth of lunar lore. Classical writers noted the druids' reliance on the phases of the moon for the timing of certain rituals. Pliny the Elder's famous account of the gathering of the mistletoe, for instance, explains that it could be done only on the sixth night after the new moon. Insofar as the druids had devised a sophisticated dating system, it was clearly based on the lunar year. The most concrete example we have of this is undoubtedly the Coligny Calendar, which we have already mentioned on many occasions. Engraved on a series of bronze tablets (some of them badly damaged), it presents sixty-two months—of which two are supernumerary, intercalary months—covering a period of five years. There are twelve recurring months, some consisting of thirty days and labeled MAT (good), others consisting of twenty-nine days and labeled ANM (for *anmatos,* not-good—i.e., inauspicious; we discussed the significance of this in chapter two). The two intercalary months, both of thirty days, occur at the beginning and at the middle of the five-year cycle. Since Diodorus Siculus—quoting from the Posidonian ethnography—reports that the druids performed special sacrifices every five years, that unit of time must have long played a basic role in Celtic tradition; and if Pliny the Elder's testimony is reliable, a druidic "age" consisted of thirty years—that is, six of the periods represented by the Coligny Calendar.

Ever since its discovery in 1897, the calendar has generated much controversy as various scholars have put forward conflicting interpretations of its structure and purpose. A good deal of the disagreement has focused on how the months of the Coligny Calendar relate to the months of the Roman calendar. Early scholars, noting that the first month was named *Samonios* (which seems to be derived from *samos,* summer) and that the seventh month was named *Giamonios* (from *giamos,* winter), assumed that they were the first months of summer and winter respectively. Of course, the modern word *Samhain* is clearly derived from *Samonios,* but unfortunately it is the beginning of winter, not summer. A later generation of students, taking extant Celtic tradition into account, have understood *Samonios* to mean end of summer and *Giamonios* to mean end of winter, and have assigned all the months to their proper seasons accordingly. Thus, according to the current interpretation, a sample twelve-month year would have the following structure:

Dark (*giamos*) half:

1. SAMONIOS (30 days) October–November
2. DVMANNIOS (29 days) November–December
3. RIVROS (30 days) December–January
4. ANAGANTIOS (29 days) January–February
5. OGRONIOS (30 days) February–March
6. CVTIOS (30 days) March–April

Light (*samos*) half:

7. GIAMONIOS (29 days) April–May
8. SIMIVISONNOS (30 days) May–June
9. EQVOS (29 days) June–July
10. ELEMBIVIOS (29 days) July–August
11. EDRINIOS or ÆDRINIOS (30 days) August–September
12. CANTLOS (29 days) September–October

The precise positioning of the months in relation to the Roman year is, needless to say, very tentative. Equally unclear are the meanings of the names of some of the months: extremely fanciful and unlikely translations have been proposed by some authors. *Samonios,* as we have seen, is "end of summer." *Dumannios* is probably the "dark month," perhaps related to the name *miz Du / mis Du* (black month) given by the Bretons and Cornish to November. *Riuros* may be the "frost month" (although it has also been related to the elements *ro-iuo-* "great feast, great libation," and thus read as "month of the great feast"; but this is unlikely, for then the term *Deuoriuos Riuri,* "great divine feast of the month of the great feast," would come across as improbably clumsy and redundant!), or it could be related to Old Irish *reo* "dense darkness," which could be descriptive of a midwinter month. *Anagantios* seems to mean "not-going," and thus has been interpreted as the "stay-at-home month," an appropriate name for a month in the dead of winter. *Ogronios* is the "end of the cold," the first month of spring. *Cutios* is of uncertain meaning, though it may have something to do with rain. *Giamonios* is the "end of winter," the beginning of the year's Light half. *Simiuisonnos* almost certainly means "halfway through summer," with *uisonnos* as a more precise term than *samos* for the quarter extending from May through July—this month being appropriately in the middle of that period. *Equos* is the "horse month" (although the persistence of the 'qu' sound here, when the Gaulish pronunciation of the word for "horse" had long ago become *epos,* has made some scholars doubtful of the meaning). *Elembiuios* has been interpreted as the "deer month," deriving it from the Old Celtic stem *eln-* "deer," though this is far from certain; instead, it may contain the elements *elu-* (many, various) and *embi* (on either side, among), with a derivational suffix of unknown meaning. *Edrinios/Ædrinios* is the "end of the heat," the first month of Harvest. *Cantlos* is the "song month," and earlier scholars thought it referred to the singing of birds in May, but it more likely reflects human chanting of *cantla* during rituals at the end of Harvest. The intercalary month is appropriately called *Antaranos* (in-between month).

Interspersed throughout the calendar are a great number of notations, most of them undecipherable abbreviations. The term *atenoux* (for *atenouxtion,* return night) clearly refers to the middle of the lunar cycle, most likely the full moon, and the word *iuos* means "feast" or "libation"; but we can make only educated guesses as to the meanings of such abbreviations as *m d, amb, exingidu, innis, petiux,* and *prinni.* The frequently occurring notation *diuertomu,* which appears

at the end of ANM-months, has, on the one hand, been interpreted
to mean "valueless" (as in Welsh *diwerth*), to indicate that the material it introduces is not part of the true sequence of days in the calendar, while on the other hand it has been thought to mean something
like "let's recapitulate" (*dê-urtomos,* "we turn back" [from], supposing
the existence of a stem *urt-* "turn" cognate to the verb *vertere* in
Latin), since it seems to label a summary of the preceding month. We
can thus appreciate that there are serious lacunae in our understanding of much of the material preserved in the Coligny Calendar.

Modern Celtic communities have by and large modeled their
months after the twelve divisions of the Roman calendar, although
as late as the nineteenth century certain areas in Gaelic Scotland
(where so much pre-Christian material survived for so long) used a
completely different system to divide up the year, very possibly inherited from the druidic past. Since some of the periods are considerably less than four weeks long, it is not entirely based on the lunar
cycle. After the month of *Samhainn*, named after the festival, there is
a long, poorly defined period entitled *an Dùdlachd* "the dark of winter," which extends into January, followed by *an Faoilteach* (the wolf
month—though some authorities think it means the carnival month,
referring to Shrovetide), which corresponds more or less to the
Coligny Calendar's *Anagantios*. This introduces a series of periods
with "animal" names: *an Feadag* (the plover), roughly a week bridg-
ing February and March, then *an Gearran* (the gelding) corresponding to the Coligny Calendar's *Cutios*, ending with the weeklong period
called *an Chailleach* (the hag) and its three-day coda, *na h-Oisgean*
(the yearling ewes). They are followed by *an Giblean* (meaning uncertain), *an Céitéin* (referring to one of the names of Bealtaine), *an
Og-mhios* (the young month), *an t-Iuchar* (perhaps an allusion to a
mythological character who opposes Lugh), *an Lùnasdal* (the period
of the Harvest festival dedicated to Lugh), *an t-Sultainn* (apparently
from *sult,* comfort, enjoyment, probably expressing the time of plenty
as the fruits of the harvest are brought in), and *an Damhar* (*damh-ghar,*
stag-rut, since it is the time when deer mate and stags joust with
each other, shortly before—like Cernunnos—they lose their antlers).
In modern Scots Gaelic usage, some of these names have come to be
applied to the Roman months. Elsewhere in the Gaelic world

months are simply identified as the beginning, middle, or end of a quarter (winter, spring, summer, or harvest), while some of them are called by their Latin names. The Brythonic traditions keep the Latin names of all the months from January through May, while giving a variety of native names to the months from June through December. Some of these names have considerable poetic charm. For instance, the name of the month of September, *Gwyngala* in Cornish and *Gwengolo* in Breton (and *Gwyngalaf* in early Welsh calendars— although the official Welsh term for September today is *Medi,* harvest), is from *Uindo-kalamos,* white stem, referring to the drying stubble left in the fields after the completion of the harvest.

As the cycle of the solar year provides an excellent framework for planned communal activity, so the space of a lunation is ideally suited to the patterning of a process within the individual human psyche. With the new moon we turn our attention to a new activity or a new form of energy; as the moon waxes we allow ourselves to become infused with that particular quality, preparing it for manifestation; and when the moon reaches its full we can indeed manifest it openly, giving the energy back to the environment through some applied activity. Each of the twelve or thirteen lunations in the year will have an ethos or preoccupation specific to it, so each cycle will deal with material different from that in the month preceding it. Again, attunement to these changing energies will require constant attention to the Land, to events in the natural environment as they correspond in time to the shifting phases of the moon, and thus further encourage the deepening of the Tribe-Land connection.

So the observance of a ritual cycle based on the moon's transformations is indeed very desirable for our circle, and for a revived Celtic consciousness in general. Yet what model should we follow for our designation of the months? The most obvious model would be the Coligny Calendar itself, since it is unquestionably Celtic in origin, and may well have, in the remote past, determined many still-extant Celtic folk concepts about the wheel of the year. Unfortunately, our knowledge of the Coligny Calendar is still too fragmentary to allow us to use its material with confidence. We can hope that further research will eventually make the picture clearer, but in the meantime we must look elsewhere for a symbolic system we can apply to the lunar cycle. As we have seen, the months used by modern Celtic communities are merely adaptations of the months of the Roman calendar, and thus too shallowly rooted in Celtic tradition to become channels for more fundamental Celtic ideas and symbols. Where, then, can we look?

There is, in fact, one item in Celtic mythological literature that is directly related to the imagery and magical form of the lunar year. This is the incantation pronounced by the archetypal druid and bard Amairgen Glúingel son of Mil when, laying claim to Ireland for his kin, the ancestors of the Gael, he first set his right foot upon the new land, as recounted in the *Lebor Gabála Érenn*. He recited a list of thirteen images (we can safely assume that *am bri a ndai* is a variant of *am brí dánae*, not a different line), affirming that he had experienced the state of being that each one implied, and that this cumulative experience had conferred a magical or spiritual authority upon him, which he used to back his claim. Most readers are familiar with this poem as "The Song of Amergin," and have first encountered it in the very free and imaginative translation Robert Graves made of it in *The White Goddess*. Although he subjected the poem to some fanciful and arbitrary interpretations—trying to relate it to the ogham alphabet, for instance, and creating in the process a "Celtic Tree Calendar" that has become a part of popular culture—Graves was surely correct in his intuition that the thirteen lines beginning with *am* (I am) represent the thirteen months of a lunar year, and that the imagery is intended to convey the special characteristics of each month. Amairgen, the speaker of the poem, makes it clear himself when he asks *Co on co tagair aesa éscai?* (Who declares the ages of the moon?), claiming that achievement as his own, among others. By passing through all the elements of the cycle he has attained a wholeness, a perspective of the entire pattern, which gives him the authority to stand between our world and the Otherworld as an interpreter and arbiter. Since he is, in Irish tradition, the idealized prototype of the bard, it follows that anyone who aspires to the bardic state must experience these thirteen conditions of existence and become conscious of the cycle in which they successively occur.

What we are about to propose is, admittedly, a complete innova-
tion, although we have tried to keep it rooted in Celtic sources. After
dividing the year into thirteen lunar months, we will (much as Graves
did, although we will not follow him in his more idiosyncratic notions) ascribe to each month a line from Amairgen's invocation. The
imagery of that line will then express the processes at work in the
month, and define the type of energy we will be dealing with as
we interact with the phases of the moon. Each moon will be identified by the period in which it is full. Of course, not every year will
have thirteen full moons: which moon is missing may, in fact, be
used to divine the overall character of a given year.

This lunar calendar was adopted by Céli Dé Circle, and therefore, like much of the ritual material in this book, has acquired a certain patina of use and can be recommended from experience. It is
not intended to supersede, or to deflect attention from, the Coligny
Calendar, which remains our primary source on the organization of
the Celtic lunar year. But it *works*: it creates a living, resonant dynamic
for relating to the lunar cycle in a Celtic cultural context. It can
therefore provide a serviceable alternative until a more practical approach to the Coligny Calendar becomes possible; it may, in fact, reveal certain mythic patterns that will be directly applicable to the
Coligny Calendar.

As it waxes and wanes with each month, we will relate to the
moon as to a personal entity that both observes and guides our activities on earth. When we see the first sliver of the new moon in the
sky we must greet it like a new-found friend, preferably focusing
that greeting with some ritual formula. The lovely salutation to the
new moon in the *Carmina Gadelica* is certainly appropriate:

> *Fàilte dhut gu brath,*
> *A ghealach ùr, a nochd:*
> *Mar is tu gu brath*
> *Lochran àigh nam bochd.*

(An eternal greeting to you, new moon, tonight: because you are
forever the joyous lamp of the poor.)

Then, while the moon's light waxes, we think as often as possible of the mythic image that is associated with that particular month, we meditate on its relation to our current activities, and we use it to give specific configurations to the energy that we are absorbing from the growing light. When the moon reaches its full, we perform a ritual to acknowledge the fullness of its energy in ourselves. This can be done by the entire circle, or in smaller, more intimate groups, or individually. One may, following folk custom, catch the reflection of the full moon in a bowl of water, and use this gesture as a magical device to trigger the assimilation of the energy by our own psyche. An invocation appropriate to the month should be recited simultaneously. If the moon is not visible, the invocation can be done without the accompanying ritual, or a different ritual can be put together according to one's needs or inclinations. Afterwards, as the moon wanes, we repeat the words of the invocation regularly to remind ourselves how the energy of that month is to be manifested on our plane, and we work to express that energy through our actions. At last the moon's shape is entirely lost in darkness, and we prepare to begin a new cycle, to encounter a new form of energy.

I. THE CLIFF

(Full Moon between October 30 and November 25)

Am fuaim mara

In this month—the first of the Celtic Year—Amairgen sings "I am a noise of the sea." Now that Celtic-speaking communities have been pushed west to the narrow "Celtic fringe" along the Atlantic seaboard, that noise echoes constantly through the Celtic consciousness and has woven itself into the songs and stories of the Celtic peoples, as the waves pound unceasingly—especially through the silence of winter—against tall cliffs in western Ireland and the Outer Hebrides, in Cornwall and southwest Wales. But even when the Celtic realms stretched far inland across regions of forests and mountains, the edge of the sea appealed powerfully to the Celtic imagination. It was the boundary between our world and the Otherworld, for if one sailed west across the ocean, the securities of earthly life would be left behind, and before long one would come to appreciate the true immensity of that ever-fluid, essentially nonhuman plane of existence—even as our everyday reality is dwarfed by the limitless potential of the Otherworld from which it came. The ancient Celts looked west toward the *Morimarousa*, the primordial ocean that had, at the beginning of time, given birth to the solid land humans live on, and they expected the dead, in their return to the Otherworld, to journey at first into the dissolution of that sea. In the famous anecdote recounted by the sixth century chronicler Procopius, we are told that certain dwellers on the Atlantic Coast were expected to serve as ferrymen for the dead. Having been awakened at midnight by a mysterious summons, they would sail west with a load of invisible passengers. After a day and a night's sailing they would reach an island where the invisible throng would disembark (perceptibly lightening the boat), while a disembodied voice called out the names and lineages of the new arrivals. Irish tradition was consistent with this model: the dead were believed to initially seek out a group of small islands off the southwest coast of Ireland called *Teach Duinn* (the House of Donn), where Donn, one of the sons of Mil (the ancestors of the modern Gael), had met his death, thus turning himself into the God of the Dead, leader and host to all who would thereafter die in Ireland. After sojourning for a period in his domain, the dead would travel on to other parts of the Otherworld—the colorful and perilous regions described in texts like *Imram Maíl Dúin*—until (if such was their destiny) they were ready to return to the world.

Life and Death—*samos* and *giamos,* summer-experience and winter-experience—are alternating stages in the process of existence, necessary and complementary to each other, and their interplay affects everything that is in the universe. We see the same pattern at work in the lives of individual humans and in the cycle of the year. As the year begins again with its return to Darkness this is linked metaphorically with the concept of a living being's death (since both are reflections of the same archetypal event), and the same mythological vocabulary is used to imagine the Other-world influences operating on both occasions. Thus the year's plunge into winter is also a plunge into the deep seawaters of Death, and the cliff on which the waves of the western ocean beat also can be seen as the boundary between the year's Light half and its Dark half. The "noise of the sea," the reverberation of the *giamos*-ocean against that boundary, serves as a timely warning to us, like a temple-gong sounding to remind us of a spiritual duty implied by the change in season.

So the waxing of the "Cliff moon" should make us conscious of the necessity of the coming change, and urge us to prepare for the new situation that the triumph of *giamos* will entail. In practical terms, this means letting go: allowing the heightened energy of the *samos*-phase, which we have been drawing on constantly to fuel many activities at the conscious level, to slip out of our control and sink back into the formless depths of the ocean-womb, there to await rebirth at the proper time. Every year we experience this form of Death, and every year the forces of life triumph anew, justifying our trust in the cycle. The absence of light will, in the meantime, bring about new modes of consciousness appropriate to it, stressing memory and reflection over observation and action. Without such a period for reprocessing and reassimilating past experience, there could be no growth to a new stage.

As the moon waxes, we listen to the "noise of the sea" grow louder, indicating our approach to the boundary between Life and Death. With the *atenouxtion* we pass the boundary, and let go of our thirst for light and action. The ebbing of the moon leads us toward the heart of the darkness, where boundaries, no longer seen, at last dissolve from our consciousness, and we become permeable to the fertilizing potential of the Otherworld. Thus prepared, we open our-selves to the experience of *giamos*.

Welcome, Moon of the Cliff! The Year crosses the boundary between Light and Dark, the forces of growth will sleep on the seas of the Other-world. We, too, turn inward, to replenish our souls in the nourishing darkness beyond ourselves.

II. THE TIDE

(November 26–December 23)

Am tond trethan

Of the second month Amairgen sings, "I am an ocean wave." This is no longer the breaker crashing against the cliff, but a wave coursing free, a part of the vast, mysterious movements of the sea-realm. In Irish tradition the expression *thar naoi dtonn* (beyond nine waves) defines the point at which the fixed laws of the land must yield to the unpredictable fluidity of the Otherworld-ocean. The ocean wave, pulling away from shore, carries us to the remotest depths, to the mysterious House of Tethra where the Fomorian powers have their true home. It is a perilous place (any place that is perceived as being underwater is by definition hostile to air-breathing human visitors, unless they take special precautions!), but it is also the source of all fertility, the first link in the great chain of life, and if one journeys there one can find the vivifying power behind the death mask. At the end of his chant Amairgen asks, *"Cia beir buar o thig Tethrach?"* ("Who will bring cattle from the House of Tethra?") An old tradition has it that these are the stars rising out of the sea, but in the context of Amairgen's invocation they are obviously more than the physical stars in the sky. A bard like Amairgen who has journeyed into the darkness of the House of Tethra and returned will be able to conjure up life-nurturing images out of the unconscious, as surely as the stars rise out of the abyss every night on their wheeling path across the heavens. The *buar Tethrach* are the ultimate reward for those willing to risk themselves in the world beneath consciousness; and legends from all over the Celtic world that speak of magical cattle emerging from deep bodies of water are reflections of this motif.

During its darkest season, with the forces of growth stilled, the year can be said to sojourn in the House of Tethra. But in order to prepare for rebirth, negative memories of the past should not be projected on the darkness. Poisons must not be allowed to remain in the soil where the seeds will sprout. The wave that carries us away from the land to the dark depths must also wash away the taint of the past cycle from us, so that we may come to the womb of rebirth purified of all that constrained us.

With the rising of the new moon we attune ourselves to the power of the dark tide, we feel the strength of the wave carrying us out into uncharted regions; and throughout the waxing period we journey farther and farther into the depths of *giamos*, having stripped the moorings that held us to the past. On the *atenouxtion* we find ourselves in the House of Tethra; and the waning of the moon will be felt as the reversal of the tidal movement, pulling away from us all memories of failure and inadequacy, leaving us in the healing darkness without fear or regret.

Welcome, Moon of the Tide! Darkness has reached its peak, and sweeps away the vestiges of the past year. We sweep away all memories of past failures and prepare ourselves for new beginnings.

III. THE STAG

(December 23–January 20)

Am dam secht ndírend

Of the third month Amairgen sings, "I am a stag of seven tines." Some early scholars also translated this as "I am a bull of seven fights," since *dam* can just as easily mean an ox or a bull as a stag. However, since it is the stag and not the bull that is a part of the quaternity of symbolic animals we discussed in previous chapters—and which is clearly present in Amairgen's poem—we can safely assume that the first interpretation is the more likely. The term *dam* originally seems to have designated the bellicose nature of these animals, and was applied metaphorically to human warriors. In modern Irish speech *damh* is almost always restricted to the meaning "ox," so that its earlier association with struggle and victory has been lost.

The Stag is the first of the four sacred animals to be mentioned in Amairgen's enumeration. We have noted the close relationship that appears to exist between the Stag and the Boar: both are creatures of the Otherworld, who cross the boundaries between the worlds with ease, and often serve as messengers or guides across those boundaries. Just as a white boar led Pryderi into the Otherworld trap laid by Llwyd ap Cil Coed in the Third Branch of the Mabinogi, so does the hunt for the White Hart inaugurate the magical events in *Geraint ac Enid* (and its Continental counterpart, *Érec*). Together with this similarity in role we have, as we have seen, a complementarity: when one of them is associated with the "Day" half of existence, the other one is given to the "Night" half. Thus when, after Bealtaine, the Boar, enthroned in the Otherworld, becomes a solar animal endowed with poetic wisdom, the power of the Stag is bound to the green, growing earth below, even as the Cernunnos, beginning to grow antlers, is driven into the forests of our world. And after Samhain, when the Boar (now a Sow) wanders over the barren earth in the guise of the fearsome *Hwch Ddu Gwta*, the Stag is in the celestial realms as a luminous presence, bringing hope.

This latter guise of the Stag is a familiar one in folklore; many local legends (notably the ones associated with Saint Eustace and Saint Hubert) speak of a wondrous Stag with luminous antlers whose apparition brings a change for the better in human affairs. In the context that concerns us, he is a most appropriate messenger for the great change that is to take place after the Winter Solstice. Although the earth remains dark and fruitless, nights are still overwhelmingly longer than days, the light has begun—imperceptibly as yet—to grow. We are still in the abyss of the *giamos*-mode, but a spark glows before us, reminding us not to lose touch with the life force, for we are eventually to live in light again. The "stag of seven tines," who has been through many cycles of waxing and waning strength and always fought his way back to triumphant life, is a guide we can trust.

While the moon waxes, then, we contemplate light—not in association with any meaning or purpose, only the pure phenomenon of light as it shines beyond the darkness in which our spirits are now quiescent. On the occasion of the *atenouxtion* we focus on the image of the Stag himself: the luminous messenger, the archetypal Changer. And as the moon wanes his receding image gives the light a direction, so that we see it positioned inevitably in our future, and begin to regard it with hope.

Welcome, Moon of the Stag! The stag of the gods leaps out of the cold forest, a spark of sunlight shining between his antlers. We set our minds to follow the light as it grows and guides us through the dark time.

IV. THE FLOOD

(January 21–February 17)

Am loch i m-maig

Of the fourth month Amairgen sings: "I am a lake upon a plain." The Celts, like many other peoples, had a flood myth; and, as in many myths of this kind, the event is portrayed ambiguously, as both a disaster and a source of good things. All water—that is, the essence of fertility—belongs to the Fomorian divinities, who hoard it in the world below. No lakes or rivers would exist to irrigate the upper world if the water had not been made, by accident or design, to escape from the Fomorian realm. Almost always it is a female figure who is the catalyst of the event. Probably the most famous version of this myth in Celtic tradition is the Irish story of the Well of Segais. This well belonged to Nechtan (great nephew), whose name is cognate to the Latin *Neptunus* (Neptune was a god of springs before he came to be assimilated with the Greek Poseidon, thus turning into a sea-god) and generally refers back to an ancient Indo-European conception of the water-ruler as "Nephew of the Waters." Nechtan's well was overshadowed by the nine hazel trees of wisdom, whose nuts fell into the water and gave it the quality of divine illumination, much sought-after by the bards (the nuts were also eaten by the salmon in the pool, impregnating their flesh with the same quality). Only Nechtan and his three cupbearers Fleasc, Lamh, and Luamh were allowed to approach the well. Then the goddess Boann (*Bó-fhionn*, the White Cow) desired to drink from the well herself, to increase her power. She came to it secretly, but the well exploded at her unauthorized presence and flooded the land, eventually flowing to the sea in the shape of the river Boyne, in which the spirit of Boann would henceforth dwell. The same story was told about the origin of other rivers (notably the Shannon), but the Boyne was clearly conceived to be the chief and type of all rivers, and even, as *Drumchla Daimh Díle* (The Roof of the Floods), the actual *source* of all rivers in the world, so that the myth of its origin is to be viewed as the myth of the origin of all waters. And although on one level the story appears to end tragically for Boann, whose plan has back-fired, in reality she has assumed the nurturing, life-enhancing role of a Land-goddess favorable to the human Tribe. She seems to play the part of a female Prometheus, stealing vital treasures from the divine realm to make them accessible to mortals.

Since it is during this lunar period that the feast of Imbolc is cel-ebrated, and since Brigit is the very type of the Land-goddess whose energy also inspires the Tribe, it is fitting to consider her mythology beside that of the flood story and to observe the cross-references that become apparent. We have seen how, in Celtic tradition, the conjunc-tion of fire and water—two seemingly polar opposites—becomes the primary symbolic representation of fertility and healing. Brigit kindles the fire in the earth (and is also the life-giving power of the sun), but she is the keeper of the Land's water table as well, and sends the rivers and springs out on their nurturing mission. She is thus equally the mistress of Fire and Water, and derives her fertility-inducing properties from this fact. One also should note that the Vedic and Persian "Nephews of the Waters"—cognates of Nechtan from other Indo-European traditions—express this same idea of "fire in water." Appropriately, then, the largely fire-centered symbol-ism of Imbolc ritual (although, as we have seen, lustration plays a major role there, as well) will appear nestled within a period gov-erned by water imagery.

The last long stretch of winter metamorphosing into spring is usually a time of heavy rain and snow. As the lengthening days pro-vide longer periods of sunlight that prevent the frost from settling deep within the earth, this abundance of waters is allowed to seep into the soil, loosening its texture, readying it to nurture the slowly awakening plants. And indeed, shortly after this moon has waned away, we begin to see the first signs of the awakening: crocuses and daffodils pushing up through the thawing loam. Translating this into the terms of our inner world, we use the watery properties of this season to thaw out our spirits, coaxing them out of their winter-induced rigidity, preparing them for the *samos*-mode of growth and expansion.

So, as the moon waxes, we make ourselves aware of the gathering waters in the amorphous, dimensionless depths of the House of Tethra, and we feel their growing pressure against the barrier of the inert soil, their yearning for conscious manifestation. Playing the role of the goddess on the occasion of the *atenouxtion,* we boldly uncap the well that keeps the waters in the Fomorian realm, and watch them gush forth over the land. And, as the moon wanes, the "lake upon the plain" spreads out all around us, floating us up into the presence of the sky, mingling its waters with our spiritual faculties, making our minds fertile even as the Land that sustains us regains its fertility.

Welcome, Moon of the Flood! Rain and snow cover the land with water, hard earth will thaw into fertile mud where seeds can sprout. Any part of us that is frozen and refuses to grow must yield to the blessed dissolution of the Flood.

V. THE WIND

(February 18–March 17)

Am gaeth i m-muir

Of the fifth month Amairgen sings, "I am a wind over the sea." As the year moves toward the equinox, high winds are expected. The "mad March wind" blows away the dead leaves and twigs that clutter the surface of the land, exposing more of the soil to the growing light, but it has a mythological significance as well. In many cultures

the concept of Spirit is linked metaphorically with that of breath—
the Latin *spiritus,* for instance, and the Hebrew *ruach*, which in the
biblical account of the Creation "hovers over the waters"—and the
wind, which resembles a living being's breath, is interpreted as being
the breath of the great Power behind the entire natural world, and
thus also a manifestation of that Power's creative spirit. The Celts
shared this symbolic language (Old Celtic *anatlon,* breath, is clearly
related to *anatiâ,* soul), so that a strong gust of wind, in the terms of
Celtic myth, suggests an ensoulment, an infusion of creative potential. In the *Lebor Gabála* the Tuatha Dé Danann, who are the gods of
conscious creativity, suddenly appear in Ireland out of the air, on
wind-borne clouds. In the *Preiddeu Annwn* the Otherworld Cauldron of creativity is fanned (inspired) by the breath of nine maidens
(*o anadyl naw morwyn*) who are, as we have seen, the Goddess in her
ninefold manifestation.

Following the sequence of imagery in our list of moons, we find
that the "wind over the sea" follows logically after the bursting-forth
of the "lake over the plain." The waters have escaped the Fomorian
abyss, bringing the essence of fertility into the light of day, but they
are as yet inert, undirected by any purpose. Now the Spirit—the
Divine Wind—must breathe itself into their fertile potential, instilling in them the ideal of growth. In terms of our own subjective response to this point in the yearly cycle, we must allow our inner selves,
thawed and irrigated by the experience of the previous moon, to
open up to the gift of the Spirit. We are ready, now, to contemplate
future creativity, the resumption of conscious action.

As the moon waxes, we become aware of gathering winds, breathing out of those regions of the Otherworld where *samos*-energy has
its source. Chasing the dark clouds of March storms before them,
they are bringing with them the gods of consciousness and personality, the gods of manifest activity. With the *atenouxtion* we feel the
full blast of the wind upon us, we savor the life it breathes into us,
the power it confers upon us, so perfectly suited to the psychic vessels we have prepared. And as the moon wanes, we continue to draw
the Spirit in with our breath, gathering strength for our coming cycle
of work.

Welcome, Moon of the Wind! Strong winds blow over the desolate land, breathing life into the waters. We open ourselves to the Spirit, making ourselves instruments of creation.

VI. THE SUN-TEAR

(March 18–April 14)

Am dér gréne

Of the sixth month Amairgen sings, "I am a tear [or a drop] of the sun." Past the equinox, in the second half of the spring quarter, the invocation of fire that had played so prominent a role in the Imbolc ritual at last finds its fulfilment. Days become (almost imperceptibly at first) longer than nights, the sun's fire gathers strength, the earth begins to respond to its warmth, and though frost may recur intermittently, the growing light will not allow it to reestablish itself for long. Although the trees are still leafless, many of the hardier spring flowers are in bloom already, informing us that the Land is awake, that *samos*-energy has begun its work within.

As the earth has, in the preceding two months, been subjected to the magic of the elements water and air, it now receives the gift of fire. Water—the necessary medium of life—has spread itself over the land, then received direction and conscious purpose from the Spirit of the divine winds, and at last opens itself to the impassioned nurturing of the sun-flame. Fire-in-water is, as we have seen, the principal metaphor for healing, life-affirming energy in Celtic tradition. At this point in the year, fire comes to vivify the inert coolness of water, to turn potential life into actual life (at a later season water will be invoked to gentle the consuming excess of fire). To specify the friendly qualities of this fire it is presented to us in a watery form, a liquid drop, a tear fallen from the sun.

The divine figure who presides over this blending of energies is, of course, Brigit, whose season is the entire spring quarter. As goddess of the rivers, of the water table that gives the Land its fertility, and as goddess of the Sun (which, in Celtic tradition, is also a feature of the Land, since it rises out of the underworld every morning), she controls both powers and knows how to balance them. She also allies the water necessary to the growth of living things with the fire of the forge, which is needed for making things in the cultural realm, so that—as we remarked in the context of Imbolc ritual—the creative activities of Land and Tribe, when under her care, are seen to mirror each other and to grow together under the influence of *samos*-energy. Our minds—agents of the Tribe's purposes—are as kindled by the sun-fire as are the seeds asleep in the ground.

The newly-awakened shoots, breaking through the thawed earth in search of the sun, are like condensed versions—abbreviations—of the plants they will become when twig, leaf, and blossom have differentiated and taken on their destined forms in due season. So our creative projects must be made to exist in imaginative form—a blueprint for our purposes—before they can take the actual shape that the interplay of our will and the world's circumstances will finally produce. What we create must express our deepest desires, what our essential nature most truly craves, what will most genuinely mobilize our talents, and to discover this we must use the power of our imagination, the Cauldron on which the ninefold Goddess has breathed and which is now heated by the flame of the sun. We now make an effort to expose the dark regions where our dreams are born to the light of Day, to the *samos* principle, so that our desires can be revealed as images, which will then become focuses of creative activity.

As the moon waxes, we become sensitive to the growing light of the sun, we feel its comforting warmth seeping into our being—despite the continued assaults of the cold—in the form of a great drop of liquid fire. On the *atenouxtion* we let ourselves be completely illuminated by that fire, we invite its clarity into the darkest recesses of our souls, fearing nothing since Brigit protects us. And in the light of the waning moon we watch the liberated images rise up out of the Fomorian depths, ready to single out the ones that must be enfleshed in our work.

Welcome, Moon of the Sun-Tear! The first days of warm light break into the cold time, the earth is awake, young shoots strain towards the sun. We draw our dreams up into the light.

VII. THE HAWK

(April 15–May 12)

Am séig i n-aill

Of the seventh month Amairgen sings, "I am a hawk upon a cliff." The Hawk is the second of the four sacred animals to be mentioned in Amairgen's recitation. In other contexts it is usually stated to be an eagle, as in the stories of Fintan Mac Bóchra and Tuan Mac Cairill, but the Old Irish term *séig* seems to have denoted a variety of birds of prey, and probably included the eagle among them. Again we are faced with the Cliff, the boundary between the Light and Dark halves of the year, since during this month we cross that boundary again. But its character has changed: instead of the gloomy sea-cliff on which waves pound, looking out to the dark uncertainty of the winter ocean, it now leads to the safety of the fertile, sunlit land, and on it perches the hawk of awakened consciousness—like the hawk that Mael Dúin and his companions, sailing on the seas of the Otherworld, saw on one of the last islands they visited, and knew that they were close to their native Ireland.

Hawks appear in a variety of roles in Celtic tradition Brigit's son by Bress Mac Elathan is named Ruadhán (red one), which can also mean "kestrel" or "sparrowhawk." There may be more than meets the eye in the sparrowhawk offered as a knightly prize in *Geraint ac Enid*; but perhaps the most significant instance relates to the name of Gwalchmai (Hawk of May), one of Arthur's principal companions in Welsh tradition. Gwalchmai assists the hero Culhwch in winning the Flower Maiden Olwen away from her father the Hawthorn Giant in one of the best-known myths relating to this season, and it is evident from the Continental romances—where he is, of course, known as Gawain (perhaps from Cornish *Gwalghwynn* or Breton *Gwalc'hwenn,* white hawk)—that he was once the main protagonist of such quests. The "Hawk of May" is perceived as the final catalyst in the change from *giamos* to *samos*: it is his decisive, willed action that liberates the Land's growth-energy from its underground confinement and allows the busy, amorous season of summer to become manifest. Whether he is in fact the Maponos or not (as usual, Celtic tradition refuses to be categorical on such a point), he provides the initial thrust that will lead to the triumph of the Maponos.

We, too, feeling the power of this vast active presence sweeping through the Land (the *marc'hek glas*—the giant green knight of springtime—that Per-Jakez Hélias, in a famous poem, presents as a tradition of his grandmother's), begin to desire action. Having been gradually empowered, during our stay in the Goddess's cauldron-womb, with the essences of water, air, and fire, we are now complete, ready to break out of our protective shells and express our own wills. Following the Land's passage into the *samos*-mode, we now manifest outwardly the energies that we had been storing within ourselves.

As the moon waxes, we become conscious of the approaching Cliff, behind which is the Land, green and beckoning, ready to fulfill our desires. On top of the Cliff the Hawk of May waits, like a sentry and a beacon. With the *atenouxtion* we reach the Cliff and come face-to-face with the Hawk, identifying ourselves with him and taking on his boundless, striving energy. And as the moon wanes we follow him on his quest to free the Summer Maiden, journeying into greener and greener lands, letting ourselves be possessed with the spirit of adventure.

Greetings, Moon of the Hawk! The Herald of Summer is abroad in the land, buds swell and burst open, winter falls back. We become warrior-champions of the Light, opening the way for a joyous triumph in ourselves.

VIII. THE FLOWERS

(May 13–June 9)

Am cain lubai

Of the eighth month Amairgen sings, "I am a beautiful flower" [or "I am a beautiful one among flowers"]. The flower is, of course, the Summer Maiden, the form that the Land-goddess takes during the season that begins on Bealtaine. We have seen how, in the world of myth, she was given a body made of flowers, and we have ourselves assisted in creating that body ritually on our plane. The Lady of Fire-in-Water, the virginal creatrix, now transforms herself into the Bride, whose floral nature speaks of sexual union and fertility, since the beauty of flowers has a reproductive purpose. *Samos* triumphs as the Maponos unites with the Flower Maiden, and throughout the natural world their union is echoed as flowers bloom and birds nest, and the forest puts on its living, breathing canopy of green.

This month is, in many respects, the high point of the year, the long-awaited time of fulfillment. It is the Divine Pair's honeymoon, and something of a honeymoon for us as well, for we have no spiritual obligation in this season save to enjoy the vivifying power of triumphant *samos*. The Land takes on its most beautiful aspect, and the contemplation of that beauty both strengthens and inspires us, motivating our imagination with new forms. Right now we need only to *be*, to glory in the energy that fills us so perfectly: the time for concentrated action will return soon enough (the Flowers, one must note, can also refer to the medicinal plants that have begun to grow in this season, but are to be harvested next month).

As the moon waxes we make ourselves pleasantly aware of the vibrant green face the Land now wears, the countless flowers, so varied in shape and hue, blooming all around us, affirming the diversity and adaptability of life, and appealing to a craving for such diversity in our own experience. On the *atenouxtion* all this beauty and freshness come together in the shape of the Flower Maiden, to whom we can now relate personally as the source of the aesthetic and sensual pleasure that keeps us involved with the things of this world. And as the moon wanes our pleasure will not be waning, but we will let ourselves be carried, in a spirit of thankfulness, on the great green tide of growth, absorbing some of its energy as we go.

Welcome, Moon of the Flowers! Summer is come, the earth blooms, the world is green, birds build their nests. We become free in the pleasure of being.

IX. THE FIERY GOD

(June 10–July 7)

Am dé delbas do chind codnu

Of the ninth month Amairgen sings, "I am a god who sets the head on fire." Fire is indeed all around us in this season: the fire of the sun which has reached its peak, driving the night to its narrowest confinement, and the fires of the midsummer celebrations, shining through even that shortest of nights. And the magical element of Fire, whose growth has fueled the triumph of *samos*, has now arrived at the limits of its growth. Soon the Dark will begin to regain its lost territory, but it will be some time before its advance is really felt. For now it is the climax of the power of fire that concerns us, and how to best put to use its influence while it is so freely available. Since fire (in the magical sense) is essential to maintaining life and growth, we must find ways of internalizing the fire of the Sun, storing it in some inner recess where it can be invoked even when the fire without has begun to weaken. This turning-in is in itself the first manifestation of the dynamics of *giamos*; yet it will provide a source of energy to be applied in *samos*-related activity all through the Harvest season, when the Sun is in decline.

So we are, in this season, trying to "set ourselves on fire" from within, and using the power of the Sun in its triumph to achieve this. Yet there is another figure who, in Celtic tradition, gives a special meaning to "setting the head on fire" at this time of the year. This is, of course, the Cernunnos, who has been driven from the Goddess's embrace by the victory of the Maponos, and now resides in the surface manifestations of the Land itself, where he becomes one with its green outburst of *samos*-growth even as he undergoes his own *giamos*-period. No longer energized by his relationship with the Goddess, he must find another source of magical fire, and discovers it within himself, within those elements that reveal the continuity of his existence with that of the Land. That fire—depicted as the ram-headed serpent—coils up along the energy-channels of his body, gaining strength as it reaches each power-node—each *coire* (cauldron), as they are called in Irish—until it bursts forth at the crown of the head, manifesting as a great illumination, usually in the form of antlers, appropriate to the god's assumption of "animal" nature. It is also the final fruit of the promise of the Stag six months earlier, at the Winter Solstice.

If we wish to learn to draw fire from the Land and store it where it can vivify us even in the absence of the Sun, Cernunnos is a good model, for he is the perfect master of fire, holding it as confidently as he holds the fire-serpent on the Gundestrup Cauldron. In one of his manifestations, Derg Corra who appears in the story "Finn and the Man in the Tree," he is called an *úa Daighre*, a "descendant of fire."

As the moon waxes, we turn our attention to the sun's heat, making ourselves conscious of the ways in which we absorb it and make it a part of our inner constitution. On the *atenouxtion* we come face-to-face with the Cernunnos at the nadir of his rejection by the Goddess and at the zenith of his personal achievement, and we identify with his mastery, allowing him to "set our heads on fire." As the moon wanes we further internalize that Fire, making it secure at the centre of our selves, so that even in the coldest and darkest depths of *giamos* it will be able to guide us toward rebirth.

Welcome, Moon of the Fiery God! The Sun at full strength bathes the long days and short nights in heat. We draw the fullness of the light into ourselves.

X. THE SPEAR

(July 8–August 4)

Am gaí i fodb feras feochtu

Of the tenth month Amairgen sings, "I am a keen spear that pours forth battle." There now comes a discontinuity within the progress of the year, a massive reversal of energies in the Land as the role of *giamos* is reasserted, and especially a new phase in the relation between Tribe and Land. Until now, the Tribe has cooperated

wholeheartedly with the *samos*-forces of growth in the Land, direct-
ing that energy to the crops; but as Harvest nears, and thoughts turn
to reaping and gathering, different needs emerge, and growth must
be checked on many levels. Although the power of the Sun has
passed its peak and days are gradually growing shorter, its heat continues unabated, to the point where it may threaten the more delicate crops. Weeds proliferate in the heat, as do generations of ever
more numerous insects and rodents, posing further dangers to the
Harvest. It is as if the Sun, waning away from the prime of its life,
had cast a destructive shadow of itself on the world it had once
warmed with a friendly fire, retaining only the power to scorch and
oppress—which, in mythological terms, is expressed by the image of
Balor of the baneful eye. To implement the needs of the Tribe new
forces must be invoked in opposition to the dominant energy of
samos, which leads quite naturally to the metaphor of "battle," represented mythologically as the "War Among the Gods."

The prime symbol of this battle for the Harvest is the Spear, one
of the Four Treasures that the Tuatha Dé Danann brought with them
from the four Otherworld cities where they learned the arts of the
Tribe. The Spear came from Goirias, the Burning Fort, where it had
been guarded by the sage Esrus (whose name is presumably derived
from that of the biblical Ezra), and it was, appropriately, given to
Lugh, the master of all skills and the Lord of the Harvest. Whoever
held it was certain of victory. It is an ambiguous weapon, for it is itself fiery in nature, and seems originally to have had the Balorian
power to suppress the Land's fertility, as in the tale of the Dolorous
Blow; but in Lugh's hands it becomes a way of "fighting fire with
fire," for it turns into the thunderbolt, the messenger of the rains that
dispel the summer heat, one of the important images associated with
Lúghnasadh, as we have seen.

The Spear has its own message for our inner life. Where before it
was enough for us to simply accumulate energy and experience as
we rode on the waxing power of the year, now we must use that energy creatively, shaping it into something that can be shared with
others, and that will exist independently of us. We must begin to set
limits in order to avoid squandering the energy we have. And here

we may confidently follow Lugh's model—for, while the Fire of Brigit, dominant in the earlier part of the year, provides the raw inspiration for any human endeavor, Lugh is expert at focusing that fire and shaping it as an artist and craftsman would. As Goddess and God of the Tribe they form a cooperative pair, the Cauldron of the one coming to bubbling, creative life when it is touched by the Spear of the other.

As the moon waxes we see, coming from afar, the menacing shape of the Spear, surrounded by an aura of strife and unbalance, but also of adventure and the hope that comes with change. We steel ourselves to accept the change that its impact on our lives will bring. On the *atenouxtion* the Spear reaches us with its thunderbolt-power, but we now perceive the God who wields it, Lugh of the Long Arm, and we accept the guidance he offers us. The thundering fall of the Spear, as he casts it, releases the cooling, shaping *giamos*-water; and with the moon's waning we begin to focus the energy we have stored, surveying those areas within ourselves that must be prepared for the Harvest.

Welcome, Moon of the Spear! The Sun's power, struck down, begins to wane and days grow shorter, but the warm green earth continues to rejoice in its fertility. We are reminded that our joy must yield fruit before the Year ends.

XI. THE SALMON

(August 5–September 1)

Am he i l-lind

Of the eleventh month Amairgen sings, "I am a salmon in a pool." The Salmon is the third of the Four Sacred Animals to be named in Amairgen's chant. The pool in which it lies is, of course, the Well of Segais, the Otherworldly source of the Boyne, where Nechtan's fountain sprang up from the Fomorian depths. Six months ago we witnessed that upwelling as a part of the energies that impelled the waxing year; now, after the explosive birth of the river, the waters have settled down as a cooling, containing influence, soothing away the fiery wrath in the summer air, establishing the benign, inward-turning atmosphere of Harvest. The hazel trees that grow at the pool's rim mirror the ripening of nuts in our own world during this season. Nuts—sweet inside, but protected by a hard shell—are obvious symbols of wisdom, which is gained only through experience. The Salmon feeds on the nuts and absorbs the magical knowledge they contain into its own flesh, so that the wisdom is reproduced and passed on.

On our own plane, we realize that only the passage of time and the hindsight it provides will allow us to gain an understanding of the true value of our actions, as we work away at our personal Harvest. The experiences we had when the energy was fresh and high within us are ripening in our memory, and when intuition (*iomas,* the faculty achieved by Cernunnos, and his human counterpart Fionn) at last reveals to us the unique, Otherworld-designated significance it was intended to have for us, we are better able to put it into a form that will enable us to communicate it to others. Like the Salmon, we ingest the ripened fruits of life's lessons, and transmute it into our own nature; like Fionn, who ate the Salmon, others who, through personal contact or contact with our works, gain a deep knowledge of our nature will also gain the wisdom that our nature has come to contain.

As the moon waxes we let ourselves feel a gentle, persistent rain falling upon us out of the Otherworld, cooling and calming us, collecting around us as a pool of still water, inducing contemplation. On the *atenouxtion* we find ourselves in the mysterious, comfortable depths of the pool, where the Salmon feeds on the hazelnuts of the world's wisdom, and where we, too, can catch hold of the crystallized fruit of our experience. As the moon wanes we treasure and analyze this fruit, securing our Harvest.

Welcome, Moon of the Salmon! Nuts ripen on the trees, symbols of wisdom; and the harvest is ready in the fields. We reflect on our achievements, letting them ripen in our hearts.

XII. THE HILL OF THE BARDS

(September 2–September 30)

Am brí dánae

Of the twelfth month Amairgen sings, "I am a hill of skilled ones." The *aes dána,* or "people of skill" were, in early Irish society, all those who followed a creative path, especially those who attended bardic schools and learned to apply their skills to the service of a tradition. The tradition was enriched and made to progress through the bards' sharing of their works with each other, as they compared ideas and techniques and learned by emulating the more experienced creators. For this purpose they held regular assemblies, like the Welsh *eisteddfodau*, where new works were publicly recited, and then praised or criticized by those who were recognized masters in their field. Usually such assemblies were held during the Harvest season—most appropriately, since the *giamos*-related energies used to reap, distribute, and store the crops are similar to those that go into making public a finished work of art. The month-name *Cantlos* (song month) in the Coligny Calendar is thought by many to be an allusion to this custom.

So after our sojourn in the pool of contemplation we must raise ourselves up on the hill of public exchange to place our work before the general scrutiny of the Tribe. Even as all the living creatures in our environment are preparing for the coming triumph of *giamos,* either by storing food, by migrating to warmer regions, or by ensuring a viable posterity through winter-hardy seeds and eggs, so does the human Tribe imitate them, not only through the physical disposal of crops, but also on a spiritual level, by pooling the results of its members' creative activities, and thus storing food for the soul. Of course, there are many different types of creative activities in a human community, and many different ways in which their results can be shared—not necessarily through a formal presentation. However, if a circle does have members who have chosen to pursue poetry or the arts in a bardic spirit, it certainly would be a good idea for them to hold an assembly during this season to share and discuss new works.

As the moon waxes, we gather to ourselves all the things that we have learned well enough to articulate consciously, and we feel the urge to climb to a high place, to expose ourselves again to the wind that breathed the creative spirit into us six months ago: now we are ready to show the fruits of that creativity. On the *atenouxtion* we open ourselves to the wonder of sharing our innermost aspirations with others, savoring the thrill of oneness—made magically palpable by the light of the full moon—that the community enjoys as a result. And as the moon wanes we appreciate the new inner richness we have gained from the sharing.

Welcome, Moon of the Hill of the Bards! Birds are flying south to their wintering grounds, and bards journey forth to assemblies. It is time to share with others what we have made and learned.

XIII. THE BOAR

(October 1–October 29)

Am torc ar gail

Of the thirteenth and last month Amairgen sings, "I am a boar in battle-frenzy." The Boar is the last of the Four Sacred Animals to be mentioned by the poet. We have already seen it in many mythological settings, especially those that deal with the "hinge" of the year, the passage across the boundary between Light and Dark. In the Cosmic Boar Hunt the creature that represents the unending continuity of divine energy is chased from one realm of energy-manifestation to the other, causing the way it expresses its nature to change, becoming by turns a dark, chthonic being of destruction and a solar teacher. Even as the Stag—the Boar's counterpart in this symbolic scheme—turns, on Bealtaine, from the fiery-antlered apparition in the Otherworld to the earth-bound power at the heart of the greenwood, so the Boar, when the hunt on Samhain drives it down into the realms of darkness, becomes the harbinger of death, dragging all the powers at work in nature with it into that darkness. The Maponos, the green energy of *samos*, who led the hunt to triumph half a year earlier with the assistance of the Hawk of May, is now killed by the Boar as the hunt replays itself. *Giamos* is victorious, the forces of growth are stilled, soon the leaves will fall from the trees, and the lengthening nights will establish the rule of the Dark.

But the Boar's descent into the Underworld is not purely a journey of destruction: because it is basically, in spite of any other roles it may play, a creature of fertility, it plants, within Death itself, the seeds of renewal. In the Welsh tale of Coll ap Collfrewi's pursuit of Hen Wen, the Old White Sow, as told in the *Trioedd Ynys Prydein*, she leaves behind her in various locations, as fruits of her own body, gifts of bees, wheat, and cattle (not to mention eagles, wolves, and cats!), which will develop into prime resources of the countries that have received them. It is as though the single, driving force of growth manifest during *samos* had been smashed, but its many fragments retain life within themselves and, buried like seeds in winter soil, they will be nurtured by the darkness of *giamos* until the next bright season.

The weakening of the sun and the cooling of the air should alert us to the waning of our own *samos*-energies and the need to face the ending of this phase of our existence. The last of the energy must be used wisely, in a way that ensures the survival of what we have already made and that facilitates the resumption of activity (by ourselves or others) at a later time. Already, from far away, we hear the boom of the Otherworld sea on the cliffs of Samhain, calling us down again into the depths.

As the moon waxes, we see the wild hunt of Death charging toward us, lighting up the Land with bright autumnal colors in its throes, and we gather up those shreds of beauty to treasure in our souls. On the *atenouxtion* the hunt has reached us, we come face-to-face with the Boar, and we hold up the gift we have prepared, the shape we have chosen to best summarize what we have achieved through this year's activity. With the moon's waning we look serenely inwards, as another year ends, and a new cycle is about to begin.

Welcome, Moon of the Boar! As the Year nears its end, and the leaves take on their dying colors, the Boar of the gods is hunted through the land, leaving a gift of fertility at each center of power. Before we welcome back the Darkness we enrich the world with a gift from the Light.

This succession of representations of the lunar months—which also reflects symbolically the pattern of a human life—will, if observed ritually, enable us to make good use of the changing energies that manifest themselves as the Celtic Year unfolds, and also will further bind the members of a circle to each other and to the Land they dwell on. It also will root us deeper in the mythological soil of Celtic tradition.

CHAPTER FIVE

The Cycle of the Tribe

All rituals, no matter how universal their intent, exist within a specific cultural continuum defined by language, community identity, and that general sense of past experience we refer to as "tradition." It is, in fact, from their continuity with a background of tradition that rituals derive their power to successfully impress consciousness with new suggestions. This dependence on the past is not an impediment to be deplored, but a reality to use. Every culture—even imperial cultures, whose influence extends over vast territories—is a limited field with a structure determined by its specific past, and is not interchangeable with other cultures. If only one culture survived of the many thousands that human history has produced, such inherent limitations would be tragic indeed; but, fortunately, the plurality of surviving cultures continues to ensure a healthy diversity within the general field of human consciousness. So above all, each culture should, ideally, be concerned with the protection and growth of its own tradition, putting its resources to the best possible use, while recognizing and tolerating the "otherness" of its neighbors, since all are differently functioning components of a great whole. Many cultures have devised rituals to affirm and celebrate the specificity of their traditions, thus strengthening their sense of identity and continuity: usually these fall within the context of "national" holidays that make a community conscious of its own

254 THE APPLE BRANCH

character and particularisms. Our circle, rooted as it is in the specificity of Celtic culture, should make use of rituals that remind us of the concrete historical reality of Celtic communities, which remain the inexhaustible source of our tradition.

Of course, as we have noted before, this goes against the "internationalist" bias that, for two centuries at least, Western intellectual elites have come to see as progressive. But we have already pointed out that the supposed "universality" of the global culture that Western militarism and commerce have created is a lie, since, far from pooling together the riches of humanity's many cultures into one superior construct, it has in fact erased all those elements that made them uniquely vital and creative. Far from being more inclusive, it is actually much more exclusive than any of the small cultures it is annihilating, since it lacks all the subtle details of tradition that make small cultures able to fine-tune their responses to situations at very specific points in time and space—details of insight that can arise only out of the relationship between a limited, localized Tribe and its Land. However, one should bear in mind that cultures are not opaque fields, that participants in one cultural tradition are not, as individuals, necessarily bound by the limits of that tradition, but can learn to function within several other cultures as well—just as one can learn to play more than one musical instrument. Multiculturalism (like multilingualism, of which it is a corollary) is already an enriching reality for many people, and is the true key to that "globalism" that Western commercialism falsely claims to represent.

The feasts of the Tribe, unlike those we have discussed so far, are not derived from readily observable cycles of change within the Land, but from chance events in the community's history that have proved significant, in communal memory, to the Tribe's identity. In the context of the Celtic Tribe, several dates have been of particular importance to the national self-awareness of the Celtic countries. Because the six modern Celtic nations, when they began to coalesce about 1,500 years ago, owed much of their cohesion to the institutions that native Christianity established on their territories, those dates tend to commemorate Christian saints who, for the most part, were active during that period. Especially during the past two hundred years, these holidays have served to focus national pride and cultural identity, as well as political demands related to such matters. Céli Dé Circle incorporated such dates into its ritual Year, using them to strengthen its link with the historical reality of the Celtic Tribe.

The adoption of a Cycle of the Tribe—conceived in the above terms—into the ritual preoccupations of a Celtic circle is likely to meet with two principal kinds of objections. First, Neo-Pagans, who will be familiar with the two ritual cycles we discussed previously, but not with this one, may be tempted to reject it as too "Christian" in inspiration. To this we may reply, again, that Christianity is a major part of the Celtic heritage, and cannot be removed without seriously distorting the whole. But more importantly, these dates have, over the years, acquired an immense power directly related to the identity of Celtic communities—a great fountainhead of energy that can be tapped into profitably by a ritual group concerned with such issues. The actual use of the energy, the design of the rituals, need not have anything to do with "vernacular" manifestations of the holiday if these are not felt to be appropriate. Our circle's celebration of Saint Patrick's Day, for instance, need not be given over to green beer, plastic leprechauns, bogus blarney, public displays of drunkenness, and such commercialized images of "Irishness." One could, if one wished, ritually use the figure of Saint Patrick, in a way that emphasized positive aspects of Irish identity; but one could just as easily dispense with all of the feast's Catholic trappings and relate it to Ireland through completely different means, since the feast's great energy traditionally has been bound up with the expression of Irishness in general, not with the specific image of the saint.

The other objection, more subtle and deeply-rooted, has to do with the "political" nature of holidays associated with national identities—especially national identities that are, for the most part, not acknowledged by state powers. For many people, the idea of national liberation movements has come to be associated with very negative imagery, long abetted by state propaganda. Apart from an understandable fear of the state's powers of repression, there is behind such negative attitudes a sense that "political" matters are somehow coarse and undignified in comparison with "cultural" or "spiritual" concerns, and that they need have nothing to do with each other. Why should someone with a passion for ancient Celtic traditions and their expression in seasonal ritual be forced to an awareness of anything as mundane as election campaigns, education board meetings, rallies, and the like?

Yet such a rejection of all "political" involvement is, in the end, a refusal to deal with the real world, the world we share with other people. The political realm is not limited to the functioning of state institutions and the antics of professional politicians: all the things we do publicly, with the potential of influencing other people's opinions and decisions, are part of the political continuum. To speak a Celtic language, for instance, is a far-reaching political act, expressing a clear opposition to the attitudes that the state has fostered through its educational and cultural policies. To *learn* a Celtic language is even more powerfully political, since it enlarges the social base of the Celtic-language community and sends a message to the public that Celtic culture is valuable enough to be acquired by choice. Any involvement with Celtic literature or art, so long as it comes to the notice of others, reminds the world at large that the culture is not as dead as it is officially proclaimed to be.

Of course, the refusal to make a public impression with one's interest in things Celtic may in fact reflect a lack of faith in the value of the culture. Indeed, this is quite common: the idea that "it's all right for me, but . . . ," that it is a harmless private hobby that must be subordinated to "real" concerns. Sometimes people who have this attitude actually go very far in their exploration of Celtic language and traditions, creating an impression of real commitment. The giveaway is usually that they refuse to pass on the language and its heritage to their children, not wishing to "burden" them with a "useless" cultural identity. Their involvement with Celtic matters, it turns out, is conceived of in terms of fantasy and playacting, and they do not allow it to impinge on state-sanctioned "reality."

But we have already ruled out such sterile dilettantism for our Celtic circle. We must accept, then, that the mere fact of our maintaining a link with the living Celtic world has an inescapable political dimension. And since, if we are sincere about our commitment, we must earnestly wish for Celtic communities to survive, we should lend our support to that whole range of activities that strengthens the position of those communities in the political arena. This will include the mundane activities that are usually labeled "political," but the heritage that we have received has taught us that magic and prayer yield results, and our circle will quite naturally concentrate on those areas, which are no less "political" in effect when they are applied to situations in the "real" world.

As we have already noted, traditional Celtic communities today survive not as part of an undifferentiated "Celtic" identity, but within six national entities, each with a well-defined historical awareness of itself. Thus, our ritual connection with modern Celtic reality—even if we have no wish to limit the world of Celtic consciousness to the current territories of those nations—must deal primarily with the mythic dimensions of the six national traditions. If anything Celtic is to survive, the six nations must be made to retain and strengthen their identities. Certain symbols, certain dates—products of historical accident—are known to reinforce those identities, and should be used to that effect in our rituals; hence the importance of focusing on the well-known national holidays, as we have proposed.

How should our circle go about creating rituals for these holidays? One hesitates to provide guidelines that are too specific, since the tastes and resources of individual circles may vary considerably, and it would be unfortunate if our suggestions came to serve as barriers against much-needed creativity. We can, however, point to some paths that it would not be profitable to follow: for instance, an exclusive focus on the most familiar (and superficial) symbols of national identity, such as flags. Flags and banners can be very effective devices for summoning group feeling (as state propagandists have discovered time and time again), and they are also a genuine and interesting part of the heritage of national groups; but all too often sterile flag-waving is allowed to take the place of a deeper exploration of one's cultural identity. It is assumed that an emotional identification with the group-symbol is enough to make one an authentic member of the group, whatever the degree of one's participation in the group's culture. At the ugliest extreme, the projection of emotions onto the flag becomes an excuse to proclaim the group's superiority (and therefore, the superiority of each individual within it) over all outsiders, refusing them the human rights one grants to those within the group.

So, while it should certainly be our circle's privilege to use national or provincial flags in its rituals, we should make sure that they don't become the most indispensable, most powerfully charged symbols in our repertory; rather than promoting a fascist uniformity of feeling, they should be reflections of an interest in heraldry and vexillology, witnesses to the rich trove of incident in the nation's history.

One also should avoid including in the ritual any of the facile, sentimental literary expressions of nationalism—usually of quite recent vintage—that are so popular in ethnic communities, especially in the Celtic diaspora. Such songs and poems usually have been composed in imperial languages by individuals who had little or no acquaintance with the Celtic languages, and thus no access to the real vigor of native traditions. Again, they hold out the temptation to remain at the surface, to indulge in an easy, ephemeral moment of shared feeling, without bothering to research the more authentic—and far more deeply rooted—elements of the culture.

As usual, the Celtic languages, and the traditions they carry, will be our touchstone. We will, wherever possible, use the six languages, both in newly created material and in quotations from their existing literary heritage. For instance, when beginning a ritual according to the pattern presented in Chapter Two, we will, on the occasion of a national feast, use that nation's language exclusively in all the invocations. Poems or other texts from that language's literature should figure in the body of the ritual, particularly if they dramatize the relationship between Tribe and Land in that country. These need not be self-conscious statements of ethnic identity, but can include descriptions of landscapes, childhood memories of places, and the like, which are often more profoundly imaginative expressions of a people's link with the Land.

Poetry, music, and visual material, coordinated according to a circle's tastes and interests, should ideally lead into some sort of group meditation. The fruit of the meditation should be a more clearly realized communion with the spirit of the nation being celebrated. One possible starting point for such a meditation might be the visual symbol that is habitually used to represent the nation in the circle's ritual space. Rather than using that symbol to induce a knee-jerk "patriotic" reaction in participants, the circle leader will explore all the complexities of the image, linking it to important elements in the nation's past history and present situation. Once identification with that Land and its Tribe is complete, the ritual will turn to a focused outpouring of supportive energy: this may be achieved through chanting, movement, or any of the other means familiar to people with ritual experience.

The feasting that will ground the participants before the close of the ritual should, of course, also evoke the individual nation through its culinary tradition—another way circle members can exercise their skills and creativity! Thus all the components of the celebration will contribute to reminding the circle members of the unique national entity they are honoring and strengthening on that day.

Interspersed among the other festivals of the Celtic Year, then, we will have at least the six dates that are associated with the individual identities of the Celtic nations. But there is no reason, of course, to limit one's Cycle of the Tribe to those six occasions; as we stated earlier, any number of other dates, important to all the Celts or only to a particular circle, can be commemorated in this way. Céli Dé also celebrated June 9, *Lá Cholm Cille*—Saint Columba's Day—as a Pan-Celtic holiday, recalling the spiritual legacy of Iona as it affected the entire Celtic world. This is the only such Pan-Celtic date included here, but there are others that might be appropriate to observe: for instance, the *Dies Alliensis* (July 18), with its image of the defeat of Rome.

We will now examine the Tribal festivals in more detail, taking them in the order in which they appear in the Celtic Year.

Là Fhéill-Anndrais

(Saint Andrew's Day—Alba, NOVEMBER 30)

Alone among the Celtic countries, Scotland does not have the feast of a Celtic saint as its national holiday. How did Saint Andrew, one of Christ's first disciples and one of the Twelve Apostles, who was martyred, as tradition tells us, at Patras in Greece, come to be associated with a territory so far removed from the area where he spent his life? According to legend, it was as early as the fourth century, long before the final, decisive spread of Christianity into the Celtic lands, that a monk from Patras named Regulus was commanded by an angel to take some relics of Saint Andrew to the very limits of the known world, to what was then Pictland. Who, exactly, Regulus (whose name was later Gaelicized to Reaghul, "Rule") was, where he came from, and how he found himself traveling in such a wild northern land, cannot be known for certain; but it is most likely that he was one of the early Oriental missionaries who helped plant the seeds of monasticism in the Celtic world, preparing it for the flowering of its Second Golden Age. Some traditions have him accompany the earliest generation of British saints in their first attempts to evangelize the Picts. In any case, the shrine near Fife where Saint Rule deposited the relics of Saint Andrew came to be recognized as the oldest Christian establishment on the territory of Scotland, and as its fame grew it became the focus of pilgrimages—especially after the relics were credited with miraculously leading King Angus of Pictland to victory in 747. At the beginning of the fourteenth century, when Robert the Bruce was successfully consolidating Scotland against the threat of Anglo-Norman domination, Saint Andrews served as a rallying-point for nascent Scottish nationalism, providing it with an attractive origin myth, and popularizing the device of the saltire (the X-shaped cross on which, according to legend, Saint Andrew was crucified), which remains to this day one of the primary symbols of Scottish identity. Saint Andrews Day is still the focus of folk celebrations in some communities, attracting to itself various elements of early-winter ritual. A singed sheep's head is traditionally served on this feast, perhaps an echo of an earlier post-Samhain sacrifice.

Scotland's cultural heritage appears far more complex than that of any other Celtic nation. The Gaelic component of that heritage, brought across by Irish settlers (Scots) early in the sixth century, took permanent root in the West Highlands and in the Hebrides, even though, with the unification of the country under "Scottish" dynasties, Gaelic influence was felt everywhere. In the South, from Strathclyde to Edinburgh, the native culture was British (that is, Welsh-speaking) until it succumbed to the assaults of the Northumbrian kingdom and, deprived of a political base, abandoned its language for a northern dialect of English. The East Highlands were the stronghold of the Picts, and many of the sacred sites relating to the sovereignty of the Land in pre-Christian times were located there, later to be recognized and taken over by the Gaels. And in the extreme North, in the Orkneys and Caithness, the Viking invasions left behind some Norse-speaking settlements—indeed, during the early Middle Ages, the Danes controlled most of Scotland's seacoast, and established themselves securely in the Hebrides, even though the islands retained their Celtic culture. Rule by a single monarchy and a common opposition to English invasion eventually led these diverse ethnic strands to share one national consciousness—a consciousness that, despite all the outside influences, remained fundamentally Celtic, and expressed itself through the medium of Scottish Gaelic.

With the close of the Middle Ages, Scotland found itself drawn into the social and economic changes that all Europe was undergoing as feudalism crumbled. This led to a major split in Scottish society: an opposition between the Lowlanders, who quickly jettisoned their Celtic heritage in favor of an "international" culture that offered them greater economic opportunities, and the Highlanders, who remained faithful to the old ways. The Reformation, taking root first in the Lowlands, further aggravated the split. However, in contrast to the situation in other Celtic countries, where those elements of the population who adopted an imperial language were quickly drawn into the mainstream of the imperial culture, the Lowlanders did not shed their Scottish particularisms or, for that matter, their national consciousness. This is because, instead of acquiring the English of London, they had originally assimilated the northern dialect spoken along their border, which was different enough from the language of the English establishment that it could be considered a "native" particularism, without, nevertheless, seriously impeding communication with the centers of economic power farther south. By speaking Lallans or "Scots," the Lowlanders had created a buffer against their full assimilation by England, and continued to identify with Scotland.

This brings us to a potential problem in designing our rituals.

Even though we are committed to using Celtic languages, would it really be all that inappropriate to use Lallans in a ceremony dedicated to Scottish identity? After all, Lallans *is* a genuine part of the Scottish heritage, and has produced cultural artifacts that would be considered fundamentally Scottish by Lowlander and Highlander alike. Robert Burns looms very large in the literary consciousness of Scotland; would it be realistic to exclude him?

The question is a delicate one, with many worthy arguments pro and con. Yet, when all is said, we should continually bear in mind that ours is a *Celtic* circle, whose rituals invoke a *Celtic* Scotland. Not that Lallans-speaking culture has brought about an irreversible rift with the Celtic culture that preceded it, or that it is necessarily hostile to the Gaelic world (quite the contrary, in the case of twentieth-century writers); but, by its very nature, it remains at the periphery of the continuum of Celtic consciousness in Scotland. By giving Lallans too great a role, we risk distancing ourselves from that continuum. We should also remember that, whenever they are used together, imperial languages tend to displace Celtic languages. While Lallans is not an imperial language, it is far more accessible to English-speakers than Gaelic. To those who do not naturally speak Gaelic, Lallans will come across as a self-sufficient vehicle of "Scottishness." Our understanding of Gaelic culture, then, would extend no further back than to the generation of Burns and Scott, seeing the Highlands through the medium of tartan kitsch but ignoring the much more ancient wellsprings of the Highland heritage, which can be approached only through Gaelic. Since our circle's purpose is ,to renew contact with the energies of the First and Second Golden Ages of Celtic civilization, we have little choice, in the Scottish context, but to identify with the Gaelic tradition; the roots of Lallans-speaking culture simply don't go back far enough.

Creating our sacred space through the medium of Scots Gaelic, then, we will construct around us a representation of the Land in all its physical variety and its historical associations. We will center ourselves on the ancient royal sites in the heart of Pictland, inherited from prehistory: Sgàin, especially, where the famous "Stone of Scone," symbol of the Land-goddess, conferred sovereignty upon the legitimate rulers of unified Scotland. This is also the midland plain, one of

the few genuinely fertile regions in the land. To the west of us will
be the Gaelic stronghold of the Highlands and the Isles, a rough
country of deep glens; to the north, even bleaker uplands pierced by
lochs, more easily accessible by sea than by overland travel, a refuge
for sea-reivers, or pirates, and adventurers from Lochlann; to the east
and south, the industrious, populous Lowlands; and further south,
mountains rising up again, the Cheviot Hills sealing the land off from
its neighbors. We may choose to invoke the seven original provinces
(Angus, Atholl, Caithness, Fife, Mar, Moray, and Strathearn) that
were governed by *morairean* at the height of the Scottish kingdom in
the Middle Ages. Thus, we will have imagined a facsimile of the
Land's physical and spiritual geography to serve as a setting for our
ritual.

Now we must evoke the consciousness of the Tribe, its image of
itself, its memory of past history, its vision of the Land. Scots Gaelic
literature offers us a wealth of material: from Alasdair Mac Mhaighs-
dir Alasdair's delightfully hyperbolic praise-poem to the Gaelic language to Somhairle Mac-'Ill-Eathain's and Ruaraidh Mac Thomais'
modern evocations of ancestral landscapes. Beside the pride and
beauty, of course, there has been grievous suffering and injustice
which must be remembered constructively, rather than repressed and
allowed to fester: the tragedy of Culloden, and the worse betrayal of
the Clearances. Coordinating the words of bards from several centuries, we will reweave the colorful web of Scottish history, leading
into a meditation on the essential nature of Scotland itself.

The thistle (*cluaran, fòghnan*) is one of the best known symbols of
Scotland, and the one we have suggested to represent the northernmost Celtic country in the context of our circle ritual. We may, if we
choose, use it to focus our meditation. The original significance of
the thistle lay with the motto it was intended to illustrate ("None
shall harm me with impunity"), but there are other ways in which it
can evoke the Scottish identity. It grows well in poor soil, and with-
stands very rough weather. From the ruggedness of its surroundings
and its need to compete fiercely with other life-forms for survival it
has evolved a rough, defensive exterior, yet it produces a beautiful
flower. Starting from such obvious elements one can build a more
subtle, multifaceted meditation—indeed, it would be good if, rather

than adopting a standard format for the meditation on each national feast, the meditation were allowed to develop spontaneously in different directions year after year.

Having made ourselves imaginatively aware of the spirit of Scotland, we are now motivated to lend our energy to movements and factors that will ensure the survival of its culture. What magic we do at the climax of the ritual (and however we choose to do it) will be directed at Gaelic play-groups for children, at Gaelic education in the Gàidhealtachd, at the growth of Gaelic business universities like Sabhal Mór Ostaig, at economic projects aimed at strengthening the Highlands and keeping the people on the Land, but most of all at encouraging confidence and self-esteem among Gaelic-speakers, and allowing them to freely express the spirit of their culture.

Tha neart agus lùth ann an Albainn fhathast, ach chàidh am falach le breug-dealbhan dhith fhéin. Feumaidh sinn an fhìrinn uimpe a nochdadh a-rithisd, agus fìor-luach a cànaine a nochdadh do dhaoine.

Gwyl Dewi

(Saint David's Day—Cymru, MARCH 1)

Dewi (whose name was Christianized as "David") was recognized as the patron saint of Wales around the twelfth century. He was one of the disciples of Saint Illtud, that "good magician" (*bonus magus*) who, at the close of the fifth century, blended Celtic magic and Oriental asceticism into the unique phenomenon that was to become the Celtic monastic movement. From his original settlements in South Wales, hosts of his students spread out to found their own communities in other parts of Wales, in Cornwall and Brittany, and eventually in Ireland. Dewi established monasteries at Henllan (though some say his father had been the abbot there), and at Mynyw, which came to be known by his name and developed into one of the main spiritual centers of Christian Wales. He was also associated with Glastonbury, that extraordinary place of mysterious origins, which was to become so important in the religious consciousness of Britain. According to one tradition he had contacts with Egyptian monks, who may have inspired some of his more ascetic practices. Indeed, he acquired the nickname *aquaticus*, ostensibly because his followers drank only water (abstaining from alcohol, which was allowed in many other communities), but probably also because—following a practice that would prove popular in the Celtic world—he liked to meditate while standing immersed in cold water. He was one of the Celtic saints whose cult was recognized and encouraged by the Roman Church. Later in the Middle Ages, as Anglo-Norman influence began to creep into Wales (especially in the form of Church administration, which tended to see Britain as a single unit centered on Canterbury), the site of Saint Davids, now a bishopric, was made the focus of demands for Welsh autonomy, a Welsh see not subordinate to the English see. Thus Saint Dewi easily gained the preeminence that established him as the patron saint of the Welsh. There is also, however, an apocryphal story that explains the origin of the national holiday. In the year 630, on the saint's feast day, Cadwallon, King of the North Britons, fought the battle of Meicaren against King Edwin of Northumbria. To confuse the Welsh, the English dressed themselves in the same red jerkins (sleeveless jackets) that their enemies favored; but the Welsh gathered wild leeks that grew by a stream and wore them as badges, enabling them to distinguish friend from foe. From then on all true Welshmen have worn leeks on Saint David's Day; although in modern times this has often been replaced by a less odorous and more colorful plant, the daffodil, which begins to bloom around the time of the feast and is referred to as *cenhinen Bedr*, "Peter's leek." (One might, of course, point to the somewhat phallic appearance of the leek, and speculate about far more ancient reasons for its use in a spring festival!)

The Welsh originally thought of the entire island of Britain as their territory, but since the end of the seventh century they have been restricted to the region now known as Wales—bound by the sea on three sides, and on the eastern side by the historically well-attested but all-too-permeable border known as Offa's Dyke. We should, as we begin our ritual, become conscious of the physical characteristics of the Land known as Cymru. Its ancient sacred center lies between the sources of the Wye and the Severn: in the most ancient traditions this is called Gwrtheyrnion, the High King's land,

and it corresponds more or less to the old county of Brycheiniog, and part of Maldwyn; and there, at its western gate, stand the five peaks of Pumlumon, symbolizing the five outer provinces. To the northwest is Gwynedd, including the island sanctuary of the druids, *Môn Mam Cymru* (Anglesey Mother of Wales), the high land of Arfon, piling up into the great peak of Eryri, the "Eagle Land," where the great redeemer-heroes of the nation (including Arthur and Owain Glyn Dwr) sleep in hope of rebirth, and the mountains of Meirionydd are rich in lore and poets. To the northeast, Powys stretches out from the Berwyn hills around Llyn Mawddwy through the border country of Clwyd and, originally, out into territories that are now English, reminding us of the fierce battles this land once knew, and of the warrior-tradition it produced. Dyfed in the southwest is where Otherworld influences have most often touched the Land: from the Bay of Ceredigion where the lost land of Cantre'r Gwaelod lies beneath the waves, to the hill of Arberth where Pwyll had the wondrous adventure that led him to becoming the Master of the Otherworld himself. And in the southeast, Morgannwg and Gwent, though rich in ancient traditions, have borne the brunt of the onslaughts of the industrial revolution and have acquired teeming urban centers with large nonnative populations, and thus have lost much of their Celtic identity.

Although Welsh-speakers are already a minority in their own country, they remain a vocal and influential minority, and since no convincing expression of Welsh identity has emerged apart from the Welsh language, they are still the main focus of the national struggle. Thus the Welsh-language community is, because of its great vitality and creativity, one of the main sources of energy and inspiration for the entire Celtic world today. Yet despite all the signs of health, the situation in Wales is precarious, and its survival is far from assured. The uncontrolled influx of English-speakers is breaking up Celtic communities and driving Welsh out of the educational system, while the continual offensive of the Anglo-American media is (despite the development of fragile Welsh-language media) loosening the hold of *Y Pethe* ("The Things," that multifaceted compendium of symbols of Welsh identity, which range from the bardic poems of Taliesin to the Methodist hymns of Pantycelyn) on the consciousness of the population. Therefore, there is ample reason to send energy back to Wales, to help re-consolidate its spiritual autonomy and cultural self-assurance. Our ritual will attempt to recharge the symbols that give life to Wales, placing them in the context of their centuries-long development and tying them firmly to the modern situation.

Perhaps one of the most ambiguous phases in Welsh cultural history was the Methodist revival of the eighteenth century, and the resulting appearance of a "chapel culture" that dominated rural Welsh life until recently. On the one hand, the "chapel culture" strengthened Welsh communities and, by using the Welsh language as a medium, gave it a new relevance and arrested its decline. On the other hand, even though the language—and through it, the continuity with the long history of the culture—had been preserved, the Methodist doctrines, promoting a new start from a *tabula rasa*, encouraged people to disregard the life-giving elements inherited from the ancient past, restricting awareness of them to scholars and intellectuals. Saunders Lewis devoted much of his life to fighting this self-imposed narrowness of vision and to restoring to his countrymen some sense of the vibrancy and cosmopolitanism their culture had enjoyed during the Middle Ages. He struggled against enormous odds—his own verdict on his life's work was *Mi fethais yn llwyr* (I failed utterly)—yet the very fact that his writings remain a highly visible part of the Welsh heritage, still subject to controversy and reevaluation, provides us with a base from which to start our own struggle in the same direction. We, too, must manage to force our way past the Protestant blockage—not by denying it, for it has been an integral part of the Welsh experience, and cannot be simply cast aside, but by focusing on those aspects of the Methodist revival that gave rise to cultural manifestations of inspiring beauty, whose roots have echoes in deeper layers of the culture. Thus we can pass beyond it, through the sectarian doldrums of the seventeenth century to the humanist flowering engineered by William Salesbury and his colleagues in Tudor times, then further back to Owain Glyn Dwr's nearly successful campaign for Welsh independence, and the golden age of Welsh poetry—polished and witty poems of love and nature like Dafydd ap Gwilym's, and dense, mysterious pieces born of trance and initiatory secrets, like the material in the pseudo-Taliesin compendium—

and finally to the colorful, multiform, creative, devout, ritual-loving, "European" world of independent twelfth-century Wales, which was Saunders Lewis's delight. But we must go even further, to the early articulations of the Arthurian legend, with its cunning interweavings of Christian and pagan themes, and its attempts to preserve the ideology of the marriage of Tribe and Land; and further still to the age of the saints, the monastic founders who brought Christianity as a bright new dream to add to the already deep-rooted dreams of an ancient people; to the tentative, temporary marriage to Roman law and order, after the failure of Caradog's and Buddug's rebellions, and the terrible end of the druids in Mona; and beyond that, at last, to the First Golden Age, the source of all the dreams, the source of life-renewal, even for our time.

And, having communed with past ages through the extremely rich resources of Welsh literature, we must indeed return to the present to knot together all the strands of Welsh experience in a single form that expresses its will to endure. Again, there are literary works that may help us to that end, like Thomas Parry-Williams' extremely well-known (and still powerful) *Hon*, or Gwenallt's spiritual appraisals of the harsh lives of the Welsh *gwerin*, or portions of Bobi Jones's mesmerizing epic, *Hunllef Arthur*. Once we feel we are one with the history of Wales, we can begin our meditation on the nature of the energy that Welsh culture gives to the rest of the Celtic world.

The symbol we have chosen to stand for Wales in our rituals is the red dragon (*Y Ddraig Goch*), which appears on the Welsh flag and is universally recognized as Wales' national emblem. Its origins are unclear, but it resembles in form the griffon-like creatures that were common in the heraldry of the countries around the Black Sea in late antiquity; most likely it was a device on the banner of a Roman legion with Oriental antecedents stationed in Britain, perhaps even of the Sarmatian horsemen who, as some scholars have speculated, helped the historical Arthur beat back the invading English. In such circumstances it would have been quite natural for the device to become a symbol for the native Britons' will to survive; but it also mixed with older mythological traditions about dragons, and acquired new meanings. In the accounts given by Nennius and Geoffrey of Monmouth, the child Myrddin Emrys, said to have been born without a father, was brought before Vortigern to be sacrificed under the foundation of the High King's fortress, which until then would always collapse before it could be completed. But instead the supernatural child explained why the fortress could not stand, revealing two dragons locked in combat in the ground beneath it: a red dragon that stood for the Britons, and a white dragon that represented the English. The two beasts fought for supremacy over the spirit of the Land, but in time the red dragon (the sign of the victorious Arthur) would win. Even today, the red dragon struggles desperately against the white one, and will require the help of all those who care about her to prevail. We may, if we choose, use the figure of the red dragon to focus our consciousness on Wales, recognizing the intimate, deadly embrace in which England has held her all these centuries.

The energy we send should be made to benefit the Welsh language movement, legislative efforts to keep the Welsh in control of their land, the survival and growth of Welsh-language media increasingly out of the control of the English state, the preservation of Welsh education and, of course, a reawakening of deeper strata in Welsh consciousness, spiritually binding the Tribe to the Land.

Rhaid i ni gofio fod gan y gwareiddiad Cymreig wreiddiau dyfnach o lawer na'r Diwygiad Methodistaidd neu'r chwyldro diwydiannol. Enaid tir Prydain yw traddodiad yr iaith Gymraeg, ac mae gwaredigaeth y Cymry fel pobl yn dibynnu ar eu gallu i ddatguddio fynnhonellau'r enaid hon.

Goel Pyran

(*Saint Piran's Day—Kernow, MARCH 5*)

Pyran (Piran) is a mostly legendary figure, said to have come to Cornwall from Ireland in the fifth century, and early on confused (because of the similarity of the names, given the P/C alternation between Brythonic and Gaelic languages) with Saint Ciarán of Saighir. Fantastic accounts have him crossing the Irish Sea on a boat of stone. In reality, he was probably yet another one of the monastic founders contemporary to Saint Illtud in South Wales, and one of the first of the missionary pilgrims who were to range far and wide across the Celtic world seeking to share their spiritual passion. During the Middle Ages his chapel became a place of pilgrimage, and he was made the patron of tin miners, who celebrated his feast-day with much pageantry, drinking, and merriment. Because the tin mines were the main source of Cornwall's wealth, and the primary focus of the Cornish economy, the celebration of Saint Piran's Day eventually acquired a national character, drawing in all the rest of the population. Today the holiday definitely celebrates the distinctiveness of the Cornish nation, accentuating its separateness from England.

Although it is the second smallest of the Celtic countries, Cornwall has an importance in tradition quite disproportionate to its size. Because of the richness of its tin deposits it was visited regularly, since the very beginning of the Bronze Age, by prospectors and merchants from distant lands to the south, and thus became Celtic Britain's main window on the rest of the world. As the western Roman Empire dissolved and the old tribes reasserted themselves on their traditional territories, Cornwall (the territory of the Cornovii) became a part of the range of the Dumnonii, which also included Devon and many regions farther east, so that even after the English confined the local Celts to the lands west of the Tamar, many sites in the old West Country (like Glastonbury) retain a Celtic cultural aura that links them to Cornwall. Within this Dumnonian matrix many of the great myths of the Celtic Middle Ages had their source. Arthur, the supreme redeemer-hero, is said to have been born at Tintagel; and Tristan and Isolde, whose story introduced the entire Western world to a new concept of love, also began as a Cornish legend. So our ritual evocation of Cornwall will not be dealing with minor traditions from a marginal area, but will touch powerful themes that are very near the core of the Celtic consciousness.

Despite its small size and its east-west elongation, Cornwall is a physically varied land whose geography can be seen to more or less fit the Celtic idea of sacred space. Its sacred center is surely in the environs of Bodmin Moor, where a great number of megalithic structures testify to an intense ritual activity extending back to the remote, pre-Celtic past. To the northeast, stretching up along Devon to meet the Bristol Channel, is the old cantref (*kevran,* in Cornish) of

Trigg, where we find the ruins of Tintagel—the old Durocorno-vium, the fortress that guarded the approaches to Cornwall—birth-place of Arthur and, by extension, of the Dark Age resistance to English encroachment. South of there, along the Tamar, stretch the welcoming fields of Wivelshire, which has lost its Celtic name, and is now the main focus of the new English invasion, as the city of Plymouth, expanding across the border, threatens to swallow it. West of the rivers Camel and Fowey we find the two *kevranow* of Pydar (in the north) and Powder (in the south), sites of Saint Petroc's great monastery at Padstow (Lannwedhennek) and of the port of Saint Austell respectively. Finally, tapering off westward into the Atlantic, we have Kerrier and Penwith, with their memory of pirates and smugglers, land-spirits and mermaids, the world of the dead just be-yond Land's End. In this region ancient traditions have survived more easily; here the Cornish language held on to life longest.

Cornwall's greatest importance to the rest of the Celtic world lies in the very fact of its survival, its resistance to being crushed by its vast English neighbor, and especially the resurrection of its language from the dead—a great source of hope to all small cultures whose languages have been driven to extinction by imperial policies. As we attempt to evoke the spirit of Cornwall ritually we will have to turn to the language-revivalists—R. Morton Nance, Caradar, Talek, Edwin Chirgwin, Tim Saunders—for literary material to use. As in the case of Wales, though perhaps even more radically here, we face a cul-tural barrier in time raised up by the Methodist revival and the Industrial Revolution, obscuring much of the earlier Celtic tradi-tion. Some writers have even seen an irreconcilable opposition be-tween the "real Cornwall" of chapel choirs, rugby matches, and pasties, and the "tourist Cornwall" of Arthurian-Celtic legend artifi-cially sustained by artists and intellectuals. In reality, of course, the two strands of the heritage must be made to harmonize in order to restore its full depth to the cultural consciousness of Cornwall and retune it to the ancient patterns of the Land; increased use of the Cornish language is the best way to accomplish that.

The symbol we have been using to represent Cornwall is the chough (*palores*), the black bird with red bill and feet that once nested on cliffs all along the sea coast, but has now become rare. In

Cornish legend, when Arthur was mortally wounded at Camlann and taken away into the West by his magical kinswomen, his spirit assumed the shape of a chough (even as, in the Mabinogi, Lleu became an eagle). As long as choughs are seen in the land, there is hope that he may again, some day, become manifest in human form. We may think of this as a metaphor for Cornwall's own survival, the long years during which the language—and the culture it carried— was hidden away in an Otherworld of unread manuscripts, until the vision and courage of a few people began to manifest it in the world again. The complete restoration of the Cornish language would be, in a sense, a supreme magical act that would greatly benefit all other struggling language movements. The energy our ritual will raise must break through all the faction-fighting that has plagued the revival, strengthen it in unity, bringing closer the time when the reawakened Tribe can be wedded anew to its Land.

An yeth Kernewek o marow, hag a veu dasserghys; mes pur wann yw-hi hwath. Res yw dhyn ri meur a nerth dhedhi, bys dhe Gernow a-hys daskavoes hy spyrys.

Lá Fhéile Pádraig

(Saint Patrick's Day—Eire, MARCH 17)

There is no arguing that Saint Patrick has become the preeminent Irish saint, to the point of eclipsing the achievements of all other saints in Irish history. Yet this is a fairly recent development. Starting in the late seventh century, the Roman Church, eager to reestablish its hold over Irish Christian communities, began to strongly promote veneration of Patrick, who it saw as one of its own, a bishop of Roman lineage representing Roman authority. Ironically, the historical Patrick who evangelized Ireland in the fifth century had not been highly thought-of by his Roman superiors. A native of Cumbria, kidnapped by pirates and kept as a slave in Ireland, he eventually escaped to the Continent and pursued an ecclesiastical career in Gaul. When the fiery soldier-bishop Germanus of Auxerre was dispatched to Britain to deal with the Pelagian movement there,

Patrick accompanied him as part of his entourage. Clearly he was thought to be lukewarm in his opposition to Pelagianism; when Christians in Ireland requested that a bishop be sent to them, he was only the Church's second choice, despite his unique Irish experience, and was sent to Ireland only after the departure of his predecessor Palladius. He did not, as modern popular tradition suggests, singlehandedly bring Ireland to Christianity; he found many well-rooted Christian communities already there, and probably did not cover all of Ireland in his missionizing. He attempted to conform to local customs, going so far as to pay young warrior-aristocrats to accompany him on his travels, as status-conscious chieftains normally did. For this, as he tells us in his *Confessio*, he came under criticism from his hierarchy who, in their prejudice against him, were eager to interpret all his doings in a negative light. However, two hundred years later, after the dissolution of the Empire had weakened the Roman Church and left the Celtic Church free to develop its own strengths in happy independence, the Roman hierarchs were grasping at straws to convincingly legitimize their authority over the Celtic lands, and seized upon the figure of Patrick. Once the writers Muirchu and Tírechán had, by conflating the events recounted in Patrick's own *Confessio* with a variety of unrelated saint-legends, established the standard outline for the saint's official biography, the stage was set for the spectacular growth of his reputation throughout the Middle Ages. Paradoxically, however, despite his having been chosen as a vehicle for Roman authority, Patrick developed into an idealized model of native Celtic spirituality—heroic, adventurous, and filled with faith—simply because he had absorbed the stories of so many other saints who had exhibited those traits. And because those saints had absorbed the roles of many local deities, aspects of the older pagan heritage also came to be associated with Patrick's persona—as when, echoing the Lord of the Harvest who subdues the Fomorian dragon of the Land, he became, in some traditions, a dragon-slayer. This is certainly the origin of the bowdlerized modern story, which has him "driving the snakes out of Ireland" (the version according to which the "snakes" are really druids is, of course, a recent Neo-Pagan invention).

Aided by the Church's approval, Patrick's feast-day became an important holiday in Ireland very early. Because it was a spring festival, close to the actual date of the equinox, it came to be associated with some of the agricultural rituals of the season, and gave rise to a variety of folk customs. Crosses of cloth or ribbon would be sown onto a quartered paper or canvas circle, each of the quarters being colored yellow, blue, green, and red respectively, depicting the regions of sacred space and the movement of the sun through the year. Such crosses were worn throughout the day and were then saved as talismans for the rest of the year, much like the *crosóg Bríde* from Imbolc. One would also wear a shamrock in one's hat, much as the Welsh wore their leeks. Although modern tradition claims that Saint Patrick used this tripartite plant to explain the doctrine of the Trinity, it is evidently an expression of the Celtic pagan predilection for triadic statements. The original *seamair* or *seamróg* was probably the wood-sorrel (*seamair choille*), but more recently it has come to be identified with yellow clover (now usually called *seamróg*), although other kinds of clover were used locally, as well as black medick. At the end of the day the shamrock would be "drowned" in the *pota Phadraig*, the mug of whiskey which was drunk solemnly to close the feast; and, after the mug was drained the soaked leaves would, in some communities, be thrown over one's left shoulder, or, in others, would be eaten—"to sweeten the breath," according to the seventeenth-century English traveler Thomas Dineley.

As, from Tudor times on, the repression of the native Irish by their English overlords grew harsher, and the persecutions came to focus specifically on the conquered people's Catholic religion, Saint Patrick's Day and its traditions acquired greater importance as a manifestation of both religious and ethnic identity. The development of political nationalism in Ireland during the nineteenth century continued this trend, giving the feast more and more of a "national" character. In the Irish diaspora the holiday acquired even more importance as a badge of "Irishness," and gave rise to great mass public celebrations, often with political overtones—although it also yielded to the coarsest form of commercialism. Even today, despite the offensive, self-deprecating silliness that surrounds so many Saint Patrick's Day observances, it is still a time when consciousness of Irish identity is at an unparalleled high, not only among people of Irish descent, but also among their non-Irish neighbors as well. It is, thus, the best possible time to enhance magically the self-confidence and vigor of Irish culture. Though we may have come to dislike the holiday's boorish associations, it will be well worth while to choose this date for our circle's ritual interaction with the spirit of Ireland.

The bardic class of Ireland—the *filí*—preserved a wealth of ancient lore concerning places and their significance, so that the sacred geography of Ireland is very well documented, and is to some extent still a part of the consciousness of native Irish-speakers. We will have no trouble, then, conjuring up for ourselves the plain of Meath, where both the High King and the druids controlled the sacred power-centers of the whole island, and the Boyne Valley, with its royal tombs and vestiges of much more ancient, pre-Celtic ritual activity, remembered as the place where the Dagda (the "good god," lord of all Ireland) ruled with his consort the White Cow, the Sacred River. Then, Connaught in the west, with Cruachan in Roscommon as its own center, but oriented towards the Atlantic Coast rather than toward its own bleak interior, where nevertheless the tireless activity of druids and bards—and, later, Christian monks—created a tradition of learning and intellectual sophistication. Then, Ulster, centered on Eamhain Macha, famous for its warrior-tradition so vividly illustrated by the adventures of Cúchulainn and his contemporaries, a warrior-tradition that continues unabated, fueled by the tragic political situation in our time. Then, Leinster, in the fertile, populous east, centered on the now uncertain site of Carman, although the expansion of Dublin has created a new center, and largely de-Celticized this once lush and tradition-rich province. And finally, in the south, the mysterious entity of Munster, an Ireland-within-Ireland closer to the Otherworld realm of the Land-goddess, centered on its very own "Tara," Teamhair Luachra (although the royal dynasty of Munster later established itself at Caiseal), a place associated with women, sweetness, elegance, and fine music.

The immense wealth of native Irish literary tradition will make it easy for us to find texts illustrating the long, intricate tapestry of Irish history, from its mythological foundations, through the reigns of exemplary rulers like Niall and Conn, the adventures of the missionary-monks, the long struggle against the gnawing advance of

Anglo-Norman feudalism, the shock of plantation in Tudor and Stewart times, the humiliation of the Penal Laws, the death-blow of the Famine, the convulsive, heroic reaction of Easter 1916, to the desperate fight for survival today in the face of an indifferent, Anglicized bureaucracy. It is significant that so many great treasures of ancient historical lore are part of the cultural consciousness of most Irish-speakers, yet are quite unfamiliar to Irishmen who speak only English. Again, it is the Irish language which defines the continuity of Irish identity, although the traumatic events of the country's recent past have made most Irishmen almost pathologically incapable of understanding the role the language plays in defining Irish culture and ethnicity, and thus of appreciating the drastic consequences of its decline, or even squarely facing the reasons for that decline. This is the morbid cultural amnesia that Seán de Fréine has called "The Great Silence," and it is the single most dangerous factor working against the survival of Celtic Ireland. The Anglicized, middle-class Irish have no wish to be reminded that their ancestors spoke a different language and belonged to a different, downtrodden culture, and are content with Roman Catholicism as an expression of their identity—even though it is a Victorian Catholicism with no roots in Irish tradition. Our main priority, then, is to strengthen the Irish-language consciousness so that people can feel confident about its vitality.

The symbol that we have chosen to represent Ireland in our circle is the harp (*cruit, cláirseach*), which appears on the provincial banner of Leinster and also, of course, on the "green flag" that was used during the 1798 rebellion and became the most widely-known national banner of Ireland until the adoption of the modern tricolor in 1937. The harp is a musical instrument of African origin, especially associated with pre-Islamic Egypt, and was not known in the Celtic world until contacts between Irish and Oriental religious communities introduced it to Ireland, probably during the sixth century; but something about its overtone-rich, reverberating sound (the early harps were metal-strung) proved immensely attractive to Celtic musicians, and it quickly established itself at the very heart of the bardic tradition. Medieval documents provide ample evidence of the importance of harpers in pre-conquest Irish society. Harps spread to other Celtic countries, acquiring the same aura of Otherworldly lore and magical power; and even today, as Celtic music becomes a major resource in the Celtic revival, the harp remains the most "Celtic" of instruments, the one best suited to expressing the most distinctive qualities of Celtic inspiration. And one should note that, even in a Pan-Celtic context, the musical tradition of Ireland is widely perceived to take precedence over all others, so that musicians from the other Celtic countries are usually eager to include Irish pieces in their repertoire. We may, if we choose, focus our meditation on this peculiarly intense vitality of the Irish muse, the way in which Ireland can be said to be the "harp" of the Celtic world as a whole, providing all Celtic consciousness with a uniquely clear and meaningful vision of itself. Although it was already ancient when it came under the English yoke, Irish culture was not in any way spent or feeble; and the sheer expressive force of the Irish-language tradition can still astonish all those who come into contact with it.

But that tradition is now under the threat of death, dwindling in the face of indoctrination from the school system, the prejudice of the Anglicized middle class, the hypocrisy of the government, the continued impoverishment of the Gaeltacht, and the massive hemorrhage of emigration. Our ritual, then, must send energy to the last pockets of Irish society where the Irish language remains a vital presence, to those who still live in the *fíor-Ghaeltachtaí*, to the families who support Irish-language schools, to the young people who choose to express their aspirations in Irish despite the seductions of the Anglo-American mass media, and to the artists and writers who are still aware of the continuity of Irish culture and its deep roots. We must work to give native Irish-speakers economic incentives to stay in the Gaeltacht, and to give them adequate representation in the media, so that the sense of isolation and insecurity in which the Irish language finds itself today can be healed. It would be a grievous blow to the entire Celtic world if it were to suffer the death of the most persuasively vital of its members.

Is gá dúinn féinmheas agus féinmhuinín na nGael a chothú in aghaidh fórsaí na himpiriúlachta atá ag brú orthu. Is obair deacair, ollmhór é sin atá romhainn, ach ní mór dúinn tosnú leis gan mhoill.

Gouel Erwan

(Saint Yves' Day—Breizh, MAY 19)

Although Brittany has more than its share of saints from the Second Golden Age of the Celts, half-legendary figures like Gwennole and Tudual and Kaourentin and Paul Aurelian of Leon, it is an individual from much later in history who has so captured the affection of Bretons that they have made him their national saint. Yves Hélory of Kermartin, born around the middle of the twelfth century in Bro-Dreger, showed such intellectual promise that he was sent to study law in Paris and Orléans. On his return to Brittany he was appointed a diocesan judge, but also put his legal skills at the service of the poor and downtrodden, with a selfless generosity one does not usually associate with lawyers! The French, ever eager to make racist jokes at the Bretons' expense, later circulated the well-known jingle:

> *Sanctus Ivo erat Brito*
> *Advocatus et non latro*
> *Res miranda populo!*

(Saint Yves was a Breton who was a lawyer instead of being a thief: a source of wonder for the people!)

But the memory of his kindness and diligence remained among the Bretons, who continued to venerate him. The Church canonized him in 1347, giving his cult an official status. His name—rendered, according to region, as either *Ivez, Ivon, Youenn*, or *Erwan*—became one of the most common given names in all parts of the country. Although Breton communities have always given priority to the feast-days of their local saints and no single figure has gained unquestioned preeminence throughout Brittany, Saint Yves comes very close to being such a figure; and while his feast does not have quite the same obvious "national" associations as, say, Saint Patrick's Day, many Bretons do think of it in such terms, and it is thus a particularly good day to focus ritually on the destiny of Brittany as a Celtic nation.

Of all the Celtic countries, only Scotland rivals Brittany in its wealth of truly ancient traditions, going back to the wellsprings of Celtic culture in its Golden Ages. In fact, there are some other striking similarities between the two countries: both involve the political reunion of people of disparate origins, who have developed a common national identity through this historical association; and in both there exists a non-Celtic language—Lallans in Scotland, Gallo in Brittany—which is nevertheless felt to be a part of the national heritage. Just as Lallans resembles English while being quite distinct from it, thus creating a buffer between the Celtic and imperial cultures in its country, so is Gallo related to, but not identical with, French. It has not, however, given rise to a prestigious literature like Lallans, and does not come close to rivaling Breton as an expression of national identity. In our circle ritual we should treat it the same as Lallans: as an unquestionable part of its country's heritage, well worth preserving and cultivating in its own sphere, but not useable as an entry into *Celtic* tradition. Breton will, of course, be the exclusive language of our communication with the spirit of Brittany.

Following the pattern we have been using for all the feasts of the Tribe, we will invoke the physical reality of Brittany by placing ourselves imaginatively at its sacred center, roughly between the rivers Elorn, Aon, Oded, and Izol, the mysterious region containing the Black Mountains in its southern part and stretching north to the Menez-Arre, with its towering high point the Menez-Mikael, and to the Yeun Ellez, the marshland which has always been thought to be the entrance to the Underworld. From there we can look northwestward to Bro-Leon, traditionally the seat of learning, the place from which priests were said to come, and whose dialect has become the Breton standard; northward to Bro-Dreger, rich with memories of contacts with Britain and of struggles to maintain Breton independence in the uncertain, early days of the Middle Ages, and with the Menez-Bre, the mountain of bardic prophecy, rising up as a guardian on its southern border; southwestward to Bro-Gerne, the land of King Marc'h and Tristan, with the triple peak of the Menez-Hom, abode of a still-potent god, looming over the bay of Douarnenez where the drowned city of Ys lies, and past which the dead of Brittany must still sail to reach their abode in the West; southeastward to Bro-Gwened, a place famous for music and song, where spectacular stone alignments remind us of the pre-Celtic past, and where the goddess Ana is still fervently venerated under the new guise of Saint Anne; and northeastward to Bro-Sant-Malo, with its memories of corsairs and adventurous voyages on all the world's seas, and beyond it Bro-Dol, Brittany's original bishopric, the seat of Celtic Christian resistance to the demands of Rome. We can then look farther east, to lands that are now outside the Breton-speaking area but are still very important in the context of Breton history and identity: to Bro-Roazhon, the site of Rennes, Brittany's modern capital, very much in the French orbit but struggling to re-Celticize itself, and where the forest of Brekilien (the "Brocéliande" of the Arthurian romances) still shades Merlin's fountain of Barenton; and, across the marshy plain on the banks of the Loire, to Bro an Naoned, where Nantes, the old capital of the Breton dukes, stands with its fortified towers on Brittany's border. The French government has recently decided that Bro an Naoned is not in Brittany, but is part of an imaginary "Pays de Loire" region, thus depriving the land of one of its most symbolically charged areas; but all Celtophiles and lovers of Brittany must refuse to accept this amputation.

Literary sources will fuel our evocation of Breton history. Although early Breton literature has, tragically, been lost, modern writers have done a great deal to fill the gap and give a mythic dimension to the historical continuity of Breton culture. We can thus draw on the ballads of the *Barzaz-Breiz*, the mystical poems of Yann-Ber Kalloc'h, the multifaceted genius of Roparz Hemon, the verve and intensity of Jakez Riou, the simple but lofty spirituality of Maodez Glanndour. We will become aware of the prosperity and sophistication of ancient Armorica, cut off by Julius Caesar's conquest and genocide; then of its subsistence as an underpopulated backwater under Roman rule; of the massive immigration from Britain, bringing new blood; the struggle against Frankish hegemony, culminating with Nevenoe's victory over the Franks at Ballon; the new prosperity with independance during the Middle Ages, which was shattered once more as French expansion cut off Brittany's economic and cultural lifelines, until it was again anemic and provincial; and finally, the modern revival, which has regained some territory despite the ferocious opposition of the French state. Today, the Breton language still has no official status and no institutional support, the nationhood of Brittany is not even recognized, every facet of public life is designed to erode Breton identity. Against such odds, survival will require intense dedication and drastic methods.

The symbol that represents Brittany in our circle is the ermine (*erminig*). This was originally heraldic ermine (the stylized representation of ermine fur), which appears on the arms of the house of Blois, one of the last dynasties to rule Brittany; but at various times in their history, Bretons have identified with the actual animal as a symbol of their nation. In the song from the *Barzaz-Breiz* called *An Erminig*, the Breton ermine appears as a Brer Rabbit-like character, using its small size, cunning, and agility to negotiate a way between its large, dangerous neighbors, the French wolf and the English bull. In many ways it seems that it is just this ermine-spirit that is best suited to ensure Brittany's survival. One can see it at work, for instance, in Diwan, the Breton-language alternative school system, which continues to grow despite all the obstacles put in its way by the French government. We can meditate on the role this spirit has played and continues to play in the Breton struggle.

It is groups like Diwan that our working will seek to support, because they are trying to keep Bretons aware of their roots, which are found in the language that links them to the Land. That link is still strong, but the intransigence of the French state is doing its utmost to break it. All the magic that the Land of Brittany still holds must be mobilized and strengthened to withstand this final assault on its ability to manifest itself.

Douar Breizh he-deus gwizioù don, met n'heller ket o tizhout heb alc'hwez aour ar yezh. Arrabat da Vreizh koll he gwizioù dre goll he yezh.

Lá Cholm Cille

(Saint Columba's Day—Keltia, JUNE 9)

Céli Dé Circle decided that, as part of its Cycle of the Tribe, it needed a feast that celebrated the Celtic world as a whole. The day finally chosen was the feast of Saint Colm Cille, because of the Pan-Celtic resonance of his role, and because of the way he exemplifies the last great period of Celtic self-confidence and creativity. It was not, of course, the Saint Columba of modern scholarship, concerned mostly with the Irish politics of his time, that we wanted to cele-brate, but the magical, bardic Colm Cille who gave such impetus to the spiritual life of Celtic Christian communities, the Colm Cille we know from Adamnan's *Vita Columbae*, from the poems in the Book of Leinster, and from the oral traditions of both Ireland and Scot-land. This was the saint who cared for the trees in the sacred grove of Derry, who proclaimed that "Christ was his druid" (in a way that made clear his profound understanding of both Christian and druidical realities), who joyfully described his contemplation of the unspoiled beauty of the seashore. The spirit that speaks through his legend, and lives on in the many traditions associated with the com-munity of Iona, is a spirit that the Celtic world needs to reawaken in itself today. This, then, will be the purpose of our ritual on Colm Cille's feast.

(It should be mentioned in passing that *Là Chalm-chille* was an important event in the ritual Year of Gaelic Scotland. It was usually celebrated not on its historical date but on the Thursday of the sec-ond week in June—hence the expression *Daorn Chalm-chille* "Thurs-day of Colm Cille." A fire of ritually appropriate woods was used to toast a cake in which a silver coin had been hidden; the lucky recip-ient of the portion containing the coin would be given some lambs. Long and beautiful invocations—some of them preserved in the *Carmina Gadelica*—would be recited, calling down the protective magic of Colm's Day upon individual households.)

Céli Dé's observance of the feast primarily took the form of a meditation. As sacred space was established, Colm Cille was invoked in four guises, each expressing a function related to one of the four quarters. In the West, he was called upon as a bard, a guardian of the magical powers inherent in the literary traditions of the Celtic lan-guages; in the North, he was a prince, a member of a prestigious lin-eage with a responsibility for the defense of his people; in the East, he was a father, an abbot who was a just and tender provider for the many monks under his care; and in the South, he was a priest, one who dealt directly with the forces of the Otherworld. Once the circle was understood to be under his protection from all sides, the sacred space was identified with Iona, and became the focus of a guided meditation. Different circles may prefer to devise meditations specific to themselves, best suited to raising a Pan-Celtic energy in their members, but we will here, by way of an example, present Céli Dé's version.

We see ourselves, then, gathered together on Iona, a spiritual center of the Celtic world, still pulsating with the energy that was awakened there by Colm Cille's presence. We are aware of the symbols of the six Celtic nations placed around the altar area, and we now perceive them to be the actual territories of those nations, six lands, each with unique characteristics of its own, facing Iona from six directions. We may take the time to get a clear impression of the individuality of each land, perhaps associating it with a particular color or texture, or a particular intensity of vibration. We should at last be perceiving all six as living entities, capable of interacting with, and reacting to, us and each other.

We then return our attention to the center, where we have visualized the reality of Iona, and thus linked ourselves with it across space and time. Deep within it we find a vast store of power, and we begin to draw it up to the surface, until it rises skyward in our imagination as a pillar of blinding light. When it appears to be fountaining freely out of the depths, we divide it into six streams, and direct each one at one of the Celtic lands. The energy sinks into the soil, awakening the native energies there, providing spiritual nourishment to all beings that live on those lands. Then we reverse the movement: we make the newly replenished energy of each Celtic land fountain up in turn, until six separate streams, each with its own characteristic attributes, meet over the center and weave together a single pillar of life that descends to reenergize the heart of Iona.

We repeat this procedure as many times as we wish, modeling it after the inward and outward motion of our breath. Each repetition will increase the energy passing in either direction; and when it has reached a certain intensity we may wish to add new elements to the visualization. At the point where the six streams meet over Iona there will appear a figure representing the activities and aspirations of the

Tribe—most likely a God—while at the foot of the pillar of light, in the depths of Iona, we will become aware of a figure personalizing the mysterious, life-giving nature of the Land—most likely a Goddess. From this Land-figure six streams of fiery, chthonic power emerge in turn and journey through the depths until they connect with the hearts of the six lands. Now a circular motion can be introduced, capable of going in two directions: up from the heart of Iona and back toward it, or down to it and then away from it. Both should be exercised at length, until there is a consensus in the circle that enough has been done. Then, the energy should be allowed to sink back into the hearts of Iona and of the six lands, and left to the care of Colm Cille.

Whether or not we choose to associate it with Lá Cholm Cille, our circle needs a ritual that brings out and strengthens the organic links between the Celtic lands, placing them together around a center. Its historical importance and the all-embracing character of its sacredness, impressive to both Christian and Pagan alike, make Iona a good choice for such a center.

Laa Tynvaal

(Tynwald Day—Mannin, JULY 5)

Like Ireland, the Isle of Man has taken Saint Patrick for its patron saint. According to medieval legend, Patrick visited the island during his missionary travels and consecrated its first two bishops, Romulus and Conindrus. Certainly many sites on the island are associated with him, notably Saint Patrick's Isle, with its numerous vestiges of religious activity, both Christian and pre-Christian. His feast has been traditionally celebrated by the Manx as one of their principal national holidays. However, if we are to have a day for our circle to focus specifically on the Manx identity, Saint Patrick's Day would be a poor choice, since it is far more widely associated with an expression of Irishness. We need to find a date that commemorates something unique to Manx tradition. If we wished to maintain our pattern of medieval saints' feasts, we might consider Saint Maughold

(*Mac Caille*) who, according to legend, was a converted pirate who was sent by Saint Patrick to the Isle of Man, where he established its greatest monastery. His feast day is April 27; but, for all his importance in Manx tradition, this is not a date that all Manx people would recognize as significant for themselves, and thus, it would not mobilize much of the energy of "Manxness."

Céli Dé chose, for its Manx-centered ritual within the Cycle of the Tribe, the date of Tynwald Day, which is probably the most important yearly event specific to the Isle of Man. This is the day on which the Manx parliament meets publicly to promulgate the new laws passed during the preceding year, and part of the ceremony is still, by custom, conducted in the Manx language. Thus, it is the day on which the inhabitants of the island are made most aware of belonging to a distinct society with its own history, culture, and institutions, and provides a heightening of national awareness into which we can tap for our own ritual purpose. The name "Tynwald" itself is, in fact, Norse (*thingvöllr*, later Celticized as *tynvaal*), a reference to the parliament (*thing*) established by the Scandinavian overlords of the island after the Norse conquest of Man in the ninth century; but many elements of the ceremony suggest that this institution was superimposed over an existing Celtic one, and that it absorbed many of the traits of its predecessor. One can therefore claim that it is rooted in the Celtic consciousness of the island.

Although it is the smallest of the Celtic countries, the Isle of Man has a varied topography, with all the sacred centers and symbolic associations we expect in a territory inhabited by a Celtic people. At its center rises the peak of Snaefell (*Sniaul Dhoo*), associated with the ancient lord and guardian of the island, Manannán Mac Lir, who is thought to have a magic castle hidden in the mists on Barrule. We should place ourselves imaginatively on that highland, and look out on either side, northwestward and southeastward. On its western side, Man faces Ireland, the source of its cultural and spiritual heritage; on its eastern side, it faces Britain, the source of much of its material prosperity, but also of all threats to its Celtic identity. The land stretches from northeast to southwest, from the defensive rampart of Purt na h-Ayryn to the separate small island called the Calf of Man (*Yn Colloo*) which, like the southwestern regions of all Celtic countries, has Otherworld associations. All around is the sea, the way to the world of the gods and the dead, Manannán's realm.

We can then begin to evoke the long and complex history of the island. Unfortunately, there is not a great store of Manx literature to draw upon: whatever was written down during the Middle Ages has not survived, and in the modern period the language has been too much under the shadow of English to inspire great literary efforts. We do, nevertheless, have a certain number of folk songs old and new that can be used to illustrate various significant episodes in the story of the nation: one about Manannán, expressing the Celtic base of the culture's self-image; one about *yn ree Orree* (King Godred Covan, who founded the independent Norse-Manx state in the eleventh century), reminding us about the Norse experience on the island; the famous lament for Illiam Dhone Christian, the Manx rebel who wrested control of the island from its tyrannous overlords, the Stanleys, during the English Civil War, and was shot in 1663; songs about smuggling, maintaining Manx independence while outwitting the English; and many songs that simply express love for the island, but are nonetheless important for pointing up the bond that has always existed between Tribe and Land. Indeed, the bond must have been very strong to ensure the survival of the Manx identity on so small a territory through so many centuries of foreign rule, under the influence of so many alien cultures.

This will lead us to consider the trinacria, the symbol we have chosen to represent the Isle of Man in our circle. This is the motif of the three legs, joined together in triskell fashion, which appears on the Manx flag and is certainly the most familiar visual symbol of the Manx nation. It originally belongs to Sicilian-Norman heraldry, but it has obvious correspondences in Celtic tradition, so much so that in folklore it has come to be associated with Manannán himself, interpreted as the gods' own "three legs," which manifest his triple (i.e., all-embracing) nature. But there is a far more obvious significance to the trinacria, readily apparent from its very structure: "However you drop me, I stand." We cannot fail to notice a connection between this trait and the durability of the Manx identity. Our meditation may well use this concept as a point of departure, and build up a concern that this adaptability continue to protect the Manx under the far more dangerous conditions that prevail today.

The energy we raise in our working will be directed at those who are struggling to replace the control of the island's destiny in the hands of the native Manx, who are now outnumbered on their own land by wealthier and more powerful foreigners, drawn to the Isle of Man by its reputation as a tax haven—a situation created by the policies of the island's often greedy and irresponsible government. We should focus especially on those who are fighting to reestablish Manx as a community language; if they succeed, the resistance to assimilation will truly have a hard core to build upon. Its central location within the Celtic world and its many links with several of the other Celtic nations could eventually give the Isle of Man an important role in the Celtic revival.

Ga dy vel Ellan Vannin beg—yn çheer s'loo mastey ny çheeraghyn Celtiagh—cha nel eh gyn scansh. Shegin da ny Manninee—as dooin ooilley—obbyr dy creoi er-son mayrnaght nyn jengey.

In these early years of the twenty-first century many profound changes are taking place in our world, not all of them favorable to the survival of the human species. The power of the state (though still very great) is gradually being eroded, but not by positive forces; it is yielding to the power of vast multinational business concerns, as the inextricable interdependence of all national economies becomes ever more obvious. This poses an even greater threat to cultural diversity; the future may well fall into the hands of a few men with no spiritual or moral ideals higher than the short-term acquisition of money, and unable to value the Land they live on, or the human and other creatures they share the world with, except as instruments toward that end. All the spiritual and cultural traditions humanity has produced would be valued solely according to their short-term success on the mass market; and, of course, judged by such standards, most of them would be forced out of existence, depriving future generations of any cultural alternatives. Crowded into an ever narrower conceptual rut, the Anglo-American-world-capitalist culture would find itself increasingly incapable of dealing with the destructive consequences of its disregard of both environmental and social balance. In the end, we would certainly witness the end of all humane civilization, if not—a likely prospect, alas!—the extinction of the human species.

We are rapidly slipping down the path that leads to such a future, yet this does not mean that we cannot resist the trend. Indeed, we *must* resist it. We have a duty to each other and to the entire living reality of our planet to do all we can to prevent such a disaster. It will, of course, require a heroic effort, and a constant, outspoken rejection of our dominant culture's most basic assumptions. We must learn to change the way we see the world, place ourselves, by a shift in language and belief, outside our culture and inside another tradition with a more life-affirming worldview.

The Apple Branch is offered as a means, for all those who have ties with the Celtic world, to effect this inner transformation. It will be a difficult path to follow, especially at the beginning, subject to ridicule and misunderstanding, even on the part of those who have genuine links with Celtic tradition. It will, above all, require a romantic approach, and therefore a rejection of the mostly negative aura the term "romanticism" has acquired in modern thought. Romanticism is dismissed as a naive projection of human emotions and desires onto an essentially meaningless, purely material world; yet it should be realized that the unquestioned assumptions which determine how we live from day-to-day—that money is the ultimate value, for instance, and that all values should be subordinated to that central fact—are just as much 'irrational' projections of subjective beliefs. Why should not the human soul perceive itself as a true "native" of the universe, and feel that its hopes, needs, and desires are intimately related to the world's deep structure? Why should "alienation" be considered the only appropriate destiny of the human mind? And for that matter, on what objective grounds does our society judge that an aggressive, macho affirmation of personal power is more respectable and "realistic" than a passionate concern for the beauty and diversity of life?

The power of ritual, as we follow the cycle of the seasons, year after year, in cooperation with other small, Land-based cultures, may yet play its part in bringing about the global transformation we so desperately need—provided we use it with full awareness of the complex political and cultural situations in which we live and do not lose sight of other aspects of the struggle. Generations will pass, no doubt, before such a transformation happens, and our own vision of the path will undergo changes as conditions around us shift—as we strive to escape destruction by either the intrusive, worldwide capitalist networks or the death-throes of the states. Yet we can still hope that someday, before it is too late, humanity as a whole will shake off its materialist blindness and look, with wonder and shame, upon the divine beauty of the Land it has defiled. We have the power, even now, to make it come to pass.

APPENDIX

English Translation of Invocations

I turn toward the North, towards Finnias, the Shining-White Fort, the Fort of the Mighty, the Fort of the Heroes, the Fort of the Spirits of Bravery, the Fort out of which comes all defense and hardihood. Home to the Lord of Victories, the Lord of Conflicts, the Lord who has power over all force and strength, whose is the Sword, the Sword that will not suffer defeat, the Sword that will not allow a loss, the Sword that answers to the Great King, and whose is the Eagle, the sharp-eyed Eagle, the heavy taloned Eagle, the hard-beaked Eagle, the broad-winged Eagle on the Winds of Heaven, O Champion, O Hero, O Brave One, O Strong One—(come tonight).

I turn toward the East, toward Morwys (a fanciful transliteration of Muirias), Ford of the Sea, Fort of the Fruitful Ones, Fort of the Beautiful Ones, Fort of the Nurturing Ones, Fort of the Ones who work to feed the earth, Home to the Lord of Riches, the Lord of birth, the Lord of growth, the Lord of blossoming and harvest, the Lord of gathering and sharing, the fat Lord of all good things, the one who has the Cauldron that gave life, the full Cauldron, the Cauldron that shall never be empty. Shelter for the salmon, the red-fleshed Salmon, the round-bodied Salmon, the Salmon from the Deep Water, the Salmon from the Fountain where the Goddess gives birth. O Abounding One, O Productive One, O Nourishing One—(come tonight).

I turn toward the South, toward Gwaloues (a fanciful Breton transliteration of Failias), the Fort of Fate, the Fort of the Wise Ones, the Fort of the Hidden Ones, the Fort of the Secret Ones, the Fort that is close to the roots of the earth, Home to the Great Lady, Lady of the Night, Lady of the Power, Lady of Authority, Lady of Winter and Summer, Who has with her the Stone, the Stone of Prophesy, the Stone of Inspiration, the Stone of Certain Choice, (giamos) Origin of the Boar, the wild Boar, the Heavy Boar, the Boar from the Hollow Hills, the Boar who is the Messenger of the Deep, (samos) Origin of the Stag, the Stag of the Twilight, the Stag of the Hidden paths, the Stag in the Sacred Forest, the Stag who leads to the World of the Dead. O Mystery, O Successor, O Beauty—(come tonight).

I turn toward the West, toward Goirias, The Fiery City, the Fort of Light, the Fort of Heat, the Fort of Knowledge, the Fort of Agility of Mind, the Home to the Many-Gifted Lord, Lord of the Sages and Poets, Lord of the Druids and the Saints, Lord of the Craftsmen and the Wrights, Whose is the Spear, the Spear that pierces the clouds, the Spear that destroys darkness, the Spear that brings victory over matter, (giamos) And whose is the Stag, the stately Stag, the Deer that is not afraid, the Stag who put the light of the Sun into his antlers, (samos) And whose is the Boar, the Boar of the Sun, the Boar of Learning, the Boar who resurrects from his own blood, O Bright-White One, O Radiant One, O Knowing One—(come tonight).

SELECTED BIBLIOGRAPHY

I. History and Archaeology

The Early Period

Brunaux, Jean Louis. *Les Gaulois: Sanctuaires et rites.* Paris: Errance, 1986.

Chadwick, Nora. *The Celts.* Harmondsworth: Pelican, 1971.

Cunliffe, Barry. *The Ancient Celts.* Oxford & New York: Oxford University Press, 1997.

Duval, Paul-Marie. *Les Dieux de la Gaule.* Paris: P.U.F., 1957.

Ellis, Peter Berresford. *Celtic Inheritance.* London: Muller, 1985.

Ferguson, John. *Pelagius.* Cambridge: W. Heffer & Sons, Ltd., 1956.

Green, Miranda. *The Gods of the Celts.* Glouchester: Alan Sutton, 1986.

———. *Symbol and Image in Celtic Religious Art.* London: Routledge, 1989.

———. *Celtic Goddesses: Mothers, Virgins and Warriors.* London: George Braziller, 1995.

Hughes, Kathleen and Ann Hamlin. *Monasticism.* New York: Seabury, 1981.

James, Simon. *The World of the Celts.* London: Thames & Hudson, 1993.

Kruta, Venceslas. *The Celts of the West.* Translated by Alan Sheridan. London: Orbis, 1985.

Loyer, Oliver. *Les Chretientes Celtiques.* Paris: P.U.F., 1965.

Macneill, Eoin. *Celtic Ireland.* Dublin: Academy Press, 1921.

Moscati (coord.), Frey, Kruta, Raftery and Szabo, eds. *The Celts.* Venice: Rizzoli, 1991.

Marnell, William. *Light From the West: The Irish Mission and the Emergence of Modern Europe.* New York: Seabury, 1978.

Powell, T.G.E. *The Celts.* London: Praeger, 1958.

Raftery, Barry. *Pagan Celtic Ireland*. London: Thames & Hudson, 1994.

Ross, Anne. *Pagan Celtic Britain*. London and New York: Routledge and Columbia University Press, 1976.

Ross, Anne. *The Pagan Celts*. Totowa, NJ: Barnes & Noble, 1986.

O'Dwyer, Peter. *Céli Dé: Spiritual Reform in Ireland 750–900*. Dublin: Taillura, 1981.

Thomas, Charles. *Celtic Britain*. London: Thames & Hudson, 1986.

Warren, F.E., Edited by Jane Stevenson. *The Liturgy and Ritual of the Celtic Church*. Woodbridge, Suffolk; Wolfeboro, NH: Boydell Press, 1987.

Webster, Graham. *Celtic Religion in Roman Britain*. Totowa, NJ: Barnes & Noble Books, 1987.

More Recent Movements

Ellis, Peter Berresford. *The Celtic Revolution*. Talybont, Ceredigion: YLofa, 1988.

Ellis, Peter Berresford. *The Celtic Dawn*. London : Constable, 1995.

Lewis, Ceri. *Iolo Morganwg*. Caernarfon: Gwasg Pantycelyn, 1995.

II. Mythology and Literature

Campbell, J.E. *Popular Tales of the West Highlands*. Hounslow: Wildwood House, 1983 (1860).

Carney, James. *Medieval Irish Lyrics*. Berkleley, CA: University of California Press, 1967.

Cath Maige Tuired. Edited by E.A. Gray. Dublin: Dublin Institute of Advanced Studies, 1982.

Culhwch ac Olwen. Edited by Rachel Bromwick and D. Simon Evans. Cardiff: University of Wales, 1988.

Cyfranc Lludd a Llefelys. Edited by Brynley E. Roberts. Dublin: Dublin Institute of Advanced Studies, 1975.

Davidson, H.R. Ellis. *Myths and Symbols in Pagan Europe*. Syracuse: Syracuse University Press, 1987.

De Vries, Jan. *Keltische Religion*. Stuttgart: V. Kohlhammer Verlag, 1960.

Ellis, Peter Berresford. *The Cornish Language and Its Literature.* London & Boston: Routledge and Keegan Paul, 1974.

Jackson, Kenneth Hurlstone. *A Celtic Miscellany: Translations From the Celtic Literatures.* London: Routledge, 1951.

Lebor Gabala Erenn 1–5. Edited by R.A.S. Macalister. Dublin: Irish Texts Society, 1938–1941, 1956.

Le Roux, Francoise, *Les Druides.* Paris, P.U.F. 1961.

Llyfr Du Caerfyrddin. Edited by A.O. H. Jarman. Cardiff: University of Wales Press, 1982.

Llyfr Gwyn Rhydderch. Edited by J. Gwenogfryn Evans. Cardiff: University of Wales Press, 1973 (1901).

MacCana, Proinsias. *Celtic Mythology.* Feltham: Hamlyn, 1967.

Matthews, Caitlin. *Mabon and the Mysteries of Britain.* London & New York: Penguin, Arkana, 1989.

———. *Arthur and the Sovereignty of Britain.* London & New York: Penguin Arcana, 1989.

O Hogain, Daithi. *Myth, Legend and Romance: An Encyclopedia of the Irish Folk Tradition.* New York & London: Prentice Hall Press, 1991.

O Tuama, Sean. *An Duanaire 1600–1900: Poems of the dispossessed.* Verse edited and translated by Thomas Kinsella Portlaoise: Dolmen Press, 1981.

Parry, Thomas. *Hanes Llenyddiaeth Gymraeg hyd 1900.* Cardiff: University of Wales Press, 1970 (1946).

Pedeir Keinc y Mabinogi. Edited by I for Williams. Cardiff: University of Wales Press, 1930.

Rees, Alwyn and Brinley. *Celtic Heritage: Ancient Tradition in Ireland and Wales.* New York: Grove Press, 1961.

Sjoestedt, Marie-Louise. *Gods and Heroes of the Celts.* Translated by Myles Dillon. Berkeley: Turtle Island, 1982 (1949).

Trioedd Ynys Prydein. Edited by Rachel Bromwich. Cardiff: University of Wales Press, 1978.

Watson, William J. Bardachd Ghaidhlig: *Gaelic Poetry 1550–1900.* Inverness: An Comunn Gaidhealach, 1976 (1918).

Williams, J.E. Caerwyn and Mairin Ni Mhuiriosa. *Tradisiun Liteartha na nGael.* Dublin: An Clochombar, 1979.

III. Folk Tradition

Courtney, Margaret Ann. *Cornish Feasts and Folklore.* Exeter: Cornwall Books, 1984 (1890).

Danaher, Kevin. *The Year in Ireland.* Cork: Mercier, 1972.

Ganachaud, Guy. *Almanach des traditions bretonnes.* Rennes: Ouest-France, 1984.

Griffiths, Kate Bosse. *Byd y Dyn Hysbys.* Talybont: YLofa, 1977.

Jenkin, A. K. Hamilton. *Cornwall and the Cornish.* London: J.M. Dent, 1933.

Le Scouezec, Gwenc'hlan. *Bretagne, Terre Sacree.* Paris: Albatros, 1977.

Mac Neill, Maire. *The Festival of Lughnasa.* Oxford: Oxford University Press, 1962.

McNeill, F. Marian. *The Silver Bough.* Glasgow: W. Maclellan, 1966.

Moore, A. W. *The Folk-Lore of the Isle of Man.* Llanerch: Felinfach, 1994 (1891).

O Duinn, Sean. *Orthaí Cosanta sa Chráifeacht Cheilteach.* Maynooth: An Sagart, 1990.

Owen, Trevor M. *Welsh Folk Customs.* Cardiff: National Museum of Wales, 1959.

Owen, Trevor M. *The Customs and Traditions of Wales.* Cardiff: University of Wales Press, 1991.

Sebillot, Pierre-Yves. *Le Folklore de la Bretagne.* Paris: G.P. Maisonneuve & Larose, 1968.

INDEX

Otherworld (*cont.*)
  owl in, 174
  Samhain feast and, 114–15, 191
  Southwest and, 85
  Stag and Boar in, 234, 250–51
  Summer Solstice and, 190–91
  time in, 104
  Wales and, 266
  weasel in, 174
  Winter Solstice and, 144
Owain Glyn Dwr, 34, 266, 267
Owen, Trefor M., 165
Owl, symbolism of, 171, 174
oystercatcher, 150

Palm Sunday, 164
Pan-Celticism, 50, 61–69, 87–88, 277
  Lá Cholm Cille feast and, 100–101, 259,
    281–84
Pantycelyn, 266
Parry-Williams, Thomas, 268
Patagonia, 42
Patrick, Saint, 21, 100–101, 272–73, 284
Paul Aurelian of Leon, 278
Pearse, Patrick, 47
Pedeir Keinc, 133
Pelagianism, 21, 272–73
Pelagius, 20–21
Penal Laws, 37, 41
Pennant, Thomas, 179
Percival, 178
Peredur, 80, 178
Perrot, Father Yann, 48
Petroc, Saint, 271
Petronius Turpilianus, 17
phallic symbolism, 177, 213
Pictland, 260, 261, 262–63
Picts, 30
Piran (Pyran), Saint, 100, 269–70
piseoga, 120–21
Planxty, 50
Plato, 33
Pliny the Elder, 222
Plutarch, 13–14
poetry and epics. *See also* bards; Celtic
    literature; mythology, Celtic
  revival of, 44–45
  written, 32
politics, Tribe and, 46–47, 56, 72, 255–57,
    274–75

Prasutagus, King of the Iceni, 16
Preiddeu Annwn, 201, 238
processions
  at Christmas/Winter Solstice, 134–38
  at Imbolc, 153, 161
  at Samhain, 118
  at Summer Solstice, 190
Procopius, 230
Protestantism, 36–37, 40–41, 62–63
Pryderi, 133, 136–38, 142, 144–45, 201,
    234
psychodynamic techniques, 79
Punic Wars, 9–10
Pwyll, 106, 136, 173, 266
Pyran, Saint. *See* Piran (Pyran), Saint

Quakerism, 40

Raven, symbolism of, 197
Reformation, 36–37, 261
Rheged, 25
Rhiannon, 106, 133, 136–38, 142, 144,
    173, 201
rhibo game, 205, 208
Rhuddlan, Statute of, 34
Rhydderch Hael, 107
Riou, Jakez, 280
Robert the Bruce, 260
Roman Church. *See also* Christianity
  Celtic community and, 62–63, 72
  Celtic saints of, 265
  growth of, 26–31
  in Ireland, 31, 36, 41–42, 47, 272–74,
    276
  in Scotland, 39
  state and, 29–31, 32
  suppression of Galician culture, 26
Roman Empire
  army of, 10, 12, 16
  atrocities and massacres of, 12, 13, 16,
    17, 280
  battles with Celts, 9–17
  collapse of, 19–21
  social institutions of, 9
  toleration of Celtic religion, 18
romanticism, 288
Rome, Celtic defeat of, 3, 9, 11, 259
Rome, Visigothic sack of, 20
Ruadhán, 241
Rule (Regulus), Saint, 260